Recent Developments
in International
Banking and Finance

Editorial Board

Recent Developments in International Banking and Finance

Volume 1

Edited by

Sarkis J. Khoury
Alo Ghosh

University of California, Riverside

Lexington Books
D.C. Heath and Company/Lexington, Massachusetts/Toronto

Library of Congress Cataloging-in-Publication Data

Recent developments in international banking and finance.

Papers from a symposium held in 1986 at the Graduate School of Management, University of California at Riverside.
Includes index.
1. International finance—Congresses. 2. Banks and banking, International—Congresses. I. Khoury, Sarkis J.
II. Ghosh, Alo. III. University of California, Riverside. Graduate School of Management.
HG203.R43 1987   332.1'5   85-46007
ISBN 0-669-13211-X (alk. paper)

Published simultaneously in Canada
Printed in the United States of America
Casebound International Standard Book Number: 0-669-13211-X
Library of Congress Catalog Card Number: 85-46007

The paper used in this publication meets the minimum requirements of American National Standard for Information Sciences—Permanence of Paper for Printed Library Materials, ANSI Z39.48-1984. ∞™

86 87 88 89 90 8 7 6 5 4 3 2 1

Contents

Figures

Tables

Preface

The Graduate School of Management, University of California at Riverside, has embarked on an academic strategy that emphasizes financial economics (domestic and international) as one cornerstone for its development in the 1980s and beyond. This strategy has led to a complete revision of the curriculum, a major campaign to hire leading scholars in the field, and the development of special programs that have depth and continuity, and are attractive to the financial community. The series of symposia on recent developments in international banking and finance are intended to demonstrate the commitment of the school to issues relating to financial economics and provide a forum for Graduate School of Management faculty to display their genuine interest in international banking and finance and to interact with scholars and financial executives within and without the United States.

The first symposium, in 1986, brought together leading scholars and practitioners in the field of international finance. The majority of the papers in this book were presented at the symposium. A series of accompanying tutorials reviewed the latest and most interesting developments in the international financial markets and in international portfolio management. The objective was to familiarize the participants, wherever necessary, with all the basics of the topic at hand and to provide a forum for discussing whatever issues arose, regardless of their level of academic sophistication.

The 1986 symposium appears to have succeeded. Comments from the participants were extremely positive, which encourages us to continue and sets the stage for the 1987 symposium. In 1986, papers and tutorials on all aspects of international finance, provided they were relevant and rigorous, were solicited. However, this does not preclude a future symposium that focuses on only one topic, such as the foreign exchange markets. For topics we will continue to solicit the opinions of our readers and participants.

This first symposium was a wonderfully enriching experience for us personally. We appreciate the support we have received from everyone, especially Chancellor Theodore Hullar and Dean Stepan Karamardian of UCR, and we trust that we will be able to count on even more support in the future. The cooperation and dedication of our editorial board were exemplary. One could hardly have hoped to work with a better group of scholars. We trust they will continue to assist us in this ambitious effort to bring scholars and practitioners to a challenging environment filled with the best ideas and conducive to cementing permanent bonds, both personal and professional.

Abbreviations

ACF	autocorrelation function
AIC	information criterion
APT	arbitrage pricing theory
ARIMA	autoregressive integrated moving average
ARMA	autoregressive moving average
BP	basis points
CAPM	capital asset pricing model
CBOE	Chicago Board Options Exchange
CII	*Capital International Indices*
CIP	*Capital International Perspective*
CIRCUS	combined interest rate and currency swap
CP	commercial paper
CRC	Capital Research Company
CTP	continuous tender panel
DM	Deutsche mark
ECU	European currency unit
F/T	foreign to total assets ratio
FDI	foreign direct investment
FRN	floating-rate note
FSA	firm-specific advantage
GCLT	generalized central limit theorem
GUN	grantor unwritten note
IBF	international banking facility
ICAPM	international capital-asset-pricing model
IID	independent and identically distributed
IMM	International Monetary Market
IOCC	International Options Clearing Corporation
IRP	interest rate parity
IRPT	interest rate parity theorem
LC	local currency
LCD	less-developed country

LIFFE	London International Financial Futures Exchange
LLR	lender of last resort
MNE	multinational enterprise
MSE	mean squared forecast error
MTS	multiple time series
OTC	over-the-counter
PHLX	Philadelphia Stock Exchange
PPP	purchasing power parity
ROE	return on equity
SD	standard deviation
SDF	stochastic dominance frequency
SHP	Sharpe performance measure
SOY	strike offered yield
STAGS	sterling transferable accruing securities
TSE	Tokyo Stock Exchange

1
Overview

The recent developments in international financial markets can only be described as revolutionary. More changes have occurred in the past ten years than in the previous history of financial markets, and the pace shows no signs of abating. Four fundamental observations emerge out of this revolutionary era.

1. There is no such thing as domestic banking. The influences of international events are felt by the entire banking sector, either directly or indirectly.
2. Stability is not the natural state, nor is it necessarily achievable through government intervention. Stability can be realized, at least in part, through competent and progressive management.
3. The future of any multinational business entity is bleak indeed, unless its information base is updated and the value of information technology is understood and endogenized.
4. Internationalism is irreversible; corporate managers must learn to cope with it.

These observations form the foundation of this book and the symposium on which the book is based.

Our mission is to make certain observations on the major developments in the international financial markets, and then to summarize and suggest any linkages among the chapters in this book.

The International Environment

The international financial environment of the 1980s can be characterized as one of:

1. Deregulation,
2. High competition,
3. Higher risk than in the past,
4. Innovations and opportunities requiring greater skills and, thus, greater education than in the past,
5. An era where the earnings of a multinational business entity, the financial one in particular, are more dependent on the human skill factor than the pure financial resource factor,
6. Increasing interdependence among product and financial markets, and
7. Increased multinationalization of the banking industry and the financial markets of every country.

The evidence of these situations abounds. One simply has to examine the current banking journals and magazines. We shall highlight the evidence, while pointing out first that the only risks we shall deal with are those of the financial type. The other risks resulting from multinational activities (such as new operating risks, cultural risks, political risks, and marketing risks) will not be discussed directly.

Deregulation and Financial Risks

The deregulatory fever began with the Eurodollar market in London during the 1950s. The first step in the deregulation of domestic markets, however, was taken by the United States in 1963. The innovator was Citicorp, which introduced negotiable certificates of deposit, effectively bypassing Regulation Q which sets interest ceilings.

The decision to gradually abandon Regulation Q was made in October 1983. The final nail on its coffin was hammered in March 1986. All rates on deposits, regardless of type, were henceforth set by market forces.

The Glass-Steagall Act, which draws the line between banking and investment banking activities, has given way to the process of development of financial supermarkets: banks moving into brokerage, insurance, corporate finance, real estate, securities trading, and other fields. The acquisition of Charles Schwab and Co. by the Bank of America in 1983 for $52 million is an example of how serious banks are about diversifying into the securities industry.

The reverse (investment banking diversifying into commercial banking) has also been witnessed. Investment banking and brokerage houses are offering bankinglike services. Merrill Lynch, for example, offers checking facilities through its check management account.

A major contribution to further internationalize the U.S. markets was the decision by the Fed to change its regulations in 1981 to allow banks to establish international banking facilities (IBFs.) On December 3, 1981, IBFs opened in the United States. Within twenty days, no less than $47 billion in assets were held at these facilities. Total assets of IBFs were $256 billion at the end of 1985.

The deregulation of other national markets such as Japan's is lagging behind that in the United States. Nevertheless, Japan's pace quickened during the 1980s, largely because of U.S. pressure and general market forces. Between 1970 and 1971, Japanese investors were allowed to buy foreign securities. In 1973, foreign companies were permitted to list on the Tokyo Stock Exchange (TSE). In 1983, the reporting requirements to the TSE by foreign companies were relaxed, thus cutting by one-third the required documentation. During January 1984, the double check requirement was eliminated. In April 1984, the Ministry of Finance reopened the swap market to private corporations to swap between the yen and foreign currencies. In December of that year, the ministry agreed to allow European financing by foreign companies. In June 1985, it allowed trading of new kinds of yen instruments such as floating rate notes (FRNs) and dual currency bonds. During October 1985, the ministry issued licenses allowing foreign banks to open trust subsidiaries. In December of that year, permission was granted to issue dual currency bonds utilizing the Samurai market. In January 1986, warrants were allowed for the first time to be traded separately. The TSE also added ten seats in 1986, with some of them going to foreign firms. During 1985, banks were permitted to sell money market certificates. The issuance of unsecured corporate bonds was allowed in 1986, and the financial futures market was opened. The deregulation process continues.

The events in the German markets were no less dramatic. Foreign issuers, including subsidiaries of German companies, floated bonds totalling DM 19 billion in the German market in 1984—up from DM 13 billion in 1982. Foreign currency bonds are being issued as well. At the end of 1984, scheduled foreign DM bond issues were running at around DM 2 billion a month. The first new issue calendar in 1985, announced on January 17, was set at DM 2.4 billion for a month. Foreign investors have also taken a great interest in German securities. Nonresidential purchases of Deutsche Mark bonds grew from DM 2.2 billion in 1982 to over DM 11 billion in 1984, during which period foreigners also bought a record DM 4 billion worth of German equities. All of these developments represent the opening of German capital markets during the 1980s.

The deregulation momentum could not be stopped even in labor-dominated Australia. A major deregulatory process has been underway since 1983, despite the fact that the Labor party came into power in 1983 on a platform that included broad opposition to financial reform.

Later, the Labor government adopted financial reforms and embraced a philosophy of deregulation. Liberal rules for chartering foreign banks in Australia were adopted, leading Japan, in turn, to open its doors to Australian banks. The deregulation of interest rates began in 1979. All deposit interest rate ceilings at banks were removed in 1980, and ownership restrictions on merchant banks were suspended. The ownership of stock brokerage firms was expanded to encourage new capital to enter the country. By November 1985, sixteen foreign banks received licenses to operate within Australia. They include the biggest names from Japan, the United States, and Europe.

Similar evidence on deregulation compiled on other countries strongly suggests a trend toward the unshackling of controls and internationalization of financial markets.

The deregulatory cycle has brought about increased competition among financial institutions and increased volatility across all markets. The increased volatility has led corporate managers to place greater emphasis on risk management. In turn, a multitude of hedging vehicles has emerged to aid international managers in coping with risk. A representative list of these includes options contracts, futures contracts, options on futures, futureslike options, swaps, caps, collars, structured portfolio strategies such as immunization and dedication techniques, and other vehicles and strategies designed to keep portfolio managers at the vanguard of efficiency. These markets and instruments have flourished largely in the United States and have been emulated elsewhere.

For instance, the London International Financial Futures Exchange (LIFFE) continues to pick up participants and volume as portfolio managers have begun to realize that futures and options are necessary hedging tools. The "casino" image of LIFFE has begun to fade, as it has with the financial futures instruments that began trading on the International Money Market of Chicago in May 1972.

Several of the markets have begun to establish links that effectively allow twenty-four-hour trading. The link between the Chicago Mercantile Exchange and the International Monetary Exchange in September 1984 (with rights to offset) and the announcement on November 28, 1985, by the London Stock Exchange and the U.S. National Association of Securities Dealers of plans to swap price quotes on about 550 British and U.S. issues are but a few examples of the multinationalization of major trading exchanges.

The internationalization process has engulfed the equity markets in addition to the bond and money markets. The equity markets are becoming truly global markets, thus providing greater liquidity to equity issues. By August 1985, $363.5 million of new international equity issues were sold compared with $386.4 million of corporate Eurobonds. Some of the corporations issuing international equity are listed in table 1–1.

Corporate treasurers and finance directors seem to have realized that sig-

Table 1–1
Some of the Firms Issuing International Equities, 1983–85

July 1983	Bell Canada Enterprises 2 million shares ($43.4 million) international offering
September 1983	Alcan Aluminum Ltd. 7 million shares ($40 million) European offering
September 1984	Esselte Business Systems 1.9 million shares ($26 million) international offering
October 1984	Swiss Bank Corporation 160,000 bearer participation certificates (Swiss franc 46 million) private placement in Japan
November 1984	British Telecom 90 million shares (£117 million) Swiss tranche of initial public offering
March 1985	Nederlandsche Middenstandsbank NV 500,000 shares (Dfl83 million) secondary offering in Switzerland
April 1985	Buhrman Tetterode NV 201,370 shares (Dfl17 million) secondary offering in Switzerland
May 1985	Thomassen & Drijver-Verblifa NV 197,323 shares (Dfl12 million) Swiss tranche of IPO
May 1985	Nestlé SA 300,000 BPC (Swiss franc 373 million) international offering
June 1985	Banca del Gottardo 65,000 bearer shares (Swiss franc 40.3 million) international secondary offering
July 1985	Student Loan Marketing Association (Sallie Mae) 1.5 million shares ($50 million) international offering
July 1985	Britoil PLC 25 million shares (£45 million) international offering
August 1985	Banca Commerciale Italiana 5 million shares L111.5 billion ($59 million) international secondary offering

Source: *Euromoney*, January 1986.

nificant additional amounts of capital could be raised internationally rather than domestically. In the process, restraints imposed by stock exchanges and securities authorities are effectively avoided.

The liquidity of the international equity market was further enhanced when a clearing system for transactions was worked out. The clearing systems for Eurobonds, Euro-Clear (Brussels), and Cedel (Luxembourg) have begun clearing equity transactions. Euro-Clear is now probably the largest securities settlement system in the world; it clears more than $1 trillion a year in negotiable securities—almost as much as the New York and Tokyo Stock Exchanges combined. "Euro-Clear and Cedel clear between them some $38 billion a week. The eight German stock exchanges take a year to transact the same volume of business." Euro-Clear cleared equities in 1985 through its network of 1,600 participating financial institutions around the world, in the process turning the equity market for blue chip stocks into a truly global market.

Innovations and Realignments in the International Financial Markets

The process of innovations in the international financial markets has been so rapid, radical, and varied that it can scarcely be covered comprehensively in this chapter. Hopefully, readers will be satisfied with tables 1–2 and 1–3's summaries of the major innovations in the Euronotes and Eurobond markets. These tables indicate that the innovations in the marketing of new issues have been substantially varied, providing in the process greater flexibility and liquidity in the marketplace.

The number of new financing features has also increased dramatically. Some of the new techniques introduced in 1985 alone were:

First mini-max (Kingdom of Denmark, February 1985)

First adjustable spread on LIBOR (Ente Nazionale per l' Energia Eletrica, March 1985)

First t-bill–priced FRN with coupon mismatch (February 1985, Svensk Export Kredit)

First securitization of interest rate cap (Banque Indosuez, June 1985)

First securitization of standby facility (Banque Nationale de Paris, 1985)

First Eurobond tap issue (Svensk Export Kredit, May 1985)

First flip-flop t-based perpetual FRN (World Bank, 1985)

First glimpse of STAGs (sterling transferable accruing securities based on stripped U.K. government gilts, August 8, 1985).

Table 1–2
Methods of Marketing New Issues

Borrowers option for notes and underwritten standby (BONUS):	Global note facility. (See *global note facility*.)
Continuous tender panel (CTP):	A compromise between sole-placing agency and tender panel. The CTP agent agrees on the issue price (the strike offered yield or SOY) with the issuer, at which price underwriting banks may request protection on their notional allocations. These allocations are calculated pro rata to their underwriting commitments, but are only exercisable to the extent that the CTP agent has not presold the issue tranche. The SOY can change during the bidding period and the underwriters may be able to increase their initial allocations by bidding at or under the SOY.
Direct bid facility (unsolicited bidding):	An increasingly common provision in tender panel facilities whereby panel members may make unsolicited bids to the issuer for particular note amounts and maturities.
Euro-commercial paper (Euro CP):	A nonunderwritten or uncommitted note issuance program where typically two or three dealers place the issuer's paper.
Global note facility:	The banks' medium-term underwriting commitment is available to back up both the issue of U.S. commercial paper and Euronotes. Should the issuer be unable to roll over U.S. CP, his will trigger off a Euronote issuance process by tender panel. Bridging finance between the time of failed U.S. CP roll-over and provision of funds from the Euronote facility is provided by a swingline.
Global commercial paper:	The growing concept of nonunderwritten Euronote issuance programs being sold on a global basis with the book moving between time zones.
Grantor underwritten note (GUN):	A floating-rate note facility akin to a Euronote facility whereby a group of banks (grantors) commits to purchase any notes put back to them by investors on any FRN interest rate fixing date. Put notes are then auctioned out to the market between the grantors.
Issuer-set margin:	Similar to continuous tender panel except that underwriters are guaranteed the protection on their pro rata allocation of paper. Should they opt not to take notes at the issuer-set margin, the lead manager will instead.
Multioption facility (MOF):	Broader than the classic underwritten Euronote issuance facility in that the banks' medium-term commitment is to backstop not only the issuance of Euronotes, but a wide range of other short-term instruments (bankers acceptances and short-term advances in a variety of currencies).
Note issuance facility (NIF):	An addition to RUF and SNIF. Now widely regarded as a general description for all *underwritten* Euronote facilities.
Prime underwriting facility (PUF):	Same as a RUF except that the maximum margin is expressed in relation to U.S. prime.
Revolving underwriting facility (RUF):	Classically, a medium-term commitment by a group of underwriting banks to purchase one-, three-, or six-month Euronotes at a fixed Libor-related margin should a sole-placing agent fail to sell the notes to investors at or under that margin. RUF has since been extended to tender panel placement facilities as well as sole-placing.

Table 2–1 continued

Short-term note issuance facility (SNIF):	Evolving after RUF as a method of distinguishing tender panel placement from the sole placing of the RUF. Otherwise, structurally the same.
Specialized tender panel:	Similar to the direct bid facility except that members of the STP are limited to a nucleus of houses with perceived note placement strength that are expected to make a market in the issuer's paper.
Stop out bid:	A refinement of tender panel bidding whereby one or more of the TP participants have an option to post a bid for all or part of an issue tranche at a price that other tender panel members must then better.
Striking price method:	The issue price for the whole tranche is set at the level of the last accepted bid that caused the tranche to be filled. That is, notes are not priced at a sequential level from the most competitive bid upward as in standard tender panel.
Swaps tender panel:	A further refinement of the tender panel whereby the issuer can ask for currency and/or interest rate swaps on a particular note issue tranche.
Swingline:	Used in a global note facility or BONUS to allow the issuer to move from the U.S. CP market to the Euronote market. Typically available for a maximum of seven days and priced over U.S. prime.
TAP basis:	The increasingly frequent method of issuance in Euro CP. The dealer approaches the issuer for paper in direct response to particular investor demand, rather than the issuer seeking bids from the dealer.
Tender acceptance facility:	Precisely the same structure as an underwritten Euronote facility using a tender panel except that the short-term instruments under auction are bankers' acceptances, not Euronotes.
Tender panel:	A group, including Euronote facility underwriters and additionally appointed banks and dealers, who are invited to bid on an issuer's paper in an open auction format. Notes are awarded to bidders in sequential order from the most competitive bid upwards, until the full tranche is allocated.
Transferable revolving underwriting facility (TRUF):	The underwriting banks' contingent liability to purchase notes, in the event of nonplacement, is fully transferable.

Source: *Euromoney,* special sponsored supplement, p. 128, January 1986.

Table 1–3
New Innovations in the International Financial Markets

Alladin bond:	A new issue offered in exchange for an old issue.
Back bond:	A Eurobond created out of the exercising of a warrant. Also known as a virgin bond.
BECS, MECS:	The two repackaged U.K. FRNs swapped into fixed-rate bearer instruments via a special purpose company.
Call protection warrants:	Long-maturity, harmless warrants that, during the initial part of their life, can only be exercised by surrendering a host bond, thereby avoiding an immediate call structure on the host bond.
Cap FRN:	An FRN with a maximum rate of interest.
CIRCUS:	Combined interest rate and currency swap.
Collar swap:	A swap of fixed-rate dollars against floating-rate dollars with the latter having a maximum and minimum rate.
Contingent swap:	A swap, the terms of which are predetermined but which is only activated on the action of a third party, such as the exercising of a warrant. Also known as an *option swap*.
Currency warrant:	A warrant exercisable by the payment of one currency into a fixed nominal amount of a security in the second currency.
Delayed cap FRN:	An FRN with a maximum rate of interest effective after an initial period.
DINGO:	A zero-coupon Australian dollar issue created by stripping an Australian government gilt.
Dual-currency issue:	An issue denominated in one currency with a coupon and/or repayment of principal at a fixed rate in another currency.
Hara kiri:	Submarket yen/dollar swap.
Harmless warrant:	A structure of warrants attached to a host bond that protects the issuers from the potential doubling up of debt in the event of warrant exercise.
Host bond:	A Eurobond issue to which is attached a warrant or similar instrument.
Income right:	An instrument that entitles the holder to an annuity cash flow.
Mini-max FRN:	An FRN with both minimum and maximum rate of interest.
Mismatch FRN:	An FRN having a coupon structure refixed more often and for different maturities than the interest period.
Naked warrants:	An issue of warrants without any host bond.
Part-paid FRN:	A part-paid FRN that can become fully paid at the option of the issuer.
Pirate issue:	An issue of Ecus done outside the queueing arrangement of the three Belgian banks.
Shogun:	A non–yen-denominated Japanese domestic issue.
STAGS/ZEBRAS:	A zero-coupon sterling issue created by stripping a U.K. government gilt.
Startrek:	A bond priced at a level previously unexplored by the market.
Sushi bond:	A dollar issue undertaken by a Japanese company from Japan and designed to be bought by Japanese institutions.
Window warrant:	A warrant exercisable on particular days or during particular periods. Also known as *European warrants*.

Source: *Euromoney,* special sponsored supplement, p. 129, January 1986.

The pace of innovation continues unabated despite some major negative developments, such as the failure of the Continental Bank of Chicago and the sovereign debt crisis. The latter problem has been patched up for the moment, but a long-term solution technique has yet to be applied. Its reemergence may well slow down, if not reverse, the process toward further integration of financial markets.

Corporate treasurers and governments continue to participate heavily in Euro markets despite some setbacks. The volume of Eurobonds increased 60 percent over 1984 by the end of 1985. The lead of this market over its U.S. counterpart is now large and firm, as shown in figure 1–1. The types of instruments issued in this market are still dominated by "straight," fixed-rate issues. (See figures 1–2 and 1–3.) Floating rate issues took a dive in 1985 because of lower interest rates and the attempt of corporate treasurers to lock them in.

Leading the way in underwriting Eurobond issues is Credit Suisse First Boston, both in number of issues and dollar amount. CSFB's share of the market was 14.1 percent in 1985, down from 16.6 percent in 1984, as shown in table 1–4.

In terms of currencies, the dollar issues accounted for almost 70 percent of all issues, with the DM- and yen-denominated issues following closely. Of particular interest is the size of the issues denominated in European currency units (ECUs). (See figure 1–4.) The forecast is for a continued vigorous growth of the ECU-denominated Eurobond market.

Euronotes proved to be reasonably popular in 1985. Euronotes issues outstanding at the end of 1985 totaled $12 billion. Euronotes were used as a cheap alternative for short-term bank loans. Their distribution by value, type of issuer, sector, and country is shown in figure 1–5.

All of these developments suggest that when markets are allowed to function freely, there is no predicting how far they will grow and who the winners and losers will be.

The flexibility, progressiveness, and maturity that the international financial markets displayed in the 1980s were somewhat tainted by the temporary frailty the markets exhibited at several time intervals as they grappled with the sovereign debt problem, the overshooting of the U.S. dollar over its long-run value as suggested by purchasing power parity (PPP), and the huge budgetary deficits accumulated by the United States.

The rush to "solve" the sovereign debt problem provided only a temporary patch to a $1 trillion problem. The problem is yet to be addressed on a permanent basis. All of the solutions that have already been applied fell far short of insuring the long-run stability of the international financial system. The dangers from potential Mexican and Argentinean default still remain. The path chosen by Peru and Cuba to deal with their debt crises does not constitute a good example for the rest of the world on either the lending or

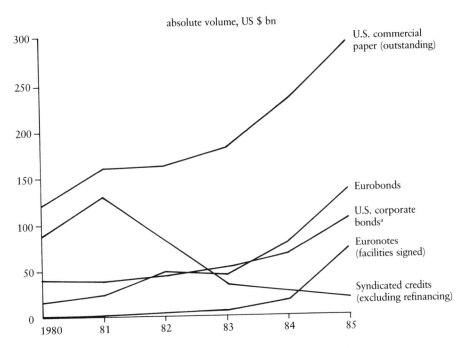

absolute volume, US $ bn

U.S. commercial paper (outstanding)

Eurobonds

U.S. corporate bonds[a]

Euronotes (facilities signed)

Syndicated credits (excluding refinancing)

Source: *Euromoney Annual Financing Report 1986*, March 1986, p. 3.

[a]All taxable publicly offered debt issued for cash and registered with the SEC on a net-proceeds basis.

Figure 1–1. The World's Capital Markets, 1980–85

borrowing side. (A comprehensive survey on the sovereign debt crises was prepared by S. Khoury and published by the University of South Carolina Business School in Columbia, South Carolina.)

The dollar overvaluation was corrected by market forces and by intervention from the European and Japanese central banks. The results were overshooting, some argue, in the opposite direction. However, the foreign exchange markets continue to evolve toward their long-run equilibrium states.

The Knowledge Advantage

Commercial banks and investment banks have long capitalized on their ability to internalize information that would otherwise have been in the public domain; on their special relationship with major clients; on their ability to innovate and automate; and, recently, on their abilities to offer flexible fi-

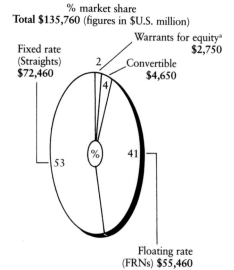

% market share
Total **$135,760** (figures in $U.S. million)

Warrants for equity[a]
$2,750

Fixed rate
(Straights)
$72,460

2

Convertible
$4,650

4

%

53

41

Floating rate
(FRNs) **$55,460**

Source: *Euromoney Annual Financing Report 1986,* March 1986, p. 16.
[a]Including both fixed rate and floating rate.

Figure 1–2. Eurobond Market by Type of Instrument, 1985

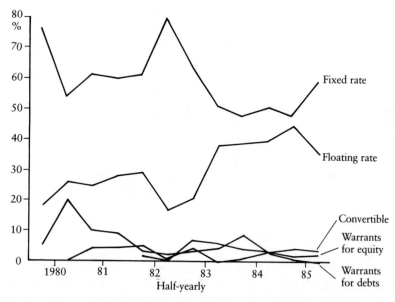

Fixed rate

Floating rate

Convertible

Warrants
for equity

Warrants
for debts

Half-yearly

Source: *Euromoney Annual Financing Report 1986,* March 1986, p. 16.

Figure 1–3. Eurobond Market Shares by Type of Instrument, 1980–85

nancing and hedging tools and to gauge the risk return characteristics of these new products.

It has been reported that Salomon and Goldman Sachs employ more Ph.D.'s in finance and in related disciplines than any university in the United States. They have huge research departments manned by the top graduates of the best universities. Their computers are continually buzzing to ensure efficient flow of information to decision-makers throughout their organizational structures.

Most of the recent financial innovations introduced by banks and investment banks are relatively more complex than the standard financial instruments available in the marketplace. The new instruments offer mainly long-to-medium–term speculative/hedging vehicles and tend to have options-like features. First of all, their longer-term maturities make them difficult candidates for pricing relative to the shorter-term instruments, which are the ones that are typically priced in organized exchanges.

Second, their optionlike features add to the complexity of their theoretical pricing. While the issuers of these instruments are interested in knowing how to strip these optionlike features and hedge against them in portfolio terms, the buyers are concerned with issues such as whether the instruments are overpriced or underpriced and how they fit into their total asset–liability portfolios in a risk–return sense. In either case, the input of computer-oriented and quantitatively oriented finance professionals is being found to be indispensable.

So convinced have financial intermediaries become of the value of the knowledge advantage that they have begun raiding the top business schools for talent. The acquisition by Goldman Sachs of Professors Fischer Black of MIT and Richard Roll of UCLA are two examples of a market that is becoming so competitive and so thirsty for technical competence. The success of Citicorp in the swap market can be attributed largely to the quality personnel it was able to assemble in order to offer a wide array of swaps while simultaneously being able to hedge its positions.

International banks and investment banks have also invested heavily in their training departments in many research centers (for example, the Salomon Brothers Center at NYU) and in many seminars and symposia. Their commitment to executive education is commendable indeed. Business schools such as Wharton are making major financial commitments to executive education; are constructing new buildings to house programs and entire administrative structures dedicated exclusively to this goal, and are unabashed about their interaction with the business community and their commitment to providing answers to real-life problems. The search for truth in the business disciplines need not be confined to abstract issues, as some leading universities are also discovering.

The new commitment to knowledge power (that is, earning assets are largely embedded in human capital in additional to financial capital) is evi-

Table 1–4
Top Eurobonds Bookrunners—All Issues, 1984–85

Rank 1984	Rank 1985	Bank	1985 Number	1985 Amount ($ million)	1985 Share (%)	1984 Number	1984 Amount ($ million)	1984 Share (%)
1	1	Credit Suisse First Boston	101	19041.2	14.1	81	13170.7	16.6
6	2	Merrill Lynch	47	7958.2	5.9	26	4295.6	5.4
2	3	Morgan Guaranty	62	7863.3	5.8	37	6107.7	7.7
5	4	Salomon Brothers	67	7833.1	5.8	32	4779.5	6.0
3	5	Deutsche Bank	75	7695.3	5.7	61	5754.7	7.3
4	6	Morgan Stanley	63	6422.0	4.8	46	5089.7	6.4
8	7	Goldman Sachs	41	6222.2	4.6	22	2468.1	3.1
7	8	Nomura Securities	61	5030.8	3.7	36	2748.5	3.5
37	9	Union Bank of Switzerland	27	3753.4	2.8	6	490.7	.6
12	10	Banque Paribas	55	3336.5	2.5	16	1497.9	1.9
17	11	Orion Royal Bank	51	3005.0	2.2	19	1162.6	1.5
13	12	Daiwa Securities	37	2937.1	2.2	25	1403.7	1.8
9	13	SG Warburg	25	2836.6	2.1	24	1937.5	2.4
15	14	Swiss Bank Corporation	23	2527.4	1.9	14	1275.0	1.6
16	15	Shearson Lehman Brothers International	16	2492.3	1.8	11	1265.0	1.6
25	16	Bankers Trust	25	2417.6	1.8	7	840.0	1.1
18	17	Commerzbank	32	2377.0	1.8	18	1139.9	1.4
20	18	County Bank	9	2327.0	1.7	5	954.0	1.2
35	19	Lloyds	9	2325.0	1.7	2	516.7	.7
23=	20	Yamaichi Securities	32	2227.3	1.6	19	910.0	1.1

14	21	Société Générale	2090.0	1.5	23	11	1292.1	1.6
23=	22	Bank of America	1983.3	1.5	9	5	910.0	1.1
30	23	Credit Commercial de France	1917.6	1.4	23	8	682.3	.9
28	24	Samuel Montagu	1911.3	1.4	7	8	699.7	.9
19	25	Nikko Securities	1866.9	1.4	32	17	1078.8	1.4

Source: "Annual Financing Report," *Euromoney*, March 1986, pp. 12–13.
Note: All bookrunners receive full amounts.

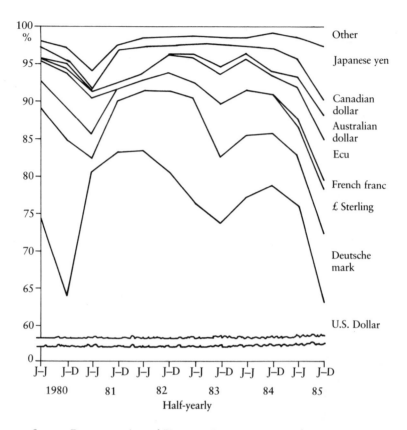

Source: *Euromoney Annual Financing Report 1986*, March 1986, p. 24.

Figure 1–4. Eurobond Market Shares by Currency, 1980–85

dent in the strategic plans of institutions such as Citicorp, Salomon Brothers, Morgan Guaranty, Bankers Trust, and Goldman Sachs. The unbundling of banking services and the expansion of human-capital–based banking business have led to a complete reexamination of the philosophy that views the size of the bank loan portfolio as the cornerstone for vigorous earnings growth.

This philosophical realignment and the reaching out across the schism that divided academia and the commercial and investment banking community underlie the series of symposia on international banking and finance sponsored by the Graduate School of Management, University of California, Riverside. The papers that we have accepted for inclusion as chapters in this book address in a significant way, we trust, some fundamental issues in the international financial markets.

Overview of Tutorials

The symposium included four tutorial sessions on topics that supported and filled gaps in the presentations of papers. G. Burghardt, Jr., of the Chicago Mercantile Exchange (CME) presented an overview of the process of risk assessment and management of option positions. In doing so, he used the vehicle of a comprehensive computer program developed at the CME under his direction. This menu-driven system (available from the CME at a modest price) operates on a spreadsheet for entering a position and graphically provides a risk analysis of the position, a table of implied volatilities, a revaluation and hedge ratio spreadsheet, a chart of theoretical versus actual prices, a graph of decay of time value of options, and a graph of the effect of volatility increasing. These analyses are available for all options on debt and currency futures. The interactive nature of the computer program and the copious graphical displays make the package an extremely useful educational and trading tool.

S. J. Khoury and A. Ghosh conducted a tutorial on interest rate and exchange rate swaps and other recent financial innovations. They first surveyed the entire area of financial swaps along with the mechanics of constructing and hedging swaps and then presented an empirical approach (based on logit analysis) to valuation of the default guarantee provided by the intermediary to the swap partners. In analyzing the recent proliferation of financial innovations in international and domestic markets, researchers (for example, Levich, 1986) have noted that swap transactions being voluntary are therefore welfare-enchancing, but since they involve bilateral trade rather than organized exchange-based trade, they must in some way be fueled by market imperfections and information asymmetries. In a realistic setting of incomplete capital markets with palpable transaction costs, information asymmetries, and regulatory frictions and barriers, brokered bilateral financial transactions are likely to coexist with exchange-traded financial instruments. Also, given the absence of legal enforcement mechanisms in international finance, the absence of liquidity in long-maturity hedge instruments, and the myriad permutations of swap transactions yet to be introduced in the market, swaps as general bilateral trade mechanisms are likely to proliferate in the future.

In such a setting, Ghosh and Khoury suggested a swap valuation mechanism that concentrates on the problem of allocation of the spread between the two instruments or cash flows being exchanged by the swap parties and the concomitant risk-sharing scheme, in the context of the Nash bargaining solution to a cooperative game. They demonstrated by using real-life numerical examples that the Nash bargaining solution provides a pragmatic mechanism for spread allocation. However, on the question of the risk-sharing mechanism, they pointed out the gaps in current research and suggested that nothing short of a full-fledged equilibrium model with stochastic interest and

Volume, 1978–Sept 1985 (signed facilities only)   Total: $58 billion, 355 transactions

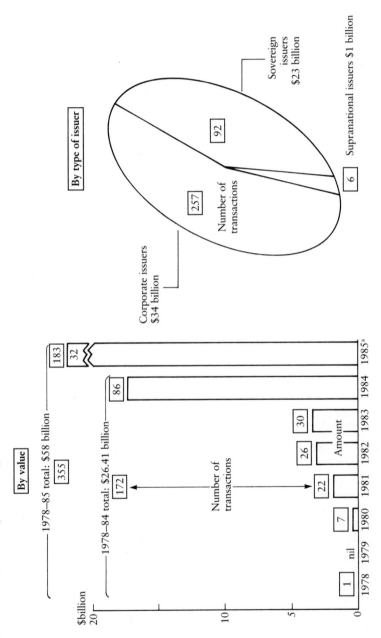

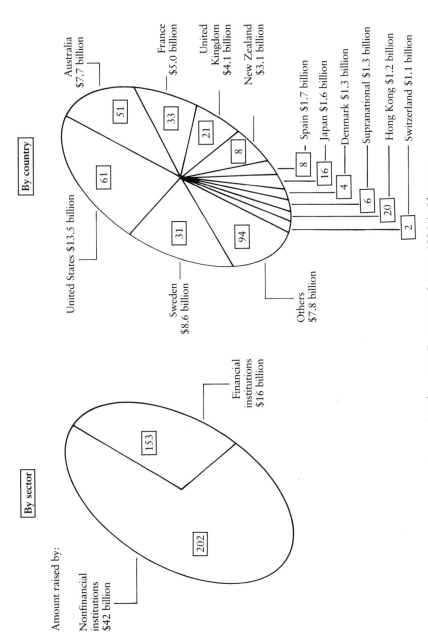

By sector

By country

Amount raised by:

Nonfinancial institutions $42 billion

Financial institutions $16 billion

202

153

United States $13.5 billion

Australia $7.7 billion

France $5.0 billion

United Kingdom $4.1 billion

New Zealand $3.1 billion

Spain $1.7 billion

Japan $1.6 billion

Denmark $1.3 billion

Supranational $1.3 billion

Hong Kong $1.2 billion

Switzerland $1.1 billion

Sweden $8.6 billion

Others $7.8 billion

61

51

33

21

8

31

94

8

16

4

6

20

2

Source: *Supplement to Euromoney*, January 1986, inside cover.

ªTo September 1985.

Figure 1–5. Charting the Market for Euronotes

exchange rates and stochastic term structures of these rates can suffice to address the interest and exchange rate risk issues. In principle, however, the Nash bargaining construct can accommodate adjustments to any risk premiums that the two parties might demand in their allocation of the spread. As far as default risk is concerned, they noted that swap partners in reality are almost always of the same risk class so that a swap in itself rarely involves additional default risk. In their future work, Ghosh and Khoury expressed their intention to attempt to value swaps and related hedge instruments as long-term forward/option contracts synthetically constructed from available short-term ones.

R. J. Sweeney and A. Ghosh reported their individual research and experience with various technical and fundamental trading rules used for speculation and hedging exchange markets. First, Sweeney outlined his extensive recent research (an example of which appeared in his March 1986 *Journal of Finance* article) on filter rules for beating the foreign exchange (and stock) markets. When filter rule profits have been detected in these studies, it has often been argued that the profits are due to risk. Early work in this area had virtually ignored risk, conducted mostly in-sample tests, and provided no satisfactory statistical significance tests of these profits. Recent research has sought to rectify these lapses and has generated a good deal of sophisticated econometrics.

Sweeney specifically summarized his work in providing an international capital-asset-pricing model- (ICAPM-) based analysis of rates of return both to buy-and-hold and to filter strategies in spot and forward markets for foreign exchange, and in developing a test of significance of filter rule profits that explicitly assumes constant risk–return trade-offs due to constant risk premiums. Although one should judge filter rule profits vis-à-vis buy-and-hold on the basis of average daily rates of return net of the interest rate differential of the two countries, Sweeney argued that this differential may be assumed to be constant and hence ignored in tests. He reported finding statistically significant excess speculative returns over a large daily data set based on his X statistic. These results might be rationalized in terms of market inefficiencies (such as those related to government interventions in foreign exchange markets) or to the possibility that risk premiums vary over time and are not constant as assumed. In the latter case, positive X statistics would reflect higher average risk borne, not true profits. While the recent work of Fama (1984) and Hodrick and Srivastava (1985) make a case in favor of time-varying risk premiums, independent research by Sweeney (1984, 1985) and Ghosh (1985) indicate that we cannot unambiguously point in that direction. In any case, Sweeney argued that in practical evaluation of portfolio performance, the manager must assume (given the ambivalences in measures of time-varying risk premiums) that these excess profits are due to market inefficiencies and thus must be exploited.

Ghosh described in brief his experience with implementation and extension of a trading rule first suggested by Bilson (1981). Since foreign exchange returns series have poor signal-to-noise ratios, to alleviate the problem, a portfolio of less than perfectly correlated forecasts of future exchange rates was considered to derive a "composite" forecast. The constituent forecasts were the spot rate (by random walk theory), the forward rate (by forward parity theory), and those by a prominent econometric service and a well-known technical service. The techniques used were a combination of Zellner's seemingly unrelated regression with Bayesian updating (involving a multivariate beta distribution). The resulting composite forecast errors for the various currencies and maturities of forward contracts were then used to form optimal portfolios by quadratic programming formulation which accounted for transaction costs, long and short positions, and upper and lower limits on these positions. Assuming that 30 percent of one's money was invested in forward contract "margins" while the remaining 70 percent went into a money market fund, the out-of-sample monthly-data–based track record for three-month portfolio decision horizons showed nearly zero average annual profits over the period 1973 to 1985. However, monthly portfolio revisions (with due regard to updated forecasts and to incremental transaction costs) resulted in average annual profits on the range of 150 to 300 percent. The results with higher frequency (weekly and then daily) data and with trades in futures and options markets instead of forward markets were reported to be nearly as encouraging. The large (although leveraged) profits above transaction costs it was felt were difficult to explain away in terms of time-varying premiums. Ghosh finally discussed his results from attempting to relate (by regression) these expected and actual profit streams with time series of fundamental variables in the economy, in the spirit of Meese and Rogoff (1983). Several consistent and statistically significant relationships between fundamental economic variables and the profit stream (expected, actual, and differences between expected and actual) were detected. No such relationships were found, however, when such financial variables as market index proxies were used as explanatory variables.

M. Eaker, in his comments on the results reported by Sweeney and Ghosh, presented his own empirical results which corroborated their conclusions. He suggested that perhaps extant economic models of exchange rate markets were preoccupied with longer-term market fundamentals whereas reality for the foreign exchange trader involves trades over much shorter intervals wherein psychological factors play a larger role than do economic ones.

M. Adler presented the fourth and final tutorial session with an overview of international portfolio choice (an area in which he coauthored with Bernard Dumas a landmark survey paper in a 1983 issue of the *Journal of Finance*). The questions that he addressed were: How must an investor choose an international stock-bond portfolio? What are the pros and cons of active versus passive international portfolio management? Is a single asset pricing model applicable in every country? Can international stock-bond portfolios be hedged against foreign exchange risk? He pointed out that the relatively low level of correlation between national stock markets and other investment instruments across the world implies that very large gains may be reaped by international portfolio diversification, but that the investment community is currently not taking full advantage of these opportunities.

When computing optimal international portfolios, it is important to recognize the inventor's habitat since consumption tastes and opportunity sets differ markedly by country. In other words, there are large deviations from PPP. Also, such PPP deviations fluctuate widely and randomly, thus strongly influencing the investor's risk perceptions. Further, these deviations are substantially a result of exchange rate variations and only slightly due to national price level dynamics. Optimal portfolio choice can be shown in this context to consist of a universal logarithmic portfolio (that corresponding to investors with unit risk aversion factors) combined with a minimum-variance or hedge portfolio representing the best hedge specific to each habitat's local brand of inflation. Adler reported empirical results indicating that hedge portfolios are typically made up entirely of the investor's home currency bank deposit (since, as pointed out earlier, stocks and foreign currencies are not good hedges against local inflation). Logarithmic portfolios tend to include stock investments that balance out the bank deposits (since stocks are about 100 percent or more exposed to local currencies) and contain large positive and negative portfolio weights (implying that the yields on the various instruments are not properly aligned).

Adler also summarized his recent empirical work on determining exchange rate exposures of international portfolios. Defining exposure in terms of a set of regression coefficients (in the same spirit as "betas") from regression of excess rates of returns on securities or portfolios on exchange rate changes, Adler reported the pre- and post-October 1979 historical exposures of major national bond and stock indices. Both bonds and stock indices were typically exposed only to their own currencies. Before October 1979, stock returns (like bond returns) were generally independent of exchange rate changes, so that their own-currency exposures were 100 percent. Also, the exposures of diversified portfolios during this period were negligible. Since October 1979, several major countries' stock indices became more than 100 percent exposed to their own-currency risks, and diversified portfolios became exposed to all major currency risks.

Since exchange rates are not fundamental state variables but are in turn driven by them, these exposure measures would perforce be nonstationary, so that exposure "betas" in practice need to be estimated periodically. Also, to hedge more completely against exchange risk, one would have to locate assets that provide hedges against unexpected movements in the underlying state variables. Many of these hedge instruments are yet to be traded in organized financial markets.

Overview of Chapters

In chapter 2, A. Rugman and S. Kamath review the motives behind international banking and the various related theories. They then review and develop the theory of internalization as it applies to the multinational banking firm. The authors argue that internalization theory explains the existence of the activities of multinational banks and possesses forecasting power for these activities. The reasons for internalization are then listed and explained. One of the reasons is risk diversification, which is a subset of internalization. The literature on this motive is then surveyed and the components of risk (systematic and unsystematic) are then examined. The argument is the well-known one: it is the systematic component that should be priced in an international context.

The authors then proceed to test the relationship between the degree of international activity by Canadian banks and the variability of their profits. The degree of multinationalism is measured in terms of the ratio of foreign to total assets. The results showed that international diversification paid off in terms of larger and more stable earnings. These results support the findings of other studies, mainly those of Khoury (cited in Chapter 1).

The authors further examine risk diversification, which focuses on systematic risk for thirty-seven multinational banks using a version of the Sharpe index model. The findings support the null hypothesis that international diversification does reduce systematic risk, albeit to varying degrees across the country groupings. The results are in agreement with the theory of internalization and the hypothesis that the motivations for diversifying international banking activities are essentially similar to those of other multinational corporations.

The Rugman-Kamath chapter, while proving that diversification of financial risk is achievable, does not imply that the international environment is more stable than the purely domestic one. In fact, in an international environment there exists a greater need for strategic planning, taking into consideration the likelihood of major shocks, such as liquidity shocks and sovereign debt crises. This is precisely the subject of Guttentag and Herring's chapter.

The Guttentag-Herring chapter represents a preliminary effort to develop principles and methods that will enable international banks to deal with infrequent events—unpredictable shocks—that may cause major damage. Drawing on the literature in cognitive psychology and decision analysis, they advance the hypothesis of "disaster myopia" to explain why a bank may inadvertently expose itself to catastrophic losses. They illustrate this hypothesis with regard to the recent pattern of lending to the major developing country borrowers.

To help counter disaster myopia, Guttentag and Herring suggest an analytical procedure that has three phases: (1) identification of those hazards that are worth worrying about; (2) estimation of the bank's existing exposure to those hazards; and (3) explicit determination of whether the exposure is excessive. Four shocks are considered—a credit shock, an interest rate shock, a foreign exchange shock, and a funding shock. It is analytically convenient to view each shock separately, although in practice they may occur simultaneously. In particular, a funding shock may be a consequence of any one of the other shocks and is a hazard that is broadly relevant to all major banks. For that reason, they illustrate the procedure for strategic planning with regard to a funding shock—an event that causes the market to question the solvency of the bank and thereby jeopardizes the bank's ability to sell uninsured liabilities.

The illustration begins with a sketch of an accounting framework that permits measurement of the bank's vulnerability to a funding shock. Vulnerability is measured in terms of the number of days the bank could sustain the shock before it incurs losses equal to the market value of its net worth just before the shock occurred. Some of the information required in the analysis is readily available, but much of the information requires subjective forecasts and careful judgments. This makes the strategic planning exercise difficult, but also extremely useful because it encourages managers to think strategically—to anticipate problems that may arise and to consider how they can influence outcomes. The process of measuring vulnerability to the shock is helpful in identifying methods of enhancing liquidity, highlighting information the bank may need but does not have, and stimulating thinking about how the bank can respond quickly and effectively should trouble occur.

The implementation problem is briefly considered. The authors advance specific proposals for overcoming ingrained disincentives to provide information and to participate in the planning exercise, for obtaining the best information available on the likelihood that a particular shock will occur, and for focusing managerial attention on exposure to shocks.

The approach developed in the Guttentag-Herring chapter also has important implications for the supervision of international banks and the division of labor between banks and supervisors in monitoring insolvency exposure. The approach would require a reassessment of some fundamental aspects of bank regulation. Traditionally, the bank supervisor has asked the question, "Is this bank unsound *now*?" From their perspective, the supervisor should pose the question, "Is this bank *unduly* exposed?" This second question requires not only a different methodology but perhaps a different organizational structure and legal basis as well as a different relationship between supervisors and banks.

The strategic planning recommended by Guttentag and Herring against uncertainty regarding major shocks is very long-term in nature and does not address the more palpable recurring risks the firm faces in the international markets. One such risk is the foreign exchange risk which can have a significant impact on the profitability of the firm and the wealth of shareholders.

The exposure to foreign exchange risk can be hedged partially or totally using various instruments which we discuss later in detail. The first step in the hedging program is the identification and measurement of foreign exchange exposure. Three additional types of exposure have been identified: translation, transaction, and economic.

Translation exposure. Sometimes referred to as "accounting exposure," translation exposure measures the impact of an exchange rate change on the recorded position of a company. It arises from the need to report consolidated worldwide operations in terms of the local currency according to predetermined accounting rules. Assets, liabilities, revenues, and expenses originally measured in a foreign currency must be restated in terms of the home currency in order to be used and compared with other home currency results.

Transaction exposure. Transaction exposure is the gain or loss resulting from the settlement of transactions denominated in a foreign currency if exchange rates change between the transaction date and the settlement date.

Economic exposure. Economic exposure is caused by a change in future cash flows resulting from a change in exchange rates. Exchange rates affect sales volume, prices, or costs which impact the value of the firm and, consequently, the wealth of shareholders.

It is economic exposure that L. Oxelheim and C. Wihlborg focus on. They offer a measure of exposure that represents an improvement over that offered by Adler and Dumas (1983) and Garner and Shapiro (1984): the ratio of the covariance between cash flows and the exchange rate in period t relative to the variance of all cash flows. The proposed measure allows for the separation between the Garner-Shapiro exposure and exposures to macro variables related to the exchange rate such as inflation and interest rates. The partial regression coefficient of interest rates on cash flows relative to the total variance of real cash flows is only one of the proposed new measures of exposure.

Their model defines exposure in terms of market price variables. Here the shareholders' real value of cash flow, the dependent variable, is regressed on the following independent variables: cash flows in period $t - 1$ and cash flow effects of unanticipated changes in the domestic price level, the foreign price level(s), the real exchange rate(s), the domestic and the foreign interest rate(s), and relative prices in the firm's commodity markets. The regression coefficients, in this case, are measures of the covariance between real cash flows and the specific regressor holding other variables constant.

This exposure measurement model is then translated in terms of underlying macroeconomic disturbances (variables) such as unexpected changes in the money supply and government budget deficits.

The drawbacks of the model are then analyzed and a disaggregation of cash flows is proposed. The results are cash flows divided into their business operation component, a depreciation shield component, and two financial cost components. The model is further adjusted to account for intertemporal relationships as well.

The Oxelheim-Wilhlborg model defines exposure on the firm level. The proposed disaggregation of cash flows can be carried further to deal with specific exposure, dealing, for example, with a specific borrowing or investment decision. The chapter does not deal with how this exposure or any other exposure should be covered.

Covering the foreign exchange exposure resulting from a specific foreign currency debt service stream is the subject of two chapters: one by W. Folks, Jr., and C. Kwok and the other by M. Granito and M. Kelley. The authors of these two chapters, unaware of the others' work, reached essentially the same conclusion: hedging in the forward market by rolling over short-term forward contracts can reduce the foreign exchange exposure significantly.

The Folks and Kwok chapter develops a methodology, "aggregate iterative covering," for covering the discounted value of the cash flow of a specific foreign currency debt service stream. The authors first demonstrate that the discounted value of the cash flows required to service the debt can be completely insulated from the effects of exchange rate fluctuations by a series of one-period–forward purchases, provided the forward premiums from period to period are assumed to be known for certain. Further, if the expected period-to-period exchange rate change equals the forward premiums, there is no reduction in the expected value of the discounted cash flow stream.

Where forward premiums are not known for certain, the methodology provides for a series of one-period–forward purchases of the discounted value of future debt service outflows, adjusted for the expected series of forward discounts prevailing in the marketplace. Since empirically the variance in forward premiums from year to year is substantially less than the variance in year-to-year rates of exchange rate change, the methodology should eliminate most of the uncertainty of the present value of debt servicing cash flows.

To demonstrate the efficacy of this methodology, a simulation model is constructed. An eight-year bullet maturity bond which is denominated in German marks and carries 6 percent annual coupon is taken as an example.

Using empirically developed estimates of the variance of year-to-year rate changes and forward premiums for the German mark, the authors show that the variance of the discounted value of bond servicing flows can be reduced by 95.3 percent under their proposed covering methodology.

Granito and Kelley start from a basis embedded in the interest immunization concept and show that the value of the exchange rate cover achieved under their hedging scheme depends on the relationship of the spot currency rate to the forward rate through time. This rate should theoretically equal the rate on a long-term forward contract should one have existed. What is being hedged is the present value of the exposed liability or asset.

Thus far, the focus has been on the issuer of securities. International investors who buy these securities (debt or equity) are motivated by the rates of return on the securities in the international markets *and* by the risk diversification possibilities these securities provide. The chapter by C. Eun and B. Resnick looks at international diversification from an interesting perspective. The authors point to a generally overlooked issue among students of international portfolio diversification: the fact that the true probability of international stock market returns are not known to the investors and thus may lead to suboptimality from using historical return data.

The authors evaluate the out-of-sample performance of the domestic and international portfolios under flexible exchange rates, and examine the actual and potential gains from international diversification. In spite of the adverse effect of the fluctuating exchange rates, every national investor can potentially benefit from international diversification. The actual gains associated with a particular investment strategy, however, tend to be substantially lower than the potential gains, and, in some cases, they turned out to be negative. This is a result of parameter uncertainty, or estimation risk. Unless investors know the "true" probability distributions of future stock market returns, they will be prevented from fully realizing the potential gains. This result emphasizes the importance of improving the accuracy with which input parameters are estimated. In fact, the existence of estimation risk may be responsible, at least in part, for the so-called "home-bias" in portfolio holdings.

The chapters by H. Schollhammer and O. Sand, and by S. Khoury, B. Dodin, and H. Takada, which were developed separately, look at the foundation of international portfolio diversification from a different perspective than that of Eun and Resnick. They attempt to measure the nature and strength of relationships across stock markets and their implications for international market efficiency, for international portfolio diversification, and for speculative opportunities and their degrees of profitability.

The Khoury, Dodin, and Takada chapter examines the dependence among five major stock markets in developed countries. National stock market indices denominated in dollars and developed by Capital Research Corporation are used to measure the relationship across the five markets. The countries considered are Canada, France, Germany, Japan, and the United States. The model used for testing the null hypothesis is the multivariate state space autoregressive moving average model developed on the basis of the Akaike information criterion. The empirical results show that the U.S. equity market leads those of Canada, Europe, and Japan. The financial markets of Europe and Japan lag behind the United States generally by one day. Significant contemporary correlation exists between the United States and Canada and also among France, Germany, and Japan. The U.S. lead is then expressed in a functional form allowing the forecast of inside prices in France, Germany, and Japan. The implications of the results are that the U.S. capital market index can be used as a proxy for world equity markets in an international capital asset pricing framework.

The Schollhammer and Sand chapter uses a much larger sample covering thirteen major industrial countries. Their research methodology is different in some respects from that employed by Khoury et al. The research framework of time series analysis employed by Schollhammer and Sand consists of identifying the univariate time series models for each of the variables in the data set (which is analogous to the first step in the Khoury et al. approach) and cross-correlating the residuals of univariate models over different time periods to investigate the lead–lag structure of the market. Their analysis does not proceed to model the dynamic relationship between the variables nor estimate parameters of the model. The major difference of research methodology between the two chapters thus lies in the step that follows the univariate time series analysis. Khoury et al. employ multivariate control analysis to investigate the multivariate relationship between the variables. This procedure allows them to identify and parameterize the model for all of the variables such that interrelationships among the variables are determined. Furthermore, the strength of various relationships is indicated by the parameter values. In summary, the Schollhammer and Sand approach may be characterized as a combined use of univariate time-series analysis and cross-correlation analysis, while the Khoury et al. approach is a multiple time-series analysis.

The Schollhammer and Sand chapter finds a significant positive correlation between inter- as well as intracontinental equity market indices. The correlations are low, however. The chapter also finds, consistent with the Khoury et al. study, that the U.S. equity market generally leads other national markets. Most lead–lag relationships documented are of one trading day or less, and consistent with acceptable the efficient market hypothesis.

The tour de force of the conference, however, involves the pricing of foreign exchange forwards, futures, options, and other more recent innovations in international financial markets. We were very fortunate in having some of the best scholars in the field present surveys and new research on these subjects. We do not exaggerate in our claim that these chapters are destined to achieve preeminence in the field.

K. Ramaswamy and S. Sundaresan have coauthored a chapter that, for the first time in the literature, considers both the spot exchange rate and the nominal interest rates in two countries as state variables in deriving explicit, closed-form pricing formulae for foreign exchange forwards and futures. The implications of these results to foreign exchange options and swaps are evident. In models that price derivative assets on foreign exchange, imposition of purchasing parity and interest rate parity (IRP) requires that the dynamics of the spot exchange rate depend on nominal interest rate differentials across the two countries. Also, the characteristics of forward and futures contracts require that the forward—futures price difference depends on the future one-period interest rates and the future spot exchange rate. While the extant literature does consider these aspects, the models (particularly those in stochastic continuous time) typically go on to assume that the stochastic processes of spot exchange rates, nominal interest rates, and price levels are independent of one another. Ramaswamy and Sundaresan account explicitly for these state-variable interdependencies, but to keep the models empirically tractable, they are forced to assume away the more indirect of these relationships. Specifically, they assume that the two nominal interest rates follow mean-reverting stochastic term structure processes (that is, short rates adjust to mean long rates at parametric speeds of adjustment), while the expected change in the spot exchange rate is assumed to be a linear function of the interest rate differential between the two countries. The variances of changes in interest rates and exchange rates are first assumed to be independent; later, they are allowed to vary with changes in local spot interest rates and spot exchange rates respectively.

The authors develop empirically verifiable expressions for the equilibrium forward exchange rate, its term structure, and the equilibrium futures exchange rate. They find when the above variances are assumed to be independent that the forward rate is a decreasing (increasing) function of the foreign (domestic) spot interest rate and of its volatility. The forward rate term structure can be upward-sloping, humped, or downward-sloping depending upon the location of the interest rate differential relative to other parameters. The futures rate is found to be affected by expected changes in the spot exchange rate (whereas the forward rate is not) as well as by the covariance between changes in the spot exchange rate and the interest rate differentials.

When the assumption of independence of the variances of spot exchange and interest rates is relaxed, the above conclusions are by and large valid, but further parametric assumptions are needed. The forward rate term structure is not easily characterized and future rates are found to have nonlinear relationships with contract maturities and interest rate differentials.

J. O. Grabbe (author of an original paper on foreign exchange option pricing in 1983) surveys the relatively young field of theoretical pricing of foreign currency options and provides an insightful and rather original framework for analyzing such contracts. He begins by classifying four types of European and four types of U.S. calls and puts: options on spots, options on futures, futures-style options on spots, and futures-style options on futures. (The latter two types involve daily mark-to-the-market types of cash flows rather than up-front premiums.) As of 1986, the last three types of European and the last category of American options on foreign exchange are not yet commonly traded.

Grabbe next discusses theoretical pricing relationships for European currency options. The argument behind them is the familiar Black-Scholes one of creating a "synthetic option" via a duplication portfolio composed of a combination of domestic and foreign currency discount bonds, which is continuously adjusted to duplicate the option payoff. An important point overlooked by Grabbe and illustrated by the work of Ramaswamy and Sundaresan is that while interest rate parity types of relationships are germane to these arbitrage-based models, the Levy-Wiener stochastic processes assumed for exchange rates are taken to be independent of interest rates; also interest rates themselves are not modeled to be stochastic or to have stochastic term structures.

Grabbe briefly discusses "range forwards" which involve the buyer in purchasing foreign currency at preset minimum and maximum exchange rates, respectively, if the future spot rate is less than either the maximum or minimum. Such a contract is equivalent to buying a European call on spot and selling a European put on the spot, where the strike price on the call is above that on the put. Options on futures and forwards are shown to be priced by the same relationships as those on spots with forwards/futures rates replacing spot rates in the formula. Again, the contractual differences between futures and forwards considered by Ramaswamy and Sundaresan are not incorporated here. Futures-style options on spot and on futures/forwards also have the same pricing formula as options on futures/forwards, except that the futures payoff states of the option are not discounted since no initial premium transfer occurs. Grabbe briefly refers to the literature on option pricing based on alternative probability distribution assumptions on spot exchange rate dynamics. He also discusses American option pricing bounds and numerical (binomial as well as other) procedures for solution of the second order partial differential equation that typically results in option pricing theory. He shows that American futures-style options on spots are the most valuable among the various types of currency options contracts. All types of American options dominate their European equivalents, except in the case of futures-style options on futures. First, passage options (which have payoffs only at the first occurrence of the underlying rate equaling the strike price) and perpetual American options (those that never mature) are also priced for foreign exchange rates. The empirical evidence on theoretical pricing models on currency spots and futures is finally summarized and the various partial derivatives of option prices (delta, lambda, gamma, theta, and elasticity) used in option position management are enumerated. By and large, the empirical tests on currency options appear to indicate that these markets (represented by the organized exchanges) are efficient, at least if nonmembers of these exchanges are assumed to do the trading. (Floor traders, on the other hand, might experience profit-making possibilities.)

J. H. McCulloch's chapter represents a major step in the direction of option pricing theory based on a fundamentally different concept on uncertainty than that embodied in the usual assumption that an option's underlying security is subject to lognormal price uncertainty. In Bachelier's time, it was believed that only the normal distribution could plausibly result from an infinite sum of independent and identically distributed (IID) random variables. Levy has since shown that the generalized central limit theorem (GCLT) leads to a much broader class of stable distributions, of which the normal is only a special case. Empirical evidence suggests that security returns (particularly in foreign exchange markets) tend more strongly to be leptokurtic (have considerably heavier tails on their probability distributions) and/or skewed than is consistent with the normal distribution. Stable distributions can encompass such distributional characteristics and, by virtue of the GCLT, can thereby play a major role in enabling option pricing theory to be more in tune with reality. Also, stable processes are infinitely divisible, so that stable returns over a discrete time interval can arise from the sum of contributing IID shocks over arbitrarily many subintervals. While the better-known call of Poisson-driven jump processes shares this property too, the stable processes are preferable as they account for both large jumps and continual movement, and use fewer parameters than the Poisson processes do.

The well-known Black-Scholes arbitrage argument cannot be applied to option pricing theory under log-stable uncertainty because of the infinite number of discontinuities that appear in the time path of the asset price. However, this characteristic implies that under log-stable uncertainty, options are no longer redundant state-contingent claims that they become under a lognormal diffusion process so that the existence of active options markets is longer a paradox. In terms of the mechanics of deriving option prices for log-stable processes, a major difficulty arises from the expected payoff on a call option being ordinarily infinite. A recent theorem by Zolotarev that overcomes this problem is used by McCulloch to derive closed-form solutions to European option prices for foreign exchange rates. Unfortunately, McCulloch in his derivation procedure has to take resort to the PPP theorem, which recent evidence shows is systematically violated. Nonetheless, his preliminary empirical results on the European formula seem to indicate that the resulting currency option prices are sometimes better approximations of reality than those resulting from European models under lognormal uncertainty (such as Grabbe, 1983).

P. Ritchken and M. Ferri present a new recursion-based model for the theoretical pricing of warrants, which are long-term options issued by the corporation. Warrants provide another application of optionlike features in international financial markets that is becoming increasingly popular, particularly in Eurobond markets. Warrants, despite possessing optionlike properties, are fundamentally different from ordinary options. Options in general are separate side bets so that their prices are independent of their volume of issuance, and they provide no specific advantage from sequential exercising strategies. Warrants, however, are securities issued by the firm and hence result in income that involves reinvestment decisions on the part of the firm as well as changes in its capital structure, which in turn have a circular impact on the value of outstanding warrants. Thus, whenever the value of the firm upon which contingent claims such as warrants and convertibles are to be priced cannot be taken to be exogenous to the pricing model, a recursive or simultaneous solution to the value of the claim and the firm is called for.

Ritchken and Ferri's model relaxes a major assumption in extant warrant pricing models: that warrant issuance does not alter the scale of operation of the firm since the warrant premiums are taken to be paid out as dividends to existing shareholders. The authors assume instead that all or part of the income from the warrants is used to increase the scale of existing projects and no dividends are declared. The options granted in exchange for this income are those on the after-conversion stock price of this larger firm. The greater is the fraction of warrant income retained by the firm, the more valuable is the warrant. This specification results in a simple closed-form solution to warrant prices using the Black-Scholes equation. A sensitivity analysis of the resulting price indicates that its value is quite sensitive to the fraction of income retained. Moreover, as the dilution factor increases, the difference between this price and those resulting from earlier models (such as that by Galai and Schneller, 1978) widens. Empirical comparisons of warrant prices with a simple dilution-adjusted Black-Scholes price indicate that warrants are significantly undervalued. The framework presented by Ritchken and Ferri is equally applicable to other forms of debt instruments, such as convertible bonds, and can be extended to the case of firms with more complex capital structures than they consider here.

M. Eaker and D. Grant address a relatively broad and important question: does trading in foreign currency futures enhance the volatility of the underlying spot exchange rate? The policy and trading implications of this question are far-reaching. They argue that since spot markets in currencies far outstrip futures markets in size (trading volume and time) and tend to be less restricted, and since the same agents trade in both markets, it is unlikely that one market is more volatile than the other or leads it in trading. If at all the volatility in the two markets is interdependent, it is because of specific circumstances linking the two. Eaker and Grant examine a sample of daily data from 1977 to 1983 to test the specific hypothesis that the means and variances of returns in spot exchange markets on the day before delivery of contracts in futures markets are greater than on other days since on these days futures-generated spot transactions proliferate; conversely, the mean and variance on delivery day and the two prior days should not differ from the mean and variance on other days. Their findings indicate that there are unusual price changes in the currency markets on the day prior to delivery. This is also the last day on which spot trades in European currencies can be transacted in order to satisfy delivery on a futures contract. The authors therefore conclude that trading in futures markets increases the volatility of spot exchange rates. It must be pointed out that the chapter does not attempt to test whether such distortionary effects are merely transitory or have a more permanent influence. After all, if such induced volatilities "smooth out" within normal hedging and speculative decision horizons and the arbitrage profit margins are low, economists can continue to claim that the ultimate effect on efficiency of spot exchange markets is negligible.

2
International Diversification and Multinational Banking

Alan M. Rugman
Shyan J. Kamath

ABSTRACT

This chapter applies recent conceptual work on the theory of the multinational enterprise to analyze the financial performance of the world's largest multinational banks in recent years. It is found that there is a significant positive relationship between the degree of multinationality and the level of profitability. It is also found that large multinational banks benefit from international diversification; that is, they have low risk in earnings, where risk is proxied by standard financial measures. While some difference in performance is detected between North American banks on the one hand and European and Japanese banks on the other, the overall benefits of international diversification are confirmed.

The profitability of the five largest Canadian banks nearly doubled between 1960 and 1980. This increased return was achieved with little increase in the risk of return, however measured. The improved performance of Canadian banking was accompanied by an increase in its multinationality, as measured by the foreign to total assets (F/T) ratio. In fact, the doubling of the return for the Canadian banks over the 1961–80 period was accompanied by a doubling of the F/T ratio. Is there a positive relationship between return and the F/T ratio in Canadian banking? What has been the relationship between return (F/T) and the riskiness of international banking? These issues will be the focus of this chapter. The return on equity (ROE), risk measures, and the F/T ratio of the five largest Canadian banks will be examined. Comparative ROE data for the largest U.S., European, and Japanese multinational banks will also be examined. The riskiness of these banks is also considered,

The research assistance provided by John McIlveen, Jocelyn M. Bennett, and Lorraine Daly is gratefully acknowledged. Helpful comments on an earlier version of this chapter were received from Arvind Jain, Jean-Claude Cosset, and Laurent Lampron.

as measured by the standard deviation of the ROE and in the degree of systematic and nonsystematic risk of a suitable proxy of bank risk.

The organization of the chapter is as follows. The first section briefly surveys the extant literature on multinational banking theory. The second section reviews and develops the theory of internalization as it applies to the multinational banking firm. The third evaluates the literature on the international diversification of bank assets in relation to other explanations of bank performance. The remainder of the chapter turns to empirical issues. The fourth section examines the increasing multinationality of Canadian banks over the 1961–80 period and the performance of these banks. The hypothesis that multinationality and ROE are positively related is investigated in this section as is the relationship between multinationality and the risk of earnings. A comparison of the return and risk performance of Canadian, U.S., European, and Japanese multinational banks is presented in the fifth section. A more technical comparative analysis of the extent of diversifiable and nondiversifiable risk is reported in the sixth section. Summary and conclusions are provided in the final section.

The Theory of Multinational Banking

A number of approaches have been used to explain the existence and growth of multinational banking. Aliber (1976) explains the growth of multinational banking by comparing the efficiency of banks in different countries. He suggests that there are two ways in which the efficiency of international banks can be analyzed. The first approach, based on international trade theory, suggests that banks located in countries with a comparative advantage in the provision of "bank products" will be more efficient and hence more competitive. Consequently, they will be more successful in international banking. Barriers to trade in money permit the persistence of spreads in different countries and the maintenance of relative efficiencies. The second approach, based on industrial organization theory, evaluates the market structure of banking in different countries by comparing the spreads between borrowing and lending rates. It predicts that bank spreads would be higher in countries where concentration ratios are high. The narrower is the spread, the more efficient a country's banking system is, and the more successful its banks are likely to be in the international banking market.

Grubel (1977) considers the source of comparative advantage in multinational banking by examination of multinational retail, multinational service, and multinational wholesale banking separately. In this analysis, multinational retail banking is predicated on the existence of firm-specific advantages (FSAs) similar to those that underlie foreign direct investment (see Rugman et al., 1985) such as management expertise and marketing know-how. Multinational service banking on the other hand is the result of long-standing relationships, contacts, and access to information at low cost built upon traditional business dealings in the home country. As multinational companies go abroad, their banks follow them. As regards multinational wholesale banking, economies of scale in funding, investing, and information gathering as well as the exemption of foreign currency banking from most domestic banking regulations provide a comparative advantage in performing this function worldwide.

Fieleke (1977) adopts a similar approach in explaining multinational banking but also attempts to test whether U.S. banks are profit maximizers, whether multinational banking leads to the diversification of risks, and therefore whether this constitutes a motive for multinational banking. He does not find evidence to support either proposition, although he does find weak support for a positive relationship between the rate of return on net worth and international involvement. His results on the test conducted to examine the relationship between the degree of multinationality and the variability of returns reveal a positive relationship, contrary to the hypothesized relationship. Fieleke attributes his results to the inadequacy of the available data. He also finds statistical support for the proposition that U.S. banks go abroad largely to serve U.S. nonbanking firms abroad.

An industrial organization approach is taken by Giddy (1983). He focuses on the exogenous market imperfections in international banking. These imperfections can take on a character that is regulatory or natural (meaning a lack of a market for information or other specific advantages). In the absence of these market imperfections, all international banking would be at arm's length. However, the costs of the regulatory environment and the lack of a market to sell country-specific prestige and the bank's brand name induce offshore banking, largely in the "tax haven" nations. Finally, these same market imperfections coupled with a low degree of regulation for a foreign bank operating in a host country (no or little territorial limits, or reserve or deposit insurance requirements) encourage host country international banking, essentially foreign direct investment (FDI). Host country multinational banking also has the added feature of internalizing or transferring abroad a set of assets, namely the knowledge skills developed at home by the banks, loan evaluation expertise and personal contacts with multinational enterprises (MNEs), home country information services, marketing skills, and the bank's brand name.

Finally, the theory of internalization has been applied to explain the activities of multinational banks. Gray and Gray (1981) examine the welfare implications of multinational banking based on the motivation for multinational banking in terms of market imperfections. Internalization theory itself focuses on market imperfections, which can be either natural or unnatural, to explain FDI. Such a version of internalization theory of the MNE was applied to multinational banking by Rugman (1979, 1981). The success of the linkage of internalization theory to multinational banking is considered in the next section.

The Theory of the Multinational Enterprise

Rugman (1981) has argued that the theory of internalization is a general theory of the multinational enterprise. This approach can be extended to provide a coherent theory of multinational banking. Internalization theory explains the existence of and provides predictive power for an explanation of the activities of MNEs. The theory focuses on variables exogenous to the MNE which can be either natural or unnatural (government-induced) market imperfections. Also central to the theory is the fact that each and every MNE has as the reason for its existence a firm-specific advantage (FSA). This FSA is usually in the form of a knowledge asset (whether it be managerial, marketing, technological, or some other area of expertise); the FSA is acquired at considerable cost.

In order to earn a reasonable return on this asset investment, the MNE is often impelled to seek out foreign markets due to domestic regulation and the rigors of global competition. The MNE has three basic modes available to assess foreign markets: exporting, licensing, and foreign direct investment. Exporting is inhibited either directly by unnatural market imperfections (such as tariffs and quotas) or indirectly by natural market imperfections (such as buyer uncertainty and exchange losses) which increase the transaction costs of conducting business across national boundaries. Licensing is frequently premature for the MNE afraid of the possible dissipation of its FSA. The lack of a market to price the FSA because of its nature as a public good and the risk of its dissipation leads to the growing prevalence of the internalization process. The MNE creates an internal market where propriety control over its FSA is maintained and it exploits the FSA by engaging in FDI, essentially monitoring the use of the FSA by organizational control in foreign markets. In this manner, the MNE is an efficient response to both natural and unnatural market imperfections. It substitutes for international trade and/or licensing when such imperfections exist.

The internal market has costs associated with it. To maintain the FSA's propriety, management of it must be centralized. Yet the MNE incurs additional costs in servicing a foreign market largely as a result of informational or regulatory requirements and this necessitates a certain degree of decentralization. The costs of governance of the internal market can negate the potentially higher returns. Internalization then, predicts that MNEs will not earn excessive profits relative to domestic firms, despite incentives for rent seeking in oligopolistic types of market structures. However, the internalization of the MNE also offers somewhat reduced risks, as offsetting market covariances across nations reduce the country-specific risk of any one nation in the MNE's investment portfolio.

The implications of internalization theory are fundamentally the same when applied to multinational banking. Table 2–1 summarizes ten of the more popular explanations for the existence of multinational banking. These explanations of international banking can be related to the four main parameters of internalization—knowledge FSAs, other intangible FSAs (both of which arise out of natural market imperfections), government regulation (unnatural market imperfections), and international diversification, a by-product of internalization.

The first three items in table 2–1 are banking FSAs in knowledge. Managerial and marketing expertise, client relationships, creditworthiness, and home national market information are all generated in the home nation. The bank faces the decision of whether to sell or internalize this knowledge. Since it cannot be sold, at least not on any open market, the bank chooses to in-

Table 2–1
Internalization Reasons for Multinational Banking

1. *Low marginal costs*—managerial and marketing knowledge developed at home can be used abroad with low marginal costs.

2. *Knowledge advantage*—the foreign bank subsidiary can draw on the parent bank's knowledge of personal contacts and credit investigations for use in that foreign market.

3. *Home nation information services*—local firms in a foreign market may be able to obtain more complete information on trade and financial markets in the multinational bank's home nation than is otherwise obtainable from a foreign domestic bank.

4. *Prestige*—Very large multinational banks have perceived high prestige, liquidity, and deposit safety that can be used to attract clients abroad.

5. *Regulation advantage*—Multinational banks are often not subject to the same regulations as domestic banks. There may be reduced need to publish adequate financial information, lack of required deposit insurance and reserve requirements on foreign currency deposits, and the absence of territorial restrictions (that is, U.S. banks may not be restricted to state of origin).

6. *Wholesale defensive strategy*—Banks follow their multinational customers abroad to prevent the erosion of their clientele to foreign banks seeking to service the multinational's foreign subsidiaries.

7. *Retail defensive strategy*—Multinational banks prevent erosion by foreign banks of the travelers check, tourist, and foreign business market.

8. *Transaction costs*—By maintaining foreign branches and foreign currency balances, banks may reduce transaction costs and foreign exchange risk on currency conversion if government controls can be circumvented.

9. *Growth*—Growth prospects in a home nation may be limited by a market largely saturated with the services offered by domestic banks.

10. *Risk reduction*—Greater stability of earnings is possible with international diversification. Offsetting business and monetary policy cycles across nations reduce the country-specific risk of any one nation.

ternalize the knowledge. The multinational bank, much like the MNE, after having incurred the costs of knowledge development at home, can now exploit this knowledge in foreign markets at a lower marginal cost than host country banking firms which are developing the knowledge in their home market.

The fourth item is an example of other intangible FSAs. The prestige of a bank embodied in its brand name or goodwill spills over into foreign markets much like the way advertising on U.S. television stations close to the Canadian border reaches Canadian markets. The MNE would not risk licensing its brand name to a licensee whose quality or service practices it could not control. The risk of dissipation of the FSA is too great. The bank and the MNE will internalize the brand name and exploit it abroad through FDI.

Items 5 through 9 represent the banking industries' efficient internal response to government regulation. The regulation advantage enjoyed by multinational banks appears to be an anomaly in that FDI is directly (unintentionally or not) encouraged by host government regulations penalizing domestic banks. It is similar to the situation when a tariff encourages FDI in order to avoid the tariff. Whether the tariff penalizes domestic producers in terms of long-run efficiency versus a captive market is debatable. However, it is clear that consumers are penalized by the tariff. Both of these types of regulation penalize domestic sectors and encourage FDI by multinationals.

Wholesale and retail defensive strategies are examples of government-induced market failures. Governments erect barriers to the free flow of funds across national boundaries; hence, there is a need to service a multinational client's foreign subsidiaries from within the host nation. In the absence of these barriers, the transactions costs of international trade in banking services would be less than the cost of FDI, in this case foreign branching. Association with foreign domestic banks to service the multinationals risks dissipation of the knowledge FSAs described in the first three items in table 2–1.

The transaction costs of the eighth item also arise out of government barriers to funds flows and attempts to regulate the exchange rate. By maintaining foreign currency balances in both the home and host nation, government barriers may be circumvented by dealing in a currency foreign to the country of origin. The ninth item contains elements of both natural and unnatural market imperfections. Limited growth prospects in a single nation may be the result of natural business cycles or market failure (that is, for knowledge), or they may be government-induced through strict monetary policy or territorial limits. In order to compensate for the investment in FSAs, banks will seek foreign markets when the home market is restricting or has failed.

Risk reduction through international diversification (item 10) has been described as a by-product of internalization. In instances where interventionist governments increase the country-specific risk to unacceptable levels, international diversification is a subset of internalization. MNEs and banks are merely reacting to government-induced exogenous variables that have placed restrictions on the use of their FSAs in the home market. To the extent that international diversification reduces systematic risk or can reduce nonsystematic risk at a lower cost than the individual investor, this may constitute a valid motivation for multinational banking. This aspect is investigated in the following analysis.

Multinational Banking and International Risk Diversification

A number of studies have examined the impact of international banking operations on the risk and return characteristics of the multinational banking firm. Several studies have used portfolio theory to explain the impact of international operations. From a portfolio perspective, the optimal policy for a multinational bank is to maximize profit for a given level of risk or to minimize risk for a given level of profit. A convergent conclusion of the empirical literature in this area (with one exception) is that the total portfolio risk of both domestic and foreign portfolio assets has been lower than the risk of a purely domestic portfolio, while the return on international assets may or may not be higher than the rate of return on domestic assets.

Khoury (1978) was one of the first to examine the adequacy of the profit maximization hypothesis in explaining the multinationalization of the banking firm. In a subsequent book, Khoury (1980) examines the idea of risk diversification as a motive for the international expansion of the multinational bank. He examines the portfolio theory hypothesis that acquisition of assets in a market whose risk is not perfectly correlated with the bank's domestic market will allow banks to improve the risk/return profile of their assets. Using data for the 1970–77 period on thirteen leading U.S. banks, Khoury (1980, chapter 7) finds that the domestic and foreign assets of these banks exhibit not dissimilar returns and risks but are negatively correlated with one another. In studying the data for the thirteen banks, he also finds that all but one achieved risk diversification through international expansion. He concludes that "limited as the data base may be, it can still be concluded that the diversification model does constitute a reasonable explanation of the multinationalization of the banking firm." Note that Fieleke's (1977) related work on thirteen U.S. banks for the 1970–76 period (discussed in a previous section) finds that the extent of foreign involvement does not affect the variance of earnings of these banks significantly, though there is some evidence to support the higher profitability of foreign operations.

Rugman (1979) tests the hypothesis that firms accept a lower rate of return from overseas because foreign investment lowers their portfolio risk.

He calculates the variations in earnings of oil, mining, industrial, and large banking firms for both the United States and Canada. His tests on 1962–76 data show that the risks of earnings for the banks (as proxied by the standard deviations of these earnings) are less than those of the other major sectors in either economy, while the mean rate of return is about the same as that for the other sectors. He therefore concludes that multinational banks benefit from stable earnings. Another measure of risk used, the beta coefficient in the capital asset pricing model context, does not perform well. He attributes this result to the data problems affecting the specification of the market factor in the analysis.

Cosset and Lampron (1982) test the influence of international banking operations on the return and risk of Canadian chartered banks, using the rate of return on assets, since this permits a distinction between international and domestic operations. They find the five major multinational Canadian banks to be more profitable than the smaller domestic banks over the 1971–79 period. However, their results also indicate that the average return on international assets is lower than the rate of return on domestic assets. They further investigate the risk of operations in the domestic and foreign sectors and find that although the standard deviation of returns on international assets is higher than on domestic assets for the 1971–79 period, the standard deviation of returns on total assets is lower than for the separate measures. They conclude that by developing international operations, Canadian banks have reduced the total risk of their operations, which is consistent with the risk diversification hypothesis.

Cosset and Lampron also find a significant negative coefficient of correlation between the percentage of assets held in foreign currencies and the standard deviation of the rates of return of the Canadian banks, corroborating Rugman's (1979) evidence on the international diversification hypothesis. They also evaluate the systematic risk of the Canadian banks using the capital asset pricing model. They distinguish between an international beta and a domestic beta. The market index they use consists of large Canadian manufacturing and financial firms. Their results reveal that the five largest multinational Canadian banks all have systematic risk less than one, suggesting that by international diversification, earnings have been stabilized over time and systematic risk reduced. Unfortunately, the results present no significance tests on the beta coefficient. In a related but purely empirical paper relating numerous financial ratios to the ROEs of Canadian banks, Peters (1985) finds a very significant statistical relationship between the ratio of foreign currency loans to equity and rates of ROE.

The issue of systematic (nondiversifiable) and nonsystematic (diversifiable) risk has been emphasized by Shapiro (1982) but it has not been considered adequately in the empirical work on international banking. Shapiro calls on modern financial theory to state that, since risk is based on the systematic component of return variability in the context of the market portfolio and investors are able to diversify away firm-specific risk, then the market will only price systematic risk. Unless the multinational bank can reduce its systematic risk through its foreign activities (and at a lower cost than its shareholders), then the bank should not be concerned with the variability of returns on individual loans or with correlations between returns on different loans in the bank's portfolio, but only with maximizing returns adjusted for systematic risk. Nevertheless, Shapiro points out that since banks can go bankrupt, other risks including total bank risk ought also to be considered. In order to determine the effect of foreign loans on the variance of the bank's earnings, the covariance between foreign loans and domestic loans must also be known. If the covariance between foreign and domestic assets returns is less than the variance of returns on domestic or foreign assets, and if the foreign assets have higher returns than domestic assets, then diversification into foreign assets reduces the bankruptcy risk of the multinational bank.

Only a few studies have attempted to deal with the issue of systematic and nonsystematic risk in the international banking context. Goodman (1981) uses proxy variables to examine the extent of these risks for individual countries on loans made to the developing countries by official and commercial agencies. This investigation is carried out in the context of the Sharpe market index model. The results show that by combining loans from different countries, a large part of the unsystematic risk can be eliminated.

Kamath and Jensen (1983) independently developed and implemented a modified Sharpe index model similar to Goodman's in the country-risk context but extended this framework to the analysis of the banks' risk using the capital-asset ratio as the relevant focus variable. Their results indicate that the major component of total risk for the world's multinational banks is nonsystematic.

Kamath and Tilley (1985) use two different ratios (namely the return on assets ratio and the capital-asset ratio) to capture different aspects of bank risk in the Sharpe index model context to rank the major multinational banks by the degree of their systematic and nonsystematic risk. Their study covers thirty-five multinational banks from ten countries over the "debt crisis" decade (1973–83). They find that, as a group, the five largest Canadian banks exhibit a low degree of systematic risk as compared to the selected group of multinational banks.

Walter (1981) focuses on some of the difficulties that arise when attempting to apply portfolio theory to international lending (and hence international banking). Some of the major difficulties are:

1. The lack of an adequate measure of expected return on a loan since returns may come in forms other than interest charges (front-end fees, for example).

2. The rate charged on a loan may reflect a bank's effort to maintain or start a relationship with a borrower rather than a market-determined rate.

3. The structure of the probability distribution of the return on a loan constrains the applicability of portfolio theory to international lending. Returns on loans are contractually limited so that the distribution of possible rates of return on a particular loan is heavily weighted on the downside. This makes it difficult to hedge one loan with another, even if the returns are inversely correlated. However, this problem is alleviated to a large extent if a broader view of expected returns including fees and possible future earnings is taken, thus creating some upside potential for a loan.

4. The low level of flexibility that a loan has as an investment creates a further difficulty in the bank's management of its loan portfolio. Since loans are not nearly as divisible as stocks and bonds and to a large extent cannot be bought and sold until maturity, this creates a certain lumpiness in the portfolio.

5. With regard to applying portfolio theory in the assessment of country risk in the international lending context, defaults and reschedulings create situations of economic loss for the lender, especially where the lender is effectively locked in and cannot restructure a portfolio out of the exposed assets in question.

In the light of these difficulties, Bennett (1984) focuses on the management of a loan portfolio and emphasizes the importance of addressing the problem of covariance between loans, which it is necessary to know in order to construct an efficient portfolio. He develops an approach of incorporating a borrower's credit rating into the risk of a loan and of adjusting the portfolio to reflect the loan's effect on the risk of the overall portfolio. Even though the method is complicated and is difficult to use for a bank with thousands of loans worldwide, Bennett presents a method of dealing with this problem by suggesting the grouping of loans into areas of high covariance, which he calls risk concentrations. Such grouping makes the analysis more manageable.

It can be seen that the literature on the international diversification motive for multinational banking is relatively new and open for further synthesis. The studies that exist tend to be limited in their scope in terms of examining one dimension of international diversification while ignoring another. This chapter attempts to integrate and extend the insights of the various papers surveyed here by analyzing these issues more comprehensively in the context of multinational banking during the 1961–80 period.

International Diversification and Multinational Banking

This section examines the relationship between the increased degree of multinationality of Canadian banks and their level and variability of profits. The role of Canadian banks as agents for international diversification is also explored.

There has been a remarkable increase in the international operations of these banks; the ratio of foreign to total assets has more than doubled over the 1961–80 period for each bank. Table 2–2 provides a summary of the growth of the international operations of Canadian banks over this period. It can be seen that international assets as a percentage of total assets increased from 18 percent in 1961 to 39 percent in 1980. Over the same period, individual Canadian banks have enjoyed the benefits of international diversification in the form of higher profits for a low and stable risk of earnings, as this section will demonstrate.

In order to examine the hypothesis of growing profitability with increasing internationalism, the following regression was run using data for the five largest Canadian banks for the twenty-year period 1961–80:

$$\pi = a_i + b_i \, (F/T) + e \qquad (2.1)$$

where:

π = profit rate (net income after tax divided by the value of stockholders' equity),
F/T = ratio of foreign to total assets,
a_i, b_i = coefficients to be estimated, and
e = error term with the usual properties.

The results obtained by running this regression were as follows:

$$\pi = 0.0899 + 41.60 \, (F/T)$$
$$(10.53) \qquad (2.2)$$
$$\text{adjusted } R^2 = 85.3\%$$

These results suggest that as Canadian banks have become increasingly multinational in the past twenty years, they have experienced a statistically significant increase (as shown by the t value) in the level of profits. Indeed, over the 1961–80 period, mean profits for the five largest banks more than doubled from 6.8 percent to 14.44 percent. However, these profits are not excessive, since they are similar to those earned in manufacturing industries. For

Table 2–2
**Multinationality of Canadian Banking: Foreign
and Domestic Assets as Percentages of Total
Assets, 1961–80**

Year	Foreign	Domestic
1980	39%	61%
1979	36	64
1978	35	65
1977	32	68
1976	30	70
1975	29	71
1974	29	71
1973	29	71
1972	26	74
1971	27	73
1970	29	71
1969	27	73
1968	21	79
1967	20	80
1966	20	80
1965	19	81
1964	22	78
1963	19	81
1962	19	81
1961	18	82

Source: Bank of Canada, *Monthly Review,* 1981.
Note: Calculated on year-end assets for all Canadian chartered banks.

example, the eighteen largest Canadian multinational enterprises earned a
12.00 percent return on equity over the 1970–83 period (and 11.64 percent
over the 1971–81 period). Where the Canadian banks have done better is in
their enjoyment of stable earnings. Over the 1961–80 period, the standard
deviation of earnings was under 2.98 percent, while for the Canadian MNEs,
it was 5.8 percent over the 1970–83 period. For the data on Canadian MNEs,
see Rugman and McIlveen (1985).

Table 2–3 reports data on the performance of the five largest Canadian
banks for 1961–80. Profits are captured by the return on equity, defined here
as net income after tax and appropriations for losses divided by the value of
shareholders' equity. These profits have increased steadily over the past two
decades as shown in tables 2–4 and 2–5, where the twenty year period 1961–
80 is divided into two subperiods. Table 2–4 divides the period into three

Table 2–3
Performance of the Five Largest Canadian Banks: Return on Equity, 1961–80

	Royal	*CIBC*	*B. of M.*	*BNS*	*TD*	*Avg. ROE Equal Wt.*
1980	11.4%	12.8%	14.6%	11.9%	13.6%	12.86%
1979	12.3	17.9	17.0	10.9	14.3	14.48
1978	12.8	16.9	16.5	11.8	13.5	14.30
1977	11.6	17.0	14.6	11.4	12.2	13.36
1976	12.6	17.3	14.0	11.4	12.5	13.56
1975	13.5	16.4	18.0	13.6	13.5	15.00
1974	12.0	12.2	11.2	11.1	14.4	12.18
1973	11.8	11.1	14.6	11.1	12.0	12.12
1972	11.6	10.7	14.6	11.5	12.9	12.26
1971	10.8	9.6	11.2	11.3	12.2	11.02
1970	11.4	10.8	11.8	9.4	11.7	11.02
1969	10.8	10.3	11.8	10.5	11.6	11.00
1968	9.8	9.5	7.8	9.6	10.3	9.40
1967	8.7	8.0	8.8	8.3	9.1	8.58
1966	8.1	7.7	8.6	7.8	8.4	8.12
1965	7.0	7.5	8.3	7.2	7.9	7.58
1964	7.3	7.7	8.1	6.9	7.4	7.48
1963	7.1	7.5	7.8	6.3	7.3	7.20
1962	6.9	7.3	7.5	7.1	7.2	7.20
1961	6.8	6.9	7.0	6.7	6.7	6.82
Mean	10.21	11.25	11.69	9.79	10.93	
Standard deviation	2.28	3.85	3.57	2.16	2.64	

Average mean: 10.77

Average standard deviation: 2.90

Source: Annual reports.
Note: Return on equity is defined as net income after tax and appropriations for losses divided by the value of shareholders' equity.

seven-year periods (with the year 1981 added in). Return on equity almost doubled between the 1961–67 period and the 1975–81 period. At the same time, the variability of earnings as proxied by the standard deviation also almost doubled, although the rate of increase falls in the late 1970s as shown in table 2–5, which consists of four five-year subperiods. It can be seen that the risk of earnings actually fell in the 1976–80 subperiod, after peaking in the early seventies. Mean earnings also stabilized in the later years.

Thus, it can be seen that the five largest Canadian banks have signifi-

Table 2–4
Performance of the Five Largest Canadian Banks: Mean and Standard
Deviation of Profits by Seven-Year Subperiods, 1961–81

	Mean	*Standard Deviation*
1975–81	13.99%	1.14%
1968–74	11.97	1.22
1961–67	7.56	0.63

Source: Annual reports.

Table 2–5
Performance of the Five Largest Canadian Banks: Mean and Standard
Deviation of Profits by Five-Year Subperiods, 1961–80

	Mean	*Standard Deviation*
1976–80	13.71%	1.05%
1971–75	12.52	1.70
1966–70	9.63	1.44
1961–65	7.26	0.36

Source: Annual reports.

cantly increased their profitability as measured by the return on equity over
the 1961–80 period, a time when they have increased the international proportion of their assets. This increase in profitability has been in line with the
increase in profitability of other sections of the Canadian economy, particularly the multinational manufacturing firms, while the multinational Canadian banks have gained from the greater stability of their earnings, compared
to the other multinationals. There has been an increasing variability of profits
over the study period, but this has stabilized in the latter quarter of the period
when the largest increases in the international proportion of bank assets took
place.

A Comparative Analysis of Canadian, U.S.,
European, and Japanese Multinational Banks

To add perspective to this analysis in this section, we compare the performance of the largest multinational banks in Canada, the United States, Europe, and Japan. Table 2–6 summarizes the performance of the twenty largest
U.S. commercial banking companies over the same 1961–80 period as was
examined for the Canadian banks. These banks are all multinational, with

Table 2–6
Performance of the Twenty Largest Commercial Banks in the United States: Return on Equity, 1961–80

	Mean	*Standard Deviation*
Citicorp	12.15%	2.23%
Bank of America	13.55	1.92
Chase Manhattan	10.94	2.00
Manufacturers Hanover	11.58	1.84
J. P. Morgan	12.23	2.70
Continental Illinois	11.99	1.70
Chemical Bank	10.67	0.91
Bankers Trust New York	11.40	2.96
Western Bankcorp	11.04	2.57
First Chicago	10.28	1.87
Security Pacific	10.38	1.87
Wells Fargo	10.83	1.89
Crocker National	11.75	1.95
Charter New York[a]	10.87	1.44
Marine Midland	9.57	3.46
Mellon National	9.78	1.20
First National Boston	10.78	1.44
Northwest Bancorp	11.96	1.66
First National Bancshares	13.31	2.32
First Bank System	12.11	1.97
Average	11.35	2.00

Source: Various annual issues of *Fortune* ("The *Fortune* Directory of the 50 Largest Commercial Banking Companies").
[a]Name changed to Irving Bank Corporation, October 17, 1979.

overseas offices and branches accounting for a high proportion of foreign assets. The mean return on equity for the twenty U.S. banks of 11.35 percent is insignificantly higher than the five Canadian banks' mean of 1 percent, while the risk of earnings at a standard deviation of 2 percent is insignificantly lower.

The U.S. bank data serve to reinforce the hypothesis that multinational banks have stable earnings (see Rugman, 1979). Over the 1961–80 period, the variation in earnings of 2 percent is remarkably low—especially in comparison to other multinational enterprises, whose risk of earnings is between 3 and 5 percent. For example, the 50 largest U.S. multinational enterprises earned 13.46 percent on equity over the 1970–79 period, but with a standard deviation of 3.28 percent. These data are calculated from *Fortune*'s annual survey of the 500 largest U.S. corporations. If the time period is extended back to 1960, similar results occur in that there is a greater level of risk but a similar level of earnings for U.S. multinational enterprises as compared to U.S. multinational banks.

Tables 2–7 and 2–8 report data for the largest European and Japanese multinational banks. Each of these banks has at least six foreign-based subsidiaries and therefore is a multinational. Difficulties in determining the values of shareholders' equity were encountered due to the different accounting methods used in each country. Wherever possible, shareholders' equity was defined as capital plus reserves plus retained earnings plus minority interests.

It can be seen from the tables that the seventeen European banks have a mean profit of 9.87 percent and standard deviation of 2.34 percent. The twelve Japanese banks perform slightly better, with a mean return on equity of 10.58 percent and standard deviation of 2.48 percent. Thus, the slightly higher risk of the Japanese banks is offset by a higher rate of return. These comments need to be qualified by noting that the performance of the European banks is not uniform. There appear to be cross-country variations, for example, those between the British and Swiss banks. Furthermore, the recent

Table 2–7
Performance of the Largest European Banks: Return on Equity, 1971–80

	Mean	*Standard Deviation*
Banque Nationale de Paris	10.69%	2.36%
Dresdner Bank, Frankfurt	9.32	1.41
National Westminster Bank Ltd., London	11.77	4.02
Barclay's Bank Ltd., London	11.04	3.08
Deutsche Bank, A.G.	9.35	1.48
Commerzbank, Dusseldorf	8.66	2.69
Bayerische Vereinsbank, Munich	7.44	1.08
Algemene Bank, Nederland, N.V.	12.88	2.59
Midland Bank Ltd., London	9.68	2.77
Amsterdam-Rotterdam Bank, Amsterdam	11.37	0.72
Lloyds Bank Ltd., London	10.20	3.34
Standard Chartered Bank Ltd., England	10.20	3.34
Bankque Bruxelles, Lambert, Brussels	7.22	2.13
Union Bank of Switzerland	7.44	0.72
Swiss Bank Corp.	7.56	0.99
Societe Generale de Banque, S.A., Brussels	12.05	5.25
Banca Commerciale, Italiana, Milan	10.64	10.05
Average	9.87	2.34

Source: Moody's *Bank and Finance Manuals*, Moody's *International Manual*.

Table 2–8
Performance of Japanese Banks: Return on Equity 1971–80

	Mean	*Standard Deviation*
Dai-ichi Kangyo Bank Ltd.	10.02%	2.94%
Fuji Bank Ltd., Tokyo	10.76	3.48
Sumitomo Bank Ltd.	8.09	1.97
Mitsubishi Bank Ltd., Tokyo	11.34	3.03
Sanwa Bank Ltd., Osaka	10.29	2.63
Industrial Bank of Japan Ltd., Tokyo	12.75	3.41
Long-Term Credit Bank of Japan Ltd., Tokyo	10.85	0.99
Bank of Tokyo Ltd.	10.47	0.83
Tokai Bank Ltd., Nagoya	14.42	6.03
Daiwa Bank Ltd.	10.11	2.73
Nippon Credit Bank Ltd.	10.09	0.88
Kyowa Bank Ltd.	7.80	0.80
Average	10.58	2.48

Sources: Moody's *Bank and Finance Manuals* and Moody's *International Manual.*

time trend of profitability is more favorable for European than for Japanese banks.

Table 2–9 compares the performance of all the banks studied. In addition, it provides a mean and standard deviation of return on equity for the five largest banks in each country over the 1971—80 period. It can be seen from the table that the five largest U.S. banks have a higher return than the Canadian banks and a lower risk of earnings, but the difference is not significant. But for the 1971–80 period, there is little difference between the two, indicating an improvement on the part of the Canadian banks. The Canadian banks show a considerable rise in mean return from 10.77 percent to 13.11 percent and a substantial decrease in risk from 2.90 percent to 1.57 percent during this period. The five largest European and Japanese banks did not perform as well as their counterparts in the United States and Canada over the 1971–80 period. Their returns are lower (10.43 and 10.10 percent, respectively) and the risk of profits higher (2.47 and 2.81 percent, respectively). These results can be explained by differences in regulation and institutional structures in the banking industries in these two areas.

These findings are supported by the results of tests of significant differences between the means. These tests were performed on the four populations of banks: Canada, United States, Europe, and Japan. The results confirmed that there was no significant difference in profit rates between the five largest Canadian and U.S. banks in the twenty-year period or in the past decade. However, the Canadian banks outperformed their European and Japanese

Table 2–9
International Comparison of Bank Performance: Return on Equity, 1961–80

	Mean	*Standard Deviation*
5 Canadian banks		
1971–80	13.11%	1.57%
1961–80	10.77	2.90
20 U.S. banks		
1971–80	12.33	1.89
1961–80	11.36	2.00
5 largest U.S. banks		
1971–80	13.55	1.46
1961–80	12.09	2.14
17 European banks		
1971–80	9.87	2.34
5 largest European banks		
1971–80	10.43	2.47
12 Japanese banks		
1971–80	10.58	2.48
5 largest Japanese banks		
1971–80	10.10	2.81

Sources: Moody's *Bank and Finance Manuals;* Moody's *International Manual;* various annual issues of *Fortune* ("The *Fortune* Directory of the 50 Largest Commercial Banking Companies"); annual reports of Canadian banks.

counterparts over the 1971—80 period since mean profits were significantly higher. Furthermore, U.S. multinational banks also earned significantly higher profits than the European and Japanese multinational banks identified in this research. There was not a significant difference in earnings between the five largest European and Japanese banks.

In conclusion, an examination of the performance of major Canadian, U.S., European, and Japanese banks does not refute the hypothesis that multinationality provides a means of efficient diversification of risks inherent in domestic asset portfolios.

Systematic and Nonsystematic Risk in Multinational Banking

As demonstrated by Shapiro (1982), investors will price only the systematic risk of a banking or industrial firm since they can diversify away any firm-specific nonsystematic risk in their portfolios. To the extent then that multinational banks can lower systematic risk through their foreign activities and reduce nonsystematic risk at a lower cost than investors can, such banks are efficient vehicles for risk diversification. To the extent that there are entry, size, and structural barriers in international financial markets and information gaps exist, multinational banks may provide a more efficient means of international risk diversification than is available to the individual investor (see Dufey and Srinivasalu, 1984).

In this section, we examine the systematic and nonsystematic components of the total risk of major Canadian, U.S., European, and Japanese banks. Related empirical work is reported in Kamath and Jensen (1983) and Kamath and Tilley (1985). The two components of risk are separated using the Sharpe market (index) model (see Sharpe, 1970). Systematic risk is the risk associated with factors affecting the asset portfolio as a whole and cannot be diversified away. Nonsystematic risk is associated with factors affecting the individual asset or firm under consideration and can be reduced or completely eliminated by diversifying the portfolio across assets subject to the differential movements of returns in the portfolio.

The Sharpe index model assumes that the return on an asset is related to the level of one or more suitable indexes. The actual level of the index is assumed to be uncertain. Thus, for the asset i, the model can be written as:

$$R_i = a_i + b_iI + e_i$$
$$R_i = \text{actual return on } i$$
$$I = \text{actual level of the index} \qquad (2.3)$$
$$a_i, b_i = \text{coefficients}$$
$$e_i = \text{error term}$$

Since neither I nor e_i can be predicted with certainty, an expected value and standard deviation are used. Under certain standard assumptions, the variance of asset i can be broken down into systematic and nonsystematic components,

$$\sigma_i^2 = (b_i\sigma_I)^2 + \sigma_{e_i}^2$$

where,

$$\sigma_i^2 = \text{ddvldgmx jr dooxb 1} = \text{total risk}$$
$$\sigma_I^2 = \text{variance of index I}$$
$$(b_i\sigma_I) = \text{systematic risk}$$
$$\sigma_{e_i} = \text{nonsystematic risk}$$

When return data on individual assets are available, equation 2.3 can be regressed for each individual bank and the systematic and nonsystematic components of risk determined. However, since such return data are not available in the multinational banking context, the Sharpe model must be modified to incorporate the availability of suitable data. Proxies related to the rates of return in that they capture bank risk (such as the capital-asset ratio) can be used to reflect the two components of risk, using the individual bank's proxy value as the dependent variables and a weighted index of the value of the proxy for all banks as the independent variable. The modified regression is as follows,

$$I_i = a_i + b_i \bar{I}_I + e_i$$
$$I_i = \text{value of ratio (index) for bank } i \qquad (2.4)$$
$$\bar{I}_I = \text{weighted index for all banks}$$

a_i, b_i, e_i have their usual meanings.

The ratio chosen to proxy bank risk in the empirical analysis used here is each multinational bank's capital-asset ratio. This ratio has been used on the grounds that it is a measure of capital adequacy which would indicate the ability of the bank to cover its loans with capital and reserves. It is therefore an indicator of the general leverage of a bank's portfolio, which is where the risks reside. Measured against an average industry index ratio, outlying banks can be isolated as taking unusual lending risks. The total risk so obtained can be subdivided into its systematic and nonsystematic components analogous to that described in equation 2.3.

The regression of equation 2.4 was implemented using annual data over the 1971–81 period for thirty-seven of the world's largest banks having considerable international operations. The results of the analysis are contained in table 2–10. An equally weighted index of the proxy was used as the right-hand side variable. The 1971–81 time period was used since data are readily available for this period from *The Banker's 500* listing.

The first column in table 2–10 gives the level of systematic risk (as measured by the systematic variance) attached to the specific bank, while columns 2 and 3 give the level of nonsystematic and total risk as measured by the respective variances. The fourth and fifth columns give the systematic and nonsystematic risk as percentages of the total risk. The last column provides an index of the banks' risk class in terms of the ratio of systematic risk to total risk. (Higher values of the index indicate greater systematic risk.)

The results show that nonsystematic risk dominates for the thirty-seven banks studied. This implies that individual banks had low systematic risk and were not risky from the point of view of depositors and investors in these banks since most of the risk could be diversified away. The Canadian banks exhibited the highest degree of nonsystematic risk as a group followed by the Japanese banks. Two out of the five largest U.S. banks demonstrated fairly high components of systematic risk as did the British banks. The performance

Table 2–10
Risk Index Rating Results for Major International Banks

Bank	Systematic Variance	Nonsystematic Variance	Total Variance	Systematic Variance as a % of Total Variance	Nonsystematic Variance as a % of Total Variance	Risk Index Rating[1]
Canada						
Royal Bank	1.7965	22.6009	24.3975	7.3635	92.6364	1
Imperial Bank	.4416	9.7643	10.2060	4.3269	95.6731	1
Bank of Montreal	.9097	38.0132	38.9229	2.3373	97.6626	1
Bank of Nova Scotia	1.1998	23.9599	25.1597	4.7687	95.2312	1
Toronto-Dominion	1.3767	260.6035	274.3714	5.0179	94.9820	1
United States						
Bank of America	.0701	10.8948	10.9649	.6397	99.3602	1
Citicorp	6.6458	9.1262	15.7720	42.1367	57.8632	5
Chase Manhattan	4.0490	24.5058	28.5548	14.1800	85.8200	2
Manufacturers Hanover	13.6006	6.7284	20.3291	66.9022	33.0977	7
J. P. Morgan	1.0257	5.6249	6.6506	15.4236	84.5763	2
United Kingdom						
Barclays	1.8361	1.3130	3.1491	58.3066	41.6933	6
National Westminster	1.5320	2.0903	3.6223	42.2934	57.7065	5
Midland	1.7951	9.6353	11.4305	15.7049	84.2950	2
Lloyds	.0009	1.4531	1.4540	.0628	99.9372	1
Standard	.4100	4.2004	4.6104	8.8943	91.1057	1
West Germany						
Deutsche Bank	.0184	1.5157	1.5342	1.2026	98.7974	1
Dresdner Bank	.2332	3.2180	3.4512	6.7595	93.2404	1
W. Deutsche Landes Giroz	.0084	4.8651	4.8735	.1726	99.8273	1
Commerzbank	8.3440	5.3901	13.7342	60.7538	39.2461	7
Bayerische Vereinsbank	26.6280	12.4681	39.0961	68.1089	31.8910	7
Japan						
Dai-Ichi Kangyo	3.0964	23.4972	26.5937	11.6435	88.3564	2

Table 2-10 *continued*

Bank	Systematic Variance	Nonsystematic Variance	Total Variance	Systematic Variance as a % of Total Variance	Nonsystematic Variance as a % of Total Variance	Risk Index Rating[1]
Fuji	.7366	20.9343	21.6710	3.3993	96.6006	1
Sumitomo Bank	2.0849	12.2988	14.3838	14.4952	84.5047	2
Mitsubishi Bank	.0594	15.9814	16.0409	.3708	99.6291	1
Sanwa Bank	.5594	10.8411	11.4006	4.9073	95.0926	1
Switzerland						
Union Bank	.5515	1.0704	1.6219	34.0040	65.9959	4
Swiss Bank Corp.	2.1811	1.5477	3.7289	54.4930	41.5069	6
Credit Suisse	1.9400	2.9365	4.8765	39.7821	60.2178	4
France						
Nationale de Paris	65.7966	874.9860	940.7826	6.9938	93.0061	1
Credit Lyonnais	2.0726	532.1396	534.2123	.3879	99.6120	1
Italy						
Banca Nazionale	16.7729	78.9812	95.7541	17.5166	82.4833	2
Banca Commerciale	22.4874	153.8314	176.3189	12.7538	87.2461	2
Netherlands						
Algemene Bank	.0255	34.7876	34.8132	.0734	99.9265	1
Rabo Bank	.0005	.5579	.5585	.1032	99.8967	1
Belgium						
Societe Generale	227.4163	119.8573	347.2736	65.4862	34.5138	7

Note: Risk index rating based on systematic risk as a percentage of total risk: 0–10%: 1, 11–20%: 2, 21–30%: 3, 31–40%: 4, 41–50%: 51–60%: 6, 61–70%: 7, 71–80%: 8, 81–90%: 9, 91–100%: 10. Lowest systematic risk = 1. Highest systematic risk = 10.

of the five largest West German multinational banks was similar. The performance of the other European banks was mixed though the majority of these exhibited a high degree of nonsystematic risk.

Kamath and Tilley (1985) have implemented this method for the 1973–83 period using equally weighted and market-weighted versions of the capital-asset ratio and return on assets proxies. Their results are broadly similar although two of the Canadian banks exhibit higher degrees of systematic risk on the capital-asset proxy. This result reflects the Canadian banking "crisis" during the 1980–83 period. The performance of the U.S. banks improves for both proxies, while the performance of the British and Japanese banks deteriorates. The other European banks exhibit the same performance. These results would seem to point toward the sensitivity of the results to the time period used and the generally poor performance of multinational banks during the 1980–83 period. Diversifiable risk still predominates.

It would seem from this evidence that not only have the world's leading multinational banks enjoyed higher profitability with stable earnings as they have expanded overseas, but also that a substantial component of the risk embodied in their operations was nonsystematic (though there was a deterioration during the international lending crisis of 1980–83).

Summary and Conclusions

This chapter examined the growing multinationality of the world's major banks during the 1961–80 period with particular emphasis on the 1971–80 decade. It was found that there exists a positive relationship between return on equity and the foreign to total assets ratio. It was also found that while the higher profitability of the world's multinational banks was in line with the trend in profitability for other MNEs, a significant difference was the stabilization in the variance of earnings that increased international operations provided. Multinational banks in Canada and the United States exhibited a lower standard deviation of earnings over the study period as compared to their nonfinancial MNE counterparts.

The profit and risk performance of Canadian, U.S., European, and Japanese multinational banks was also compared. It was found that the Canadian and U.S. multinational banks outperformed their European and Japanese counterparts. It was conjectured that domestic regulations and reporting requirements in such areas may affect performance.

The extent of systematic and nonsystematic risk embodied in the operations of thirty-five multinational banks was investigated using a modified Sharpe index model framework. It was found that the major component of multinational bank risk was diversifiable, though performance among different country groups varied. Canadian banks seemed to perform best on this criterion, in contrast to a recent study by others, which revealed a deterioration in their performance vis-à-vis the other banks in the 1980–83 period.

Overall, the conclusions of the chapter confirm the strength of the risk diversification hypothesis and internalization theory as good explanations of Canadian and other countries' banking performance—ideas first examined by Khoury (1980) and Rugman (1979). There is considerable incentive for the further application and testing of internalization theory to explain the performance of multinational banking firms.

References

Aliber, Robert Z. "Towards a Theory of International Banking." *Federal Reserve Bank of San Francisco Economic Review* (Spring 1976), 5–8.

Bank of Canada. *Bank of Canada Review*. Various issues.

Bennett, Paul. "Applying Portfolio Theory to Global Bank Lending." *Journal of Banking and Finance* 8 (1984), 153–69.

Cosset, Jean Claude, & Laurent Lampron. "Returns, Risk and International Diversification of Canadian Chartered Banks," in Alfred Kahl, ed., *Proceedings of Administrative Sciences Association of Canada* 3, no. 1 (1982), 117–27.

Dufey, Gunter, & S. L. Srinivasalu. "The Case for Corporate Management of Foreign Exchange Risk." *Financial Management* 12, no. 4 (1984), 54–62.

Fieleke, Norman S. "The Growth of U.S. Banking Abroad: An Analytical Survey." *Key Issues in International Banking.* Proceedings of a conference held in October 1977. Federal Reserve Bank of Boston, 9–40.

Giddy, Ian H. "The Theory and Industrial Organization of International Banking" in Robert G. Hawkins et al., eds., *The Internationalization of Financial Markets and National Economic Policy.* Research in International Business and Finance, vol. 3. JAI Press (1983), 195–243.

Goodman, Laurie S. "Bank Lending to Non-OPEC LDC's: Are Risks Diversifiable?" *Federal Reserve Bank of New York Quarterly Review* (Summer 1981), 10–20.

Gray, Peter H., & Jean Gray. "The Multinational Bank: A Financial MNC." *Journal of Banking and Finance.* 5, no. 1 (March 1981), 33–64.

Grubel, Herbert G. "A Theory of Multinational Banking." *Banca Nazionale del Lavoro Quarterly Review* 123 (1977), 349–63.

Kamath, Shyan J., & Keith C. Jensen. "Models of International Bank and Country Risk: A Survey of the Literature and a Portfolio Model." Simon Fraser University Discussion Paper 83-02-03. Burnaby, B.C., Canada: February 1983.

Kamath, Shyan J., & Roderick J. Tilley. "Canadian International Banking and the 'Debt Crisis.'" Dalhousie Discussion Paper in International Business no. 49. August 1985.

Khoury, Sarkis. "International Banking: Its Scope and Raison d' Être—A Special Look at Foreign Banks in the United States." Ph.D. dissertation. Philadelphia: University of Pennsylvania, 1978.

————. *The Dynamics of International Banking.* New York: Praeger, 1980.

Peters, David W. "Canadian Bank Profits as Viewed from Financial Theory." Queen's University School of Business Working Paper no. 83-5 (June 1985).

Rugman, Alan M. *International Diversification and the Multinational Enterprise.* Lexington, Mass.: D. C. Heath, 1979.

————. "Multinational Banking and the Theory of Internalization." Alan M. Rugman, *Inside the Multinationals.* New York: Columbia University Press, 1981.

————, Donald J. Lecraw & Laurence D. Booth. *International Business: Firm and Environment.* New York: McGraw-Hill, 1985.

Rugman, Alan M., & John McIlveen. *Megafirms: Strategies for Canada's Multinationals.* Toronto: Methuen, 1985.

Shapiro, Alan C. "Risk in International Banking." *Journal of Financial and Quantitative Analysis* 17, no. 5 (December 1982), 737–39.

Sharpe, William F. *Portfolio Theory and Capital Markets.* New York: McGraw-Hill, 1970.

Walter, Ingo. "Country Risk, Portfolio Decisions and Regulation in International Bank Lending." *Journal of Banking and Finance* 5, no. 1 (March 1981), 77–92.

3
Strategic Planning to Cope with Uncertainty

Jack Guttentag
Richard Herring

ABSTRACT

This chapter is a preliminary effort to develop principles and methods that will allow international banks to deal with uncertainty regarding major shocks. When a bank fails or suffers enormous losses, this is often because it paid insufficient prior attention to a hazard that it might have avoided or mitigated. We believe the strategic planning function should include responsibility for anticipating and developing defensive strategies against such hazards. In this chapter we consider how this can be done.

Following Alex J. Pollock (1984), we define strategic planning as "identifying the relatively few things which really matter to the future of the company, figuring out what to do about them, and making sure that it is done." The "few things that really matter" fall into two broad categories: opportunities and dangers. This chapter focuses on dangers of a special type—unpredictable shocks that would cause major damage to the bank. Banks typically do not have institutionalized mechanisms for dealing with dangers of this

From *Strategic Planning in International Banking,* edited by Paolo Savona and George Sutija. © Paolo Savona and George Sutija, 1986, and reprinted by permission of St. Martin's Press, Inc. This is a revised version of a paper that was prepared for a May 1984 seminar of the Permanent Advisory Committee on Eurodollars in Rome. Research for this chapter was supported by a grant from the National Science Foundation to the Brookings Institution for an experimental study program of research on international economic policy. The views expressed here should not be attributed to the officers, trustees, or other staff members of the Brookings Institution. The authors are grateful to officials from the following institutions for useful discussions concerning liquidity management: Bank of England, Bankers Trust, Chase Manhattan Bank, Citibank, Continental Illinois National Bank, Federal Reserve Board, Federal Reserve Bank of New York, First Pennsylvania Bank, Marshall Woellwarth, Morgan Guaranty Trust, and Philadelphia National Bank. We are grateful for Robert Mundheim's comments on an earlier draft.

type, as they do for opportunities. The typical bank, especially in the rapidly changing financial environment of today, will have departments responsible for developing new market opportunities. This responsibility may be concentrated in a separate product development department, ot it may be split among several operating departments, each responsible for finding its own opportunities. But wherever the function is located, it is institutionalized and constitutes a major responsibility of persons with access to top management.

Dangers, in contrast, seldom receive attention until they become clear, present, and unavoidable. Often no one has clear responsibility to identify them and alert the bank in time to avoid serious damage.

When a major shock actually occurs, substantial attention and resources are shifted to dealing with it. The realization hits that—to use the words of Bank of America Chairman Leland Prussia (1983)—"excess optimism prevailed." In reaction, exposures to shocks are reduced as rapidly as possible. After the shock, excessive optimism becomes excessive caution.

This sharp swing in perceptions is counterproductive in two ways. In the broader picture, the excessive caution can lead to credit rationing or a partial breakdown in financial markets in circumstances that do not warrant such responses, creating problems in resource allocation and macroeconomic policy. From the standpoint of the individual bank, excessive caution may cause the bank to forgo profitable opportunities and over the longer term may lead it to make the same mistake again!

This seeming paradox arises from the fact that excessive caution makes institutional reform redundant in the short run. With memories fresh, no other safeguards are needed. Besides, managerial attention (perhaps the scarcest of resources) is preoccupied with crisis management, that is, with minimizing the losses from the shock that has occurred.

Over time, however, memories fade, losses are written off, old hands retire, and excessive caution fades. Gradually, conditions reemerge for another round of excessive optimism. There is never a good time for reform.

This has been the pattern in international lending ever since the fourteenth century. Long periods of profitable lending have been followed by short periods of very heavy losses, trauma, and often failure. It is a history of banks learning their lessons all too well in the short run and then unlearning them over time because the lessons are not effectively institutionalized.

It is the responsibility of the strategic planning function of the bank to avert potential disasters as well as to exploit opportunities. This implies that when a disaster occurs, the strategic planning function should reevaluate the decision-making procedures, incentive systems, and analytical methods that allowed it to happen, and see to it that the appropriate lessons are institutionalized. But the more important responsibility of strategic planning is to prevent the disasters that have not yet occurred, and this is the main focus of our chapter.

The Risk–Uncertainty Spectrum

A venerable and useful tradition in economics which we follow is to view hazards in terms of risk and uncertainty. Suppose p_i is the probability that the *ith* event will occur. "Pure uncertainty" pertains to the situation where we know nothing whatsoever about the magnitude of p_i. "Pure risk" describes the situation where p_i takes on a value between zero and one that is known with complete confidence.[1] With regard to most events, our knowledge is intermediate between pure uncertainty and pure risk. We do not know p_i, but we have some evidence that allows us to formulate an estimate. The greater our confidence in that estimate, the closer we approach the case of pure risk. The lower our confidence, the closer we approach the case of pure uncertainty.

Two major factors determine the extent to which our knowledge about an event is characterized by risk or uncertainty. The first is our knowledge regarding the causal structure underlying the event. The result of a fair toss of a coin or die is governed entirely by risk, for example, because our prior knowledge of the mechanism that determines outcomes allows us to specify the exact probability, even if no evidence exists on the result of prior tosses.

The second determinant is the frequency with which the event occurs relative to changes in the underlying causal structure. If that structure changes dramatically every time an event occurs, the events do not generate evidence regarding probabilities. But if the event occurs many times while structure is stable, evidence regarding probabilities accumulates over time. For example, if floods over a given plain occur on average only every twenty-five years, but the underlying topography and climatic conditions generating the floods are stable, and if a historical record is available over several hundred years, good estimates of flood probabilities can be generated. The situation is closer to risk than to uncertainty, despite the low probability over any short period.

We emphasize the distinction between risk and uncertainty because we believe that decision making in regard to anticipating potential events that would affect the decision-maker depends on the extent to which knowledge regarding the event is characterized by risk or uncertainty. The reasons underlying this belief will be discussed later.

Events that potentially have very large effects and occur very infrequently we term "shocks." In general, low-probability events may be described as risky or uncertain, but economic shocks are inevitably better characterized as uncertain than as risky. Our a priori knowledge of the causal structure determining economic outcomes is inadequate to enable us to specify probabilities without empirical evidence, while the causal structures determining economic outcomes seem to change too rapidly to enable us to formulate reliable statistical estimates of the probability of infrequent events. There is no economic analogue to infrequent, natural phenomena such as a flood or an earthquake for which the causal structure is so stable that evidence accumulated over the centuries is empirically useful to estimate the probability of an occurrence with considerable confidence. Since our concern is with economic shocks, in the remainder of this chapter we will confine our attention to uncertain, low-probability events.[2]

Risk, Uncertainty, and Insolvency Exposure of Commercial Banks

Banks engage in a variety of actions whose outcomes cannot be known in advance. Some of these actions are best described as subject to risk; others, as subject to uncertainty. Defaults on consumer loans and mortgages are largely subject to risk as shown by a long statistical record reflecting a variety of economic conditions. Although it is not possible to predict which borrower in a particular category will default, risk analysts can estimate with reasonable confidence that over a long period, a specified percentage of borrowers in a given category will default. This estimate enables banks to charge an appropriate default premium and establish reserves so that the ex post return on the category of loans will be at least as great as the return on a safe investment.[3]

In contrast, it is difficult to price uncertain activities appropriately, because there is insufficient evidence to permit an estimate of the probability of a default (or, in the case of trading activities, of a loss) in which we can place much confidence. The events that produce unfavorable outcomes do not occur frequently enough to enable us to estimate probabilities and we do not have an adequate understanding of the causal structure to enable us to make convincing a priori estimates. Examples of uncertain activities would include taking a position to benefit from a drop in interest rates or lending large amounts to a developing country.

Risky activities are less likely to give rise to insolvency exposure than uncertain activities. If the probability of loss is known, rates can be adjusted to compensate for the risk of loss and reserves accumulated. Thus, even if unfavorable outcomes occur rather frequently (as, for example, in consumer lending), so long as they are properly anticipated, they do not pose a threat to the solvency of the bank. The main qualifications to this statement—qualifications generally of trivial importance—are that the bank's capital be sufficient to absorb losses from a run of bad luck, or that the portfolio be diversified.

To be sure, default probabilities do not announce themselves. An investment in information and analysis is required; until this is done, uncertainty prevails. Converting such uncertainty into risk constitutes a large part of what is commonly referred to as "risk analysis" or "risk management." But in such cases, the basic conditions exist for the conversion, and, therefore, we can refer to it as a risky situation whether the conversion is made or not.

Insolvency exposure of banks is associated mainly with uncertainty regarding the occurrence of shocks for which insufficient provision has been made. Banks engage in a variety of actions that expose them to potential shocks characterized by uncertainty. Such actions include (1) the granting of certain kinds of loans, (2) taking an overall asset—liability duration position, (3) taking net foreign exchange positions, and (4) taking a liquidity position.

The strategic planning function should have major responsibility for positioning the bank to avoid or minimize damage from major shocks. Events affecting the bank that are governed by risk are very likely to be handled adequately in operating departments and, therefore, generally need not concern the strategic planner. But uncertainty regarding major shocks is seldom handled adequately. On the contrary, there is good reason to believe that bank decision making under uncertainty is subject to some systematic biases resulting in what we call "disaster myopia." We believe that the buildup of heavy concentrations of country exposure that led up to the banking crisis that erupted in August 1982 is explained in large part by disaster myopia.

Disaster Myopia under Uncertainty: An Illustration

Prior to the recent crisis, the danger that a country would be unable to service its international debt fell near the far end of the risk—uncertainty spectrum. Unlike car loans, mortgages, and many categories of domestic, commercial, and industrial lending, events that cause losses on country loans are infrequent. Moreover, the underlying causal structure that generates losses is not well understood. In addition, the market structure had changed drastically since the previous major episode of country defaults in the 1930s. Bank loans had replaced bonds as the principal financing vehicle, while important official international financial institutions had been created. Hence, the earlier experience was not viewed as very relevant in assessing future probabilities of default. Assessment of the dangers of country default was thus subject to uncertainty, and we shall argue that banks were myopic about it in the sense that they tended to disregard it.

Specialists in cognitive psychology and decision sciences have found that decision-makers confronted with low-probability, high-loss hazards are often disaster myopic because their judgments regarding the probability of an event are subject to several types of bias. These biases arise out of what are called the "availability" heuristic, the "threshold" heuristic, and "cognitive dissonance." We believe that the behavior of banks with regard to the possibility of country defaults reflected such biases.

The availability heuristic is a psychological mechanism by which people evaluate the likelihood of an event. In the terminology of Tversky and Kahneman (1982), the availability heuristic is employed whenever a person "estimates frequency or probability by the ease with which instances or associations can be brought to mind." Frequent events are usually easier to recall than infrequent events. But ease of recall is also affected by such factors as the emotional intensity of an experience or the time elapsed since the last occurrence, and these factors can lead to an "availability bias." This bias is easily illustrated by the common experience of driving more cautiously after witnessing an automobile accident, as if in response to a sharp increase in the subjective probability of an accident. Normal, less cautious driving habits usually return quickly as the image of the accident recedes from memory.

Tversky and Kahneman (1982) report results of ten controlled experiments performed with 1,500 subjects which demonstrated that even when probabilities could be objectively determined, people tended to employ the availability heuristic. They argue that their results are equally applicable to very infrequent events where probability cannot be based on a tally of relative frequencies.

Our view is that banks were subject to this bias in assessing the probabilities of defaults by developing countries. As the period since the previous major incidence of country defaults in the 1930s lengthened, the ease with which decision-makers could imagine such an event declined and, thus, so did the subjective probability. Over time, moreover, the managers who had lived through the 1930s were replaced by managers who had not, and finally they were replaced by managers who did not even have indirect experience through personal contact with managers who had.

The second bias generating disaster myopia is a tendency, when the subjective probability of occurrence falls below some threshold level, to treat that probability as if it were zero. This is an application of the threshold heuristic—an implicit decision rule through which decision-makers allocate their scarcest resource—managerial attention. This heuristic is necessary for a decision-maker to get through the day, since there are always a large number of low-probability hazards and even cursory attention to all of them would not be possible. This heuristic becomes an impediment to effective decision making, however, when it leads to the neglect of those few potentially costly hazards that might have been identified and avoided. In a sense, the core problem of strategic planning is to create procedures and mechanisms for distinguishing those few hazards that are worth worrying about from the many that are not.

The availability and threshold heuristics, drawn from the descriptive approach to decision making under uncertainty, are at variance with conventional rational expectations assumptions that characterize the normative approach to decision making. The principal argument in favor of the rational expectations approach is that market discipline will ensure that decision-makers form expectations correctly. Those who make systematic errors will incur losses and go out of business. But this argument has little force with regard to expectations concerning low-probability hazards that occur so infrequently that they may be disregarded with impunity for long periods.

Indeed, under such conditions, competition may drive prudent lenders from the market. A bank that attempts to charge an appropriate default premium for low-probability hazards is likely to lose business to banks that are willing to disregard the probability of a default. If there is a long period of time between defaults, market discipline may be delayed for so long as to become completely ineffectual. We believe this has been an important factor in international banking.

Tendencies toward disaster myopia are exacerbated by incentive systems within banks that reward performance over short periods using current income (which may be heavily front-loaded with fees) without adequate adjustment for potential future losses. Concern for future consequences is further reduced by high job mobility among lending officers. A lending officer who does not expect to be at the current position very long may have little concern for future losses.

The third cognitive bias that encourages disaster myopia comes into play when new information becomes available to suggest that, contrary to prior assumptions, a serious hazard does exist. In 1980 and especially in 1981, for example, a considerable amount of evidence accumulated that many less-developed country (LDC) borrowers were going to have trouble. Yet, most banks ignored the signs or otherwise explained them away.[4] They supported their opinions, furthermore, with new loans.[5]

Psychologists call this "cognitive dissonance." This is a psychological mechanism designed to protect the decision-maker's self-esteem when information arises that casts doubt on the wisdom of past decisions. Such information is likely to be ignored, rejected, or accommodated by changes in other beliefs that justify the past decisions. Cognitive dissonance is a fundamental proposition in social psychology that has been verified in a number of experiments. It seems likely that it applies as much to bankers as to, say, university professors or international civil servants.[6]

In summary, the disaster myopia hypothesis suggests that banks assumed heavy concentrations of country risk exposure because the risk of default was perceived to be negligible. The availability heuristic may have led to a decline in the subjective probability of defaults; the threshold heuristic may have contributed to the effective disregard of default probabilities that were believed to be very low; and cognitive dissonance may have impeded the response to evidence that the probability of a default was rising.

Although we have illustrated disaster myopia with regard to heavy concentrations of country exposure, the hypothesis has potential relevance to any high-loss hazard characterized by uncertainty that confronts the bank.[7] In the following sections of this chapter, we develop an approach to help the strategic planner counter disaster myopia in order to ensure that the bank does not inadvertently expose itself to catastrophic losses. After a discussion of the appropriate division of labor between the bank and the bank's supervisor, we consider some of the general problems involved in implementing the procedure within a bank. This is followed by an application of the procedure to one type of major hazard facing every bank: a liquidity crisis.

An Analytical Procedure for Identifying Exposure to Major Hazards

It is instructive to consider how a bank would develop a strategy for dealing with potential shocks *if* it had information regarding shock probabilities. Suppose the bank knew the probability of credit shocks of every magnitude, and also the probability of the joint occurrence of all combinations of all types of shocks. The bank would then (1) estimate the loss it would incur for varying magnitudes of each shock and (2) stipulate a maximum overall probability of insolvency that the bank would tolerate as a policy objective. The bank could then adjust all exposures in the least costly way that was consistent with the policy-determined constraint on the probability of insolvency.

This approach is not feasible however, because shock probabilities are not known. But beyond this, it is not even useful in indicating the direction in which strategic planning should proceed. It would focus attention on the estimation of shock probabilities as the first step whereas, in our view, disaster myopia is best countered by making the consideration of shock probabilities part of the last step, at a point where policymakers are involved.

The approach proposed here involves three major steps: (1) identifying those hazards that are worth worrying about, (2) estimating the bank's existing exposure to those hazards, and (3) making an explicit determination as to whether the exposure is excessive. The first two steps are very closely related in the sense that a hazard to which the bank is not exposed is not worth worrying about. Yet, it is useful to treat step 1 separately as a means of classifying hazards with sufficient rigor and clarity that exposures to them become measurable.

Classifying Relevant Hazards

We define a hazard in terms of a particular type of crisis scenario—a sequence of events that begins with a major shock and that would cause loss for the bank if it occurred, depending on the bank's exposure. A crisis scenario may run its course in a matter of weeks or may stretch out to years. The end is typically less well defined than the beginning but essentially the end is reached when no more high-level managerial decisions are required and the problem falls off the planning agendas of the bank and the regulator.

Crisis scenarios can be classified by the type of shock that initiates them. An exogenous development that mainly affects loan losses is a "credit shock." Similarly, a marked change in market interest rates that would affect income or capital values, depending on a preexisting difference in the duration of assets and liabilities, is an "interest-rate shock." A sudden increase in the severity of credit rationing, which might result in an inability to meet maturing liabilities, is a "liquidity shock." A marked change in foreign exchange rates that might affect capital values and income, depending on a preexisting net foreign exchange position, is a "foreign exchange shock."

It is analytically convenient to view each type of shock separately, although in practice they may be causally connected. In particular, a liquidity shock may be a consequence of one of the other types of shocks. We defer discussion of potential interconnections.

A key element in the construction of crisis scenarios is the scaling of crisis magnitudes, which may involve two or even more dimensions. A credit crisis can be scaled by the scope of the shock (as measured by the number and size of asset categories affected) and by the depth of the shock (as measured by loss rates). Interest rates and foreign exchange shocks can be scaled by the magnitude of interest rate and exchange rate changes and perhaps by time. Liquidity shocks can be scaled by the severity of rationing and by the length of the period over which credit rationing persists.

Measuring a Bank's Exposure to a Crisis Scenario

We would measure a bank's exposure to a crisis scenario in terms of the largest crisis of that type that the bank could withstand at the bank's current exposure. If crisis magnitude is scaled along two dimensions, exposure would be measured along one while the other took "predicted" or varying projected values. Anticipating the discussion in the section "An Illustration of the Scenario Approach," assume, for example, that the severity of a liquidity crisis is measured by the percent of net cash requirements that can be met by issuing liabilities at precrisis rate relationships (indicating the "intensity of rationing) *and* by the number of days that rationing persists. Then, the intensity of rationing can be specified and exposure measured by the number of days this could persist before it would cause the bank to fail. Alternatively, a rationing period could be specified and exposure measured in terms of the severity of rationing that would cause the bank to fail over that period. The first approach is used in our later illustration.

In principle, the "largest loss a bank can absorb" should be measured by the bank's true net worth at the time of the exercise—or by some fraction of true net worth, since a bank needs some worth to be a viable entity. If there is an effective market for the equity shares of the bank and the market considers the probability that true net worth is negative to be negligible, the market value of equity would be a good proxy for true net worth.[8] Other proxies also could be used—for example, the book value of equity (which might be of more interest to supervisors) or the market value of equity plus the book value of preferred stock and subordinated debt (which might be of interest to deposit-insuring agencies).

Determining Whether Exposures Are Excessive

The third step in the process is determining whether or not existing exposures are excessive. Whereas the first two steps are heavily technical, the third is policy-oriented in the sense that the top management of the bank should be involved, and explicit decisions regarding exposure should be made. It is at this stage also that strategic planning to counter disaster myopia should be integrated with the broader strategic plan of the bank. For top management to confront effectively the question of whether existing exposures are excessive, they need to know not only how large are the shocks that the bank can withstand, but also the costs of reducing the various types of exposures in terms of income forgone.

The third step in implementation also involves bringing to bear the best information available on the likelihood that specified crisis scenarios will develop. Top management should participate in this stage of the planning process. Persons outside the banking including the regulators may have important insights to contribute, and ways must be found to tap such sources of expertise. This can be done in a variety of ways such as informal brainstorming sessions and consulting projects.

The regulators' views on crisis scenarios are likely to be biased toward high likelihood, reflecting their asymmetrical attitude toward the risk–return trade-off of the bank. Knowledgeable persons inside the bank are likely to be biased in the opposite direction for reasons discussed later. In such situations, a dialectic process is often very useful in getting the best possible information base for final decision by management.[9]

In this process one party would make the best possible case for the scenario occurring and the other party would make the best case against it. Both parties must have access to the same information so that differences between them are based only on inferences from this information. Hence, if one party has information not initially available to the other, that information must be shared and the party receiving the information given the opportunity to revise its case accordingly. Differences of opinion concerning questions of fact should be resolved by the planner who serves as umpire. In the interchange between the two parties, the planner seeks to identify and challenge any questionable assumptions that are made by both parties and invites them to provide their best defense of these assumptions. The parties are encouraged to revise their views as a result of such challenges. The result of this dialectic process is delivered to the top management for a final decision.

The purpose of the exercise described above is to formulate and develop scenarios that constitute important dangers to the bank; to determine the extent to which the bank would be impacted if the hazards occur; and ultimately to force both the bank and supervisor to consider whether exposure is excessive.

Of course, this does not assure that the optimal decisions regarding exposure will be made. Nor does it imply that the regulator and the bank may not have different views on what constitutes excessive exposure. Indeed, there is every reason to believe that they will have different views. Arguing it out could be a useful dialectic exercise, as we noted above. The purpose of the strategic planning exercise is not to find the "right" answer (since when probabilities are not known, there can be no "right" answer), but to make sure that both banks and regulators consider the question.

Division of Labor between the Bank and the Regulator

In a well-ordered world it would be the responsibility of the bank regulator to define the crisis scenarios in detail, including the ways in which the magnitude of the crisis is to be scaled, and to specify how the maximum shock the bank can withstand is defined. The responsibility of the bank would be to estimate the maximum shock of each type.

There are two reasons why it makes sense in principle for the supervisors to define the crisis scenarios and the way in which the impact on the bank is measured. First, from the supervisor's standpoint, it is obviously desirable to have uniform benchmarks that allow peer group comparisons of bank exposures. We hasten to add that it is treacherous to rely on such comparisons in determining what constitutes an "acceptable" exposure since the entire group can march to the precipice together; nevertheless, comparable information is extremely useful.

The second reason that it makes sense for the supervisor to define the crisis scenarios is that the scenarios with which they are mainly concerned are those that would affect all or a major segment of the banking system. It is economical to centralize responsibility for what is essentially a common function. This does not preclude the possibility that individual banks may "improve" the supervisor's scenarios to make them more relevant to that bank or even to develop scenarios that are applicable only to the individual bank.

The supervisory agencies, however, are not yet prepared to assume this responsibility. In anticipating the two most costly and dangerous recent threats to the solvency of large numbers of financial institutions in the United States—the collapse of the thrift industry under rising interest rates during 1979–82, and the payments crisis affecting Latin American creditors of major international banks beginning in 1982—the agencies with responsibility for prudential regulation were almost as myopic as the affected firms themselves. And while some supervisors had sufficient foresight to be seriously concerned, strong institutional impediments within the agencies prevented any forceful measures from being taken.

The regulatory process as it has evolved over the decades is simply not well designed to deal with exposure to major shocks of unknown probability. The major thrust of supervision has been to assess the condition of an institution under current conditions. It is intrinsically very difficult for supervisors to deal with a firm in good condition that would be seriously damaged if a shock of unknown probability occurred, the probability being one about which reasonable persons could easily disagree. Indeed, it is not even clear that under existing laws supervisors have the legal authority to take forceful measures to deal with problems of this type even if they are otherwise prepared to do so.

Since the division of labor we have proposed is not possible at this time, we shall proceed on the assumption that the bank will conduct the exercise on its own. It would not be the first time that banks have educated supervisory authorities on how the banks ought to be supervised.

Implementation within the Bank

There are important barriers within the bank to effective planning of the type described. If there is to be any chance of success, these barriers must be recognized in order to be overcome.

First, some of the people in the bank who are most knowledgeable about potential hazards to the bank are likely to have the least incentive to place such hazards on the agenda. This is an important factor encouraging disaster myopia. The head of a profit center, for example, will assume that any actions on the profit center's part that create a perception that it is exposing the bank to a substantial hazard will redound to the head's disadvantage. Depending on the accounting conventions used, either the required capital to be allocated to the function or reserve allocations out of income will be increased, which will worsen bottom-line measures of the center's performance.[10] Alternatively, the allowable scale of activity of the center may be reduced.

The approach described earlier was designed in part precisely to deal with this problem. Department heads are asked to develop loss estimates contingent upon scenarios presented to them. They are not asked to assess the likelihood that the scenarios will occur. Hence, their defensiveness regarding performance is less likely to be engaged.

It can be argued, of course, that if existing measures of performance create disincentives to constructive behavior, there must be something wrong with the performance measures and they should be changed. In fact, the underlying problem is not the measures used (although they *could* be dysfunctional) but the period of time over which performance is assessed. Performance must be measured over a period short enough to motivate those covered by it, but such periods are too short to deal with low-probability hazards of the type discussed in this chapter. For example, it is not feasible to tie the compensation of international banking loan officers to profit performance over thirty years, yet this may be the order of magnitude of the length of time required to take account of low-probability hazards.

The second problem is getting the attention of top management. How does the planner arrange to place low-probability, high-cost hazards onto an agenda that is already crowded with the important problems of the moment, especially if the hazards are not likely to occur any time soon? How can the attention of top management, perhaps the scarcest resource in the bank, be directed toward the problem (or "nonproblem" as many would view it)?[11] If success is somehow achieved in placing the issue on the agenda at a stage early enough for constructive planning, how can interest be maintained over a long period when the shock does not occur?

To get the attention of top management, planners must establish credibility in the planning process (and therefore in themselves). To establish credibility, planners must avoid predicting the unpredictable or attempting to attach probabilities to crisis scenarios, implicitly or explicitly. The role of the strategic planner is not to convince a bank's managers that the planner knows more about the future than they do. Rather, it is to convince the managers that the planning process can generate useful information for them to make decisions regarding what exposure is appropriate.

To sustain the interest of management, the process of planning to avert disasters must be integrated into the overall strategic planning exercise as a matter of routine. Then the process of evaluating opportunities with hazards at the same time will become routine.

We next illustrate the procedure of developing a crisis scenario with one kind of scenario that is broadly relevant to all major international banks.

Liquidity Crisis Scenarios

The common element in liquidity crisis scenarios is a sudden and marked increase in the severity of credit rationing. Several categories of liquidity crisis scenarios should be distinguished, even though it is possible for them to occur together. A general crisis scenario affects all banks to some degree and arises out of general market forces. A general liquidity crisis scenario may reflect an attempt by the central bank to combat strong excess demand with an extremely tight monetary policy. An explosive rise in interest rates could cause dealers suddenly to become apprehensive regarding the possible downside risk in holding securities and to refuse to increase their positions. At this point, dealer markets would cease to function, and what were considered to be liquid assets would be transformed into illiquid assets. This would result in extraordinary demands for bank loans and might possibly lead commercial banks to renege on their loan commitments, which in turn would stimulate even more demand—a run on bank loans in order to stockpile cash. For a short period in the fall of 1966, such a scenario developed in the United States, but it was aborted before cash stockpiling began. (See Guttentag, 1969, and the sources cited there.)

A market-specific liquidity crisis scenario is a less serious problem because it is less general. It can arise in a specific market when major defaults cause a wholesale flight from a particular category of asset. This happened in the commercial paper market following the Penn Central default in 1970. Again, however, prompt action by the Federal Reserve made it possible for borrowers heavily dependent on that market to shift to other sources.

A bank-specific liquidity crisis scenario, in contrast, involves only a single bank (or a small group of banks). The shock consists of some event that raises a concern about the solvency of specific banks and thereby affects their ability to borrow. Banks with large amounts of uninsured liabilities that become insolvent (such as the Franklin National Bank in New York) invariably encounter a liquidity crisis. But it can happen also to a solvent bank that is hit by very bad news that undermines market confidence in the bank's solvency. This happened to the Continental Illinois Bank in June 1982, following the failure of the Penn Square Bank from which it has purchased a large volume of loans of questionable value. Continental Illinois survived the 1982 shock, although at a heavy cost that increased its vulnerability to the 1984 shock which brought it down.

Of these three categories of liquidity crisis scenarios, we focus on the third because it is the likely consequence of a credit shock, interest rate shock, or foreign exchange shock, and because it is potentially the most dangerous to the individual bank. General liquidity crisis scenarios engage the attention of central banks which will use their powers to create liquidity to prevent illiquidity-induced failures, even when prior actions by the central bank itself were responsible for the crisis. So long as there are no concerns about bank solvency, moreover, the general provision of liquidity through open market operations or relaxation of reserve requirements will suffice to ease the crisis since markets can be depended upon to shift funds to the banks with greatest need. For this reason, insofar as general liquidity crises are concerned, the

Federal Reserve can be viewed as the lender of last resort (LLR) in meeting the U.S. dollar needs of all banks throughout the world.

A bank-specific liquidity crisis scenario is a different matter altogether. When a bank depends heavily on liability management for its liquidity, its survival will depend on its ability to place new liabilities equal at least to maturing liabilities in excess of maturing assets. LLR assistance in this situation requires direct lending to the affected bank, and such assistance may or may not be available. Not all central banks accept this type of LLR responsibility (as opposed to responsibility for general liquidity provision); sometimes a central bank accepts this responsibility only for specified categories of banks or subject to various types of constraints such as strict collateral requirements.[12] Some banks, therefore, do not have clear access to an LLR.

Even when a bank does have clear access to an LLR, furthermore, such access may not be very useful. The LLR to a specific bank, when this responsibility is accepted, commits itself to provide whatever direct support is needed in pressing and exigent circumstances, *provided that the bank is solvent.* An LLR of this type requires, first, access to current and reliable information on the bank's condition, and, second, the ability, directly or indirectly, to monitor the bank's activities. In theory, an LLR's decision to extend credit to a bank from which other lenders are running would constitute a signal to the market that the bank is sound. By dampening adverse expectations regarding the bank's condition, the amount of credit required of the LLR would be very small.

Unfortunately, this favorable impact on expectations may not occur. In recent years, central banks have often lent to sustain insolvent banks pending an orderly disposition by the relevant regulatory and/or insurance agency. Thus, assistance from the lender of last resort may intensify concern about the bank's condition.

Because of the possibility of this perverse signaling effect, we believe that banks should develop bank-specific liquidity crisis scenarios on the assumption that there will be no recourse to official institutions for emergency liquidity assistance. Moreover, a bank should have a clear understanding of its own options for dealing with a liquidity crisis in order to evaluate when recourse to official assistance is worth the cost.

An Illustration of the Scenario Approach: A Bank-Specific Liquidity Crisis

The scenario begins with a shock, in this illustration, an event that causes the market to question the solvency of the bank and jeopardizes its ability to sell uninsured liabilities. In the first scenario we shall assume the shock is so severe that the bank cannot rollover any of its uninsured liabilities. This extreme assumption is a useful benchmark from the perspective of both the bank's management and the supervisory authorities. It is a worst-case scenario against which other less severe shocks can be compared.

To facilitate the exposition and highlight the characteristics of a *pure* liquidity crisis, we assume that the bank is actually solvent, but that the bank's managers must persuade the market that this is the case. The bank's vulnerability to a bank-specific liquidity crisis will be measured by the number of days the bank could sustain the shock before it incurred losses equal to the market value of its net worth just before the shock occurred.

The accounting format depicted in table 3–1 provides a convenient framework for organizing thinking about a bank-specific liquidity crisis. Admittedly, the procedure we propose generates more questions than answers, but we consider that an advantage. The procedure encourages managers to think strategically—to anticipate problems and consider how they can influence outcomes. As de Leon (1975) emphasizes, the purpose of scenario building "is not to predict the future perfectly: it is to organize verisimilar crisis situations in such a manner that one can study the reactions of . . . participants—and more important—the options they generate."

First, we will take an overview of the framework and then take a closer look at some of the most problematic features. The left margin of table 3–1 lists each day that has elapsed since the shock, which is assumed to occur just before the opening of business on day 1. The first column sets out the magnitude of the challenge facing the bank. It lists the net cash flows that are the consequence of the bank's current position under the extreme assumption that it will not be able to roll over *any* uninsured liability. These cash flows should reflect not only the interest and amortization schedules of assets and liabilities currently on the bank's books, but also those assets and liabilities for which the bank has made binding commitments that do not yet appear on the balance sheet. Any bank that depends on liability management for its liquidity will register negative cash flows in this column. For the most part, these data can be generated from existing accounting reports that classify assets and liabilities by final maturity and distinguish insured from uninsured liabilities.[13]

Column 2 defines the severity of credit rationing that the bank may face. It shows estimates of the amount of uninsured liabilities the bank would be able to sell after the shock. In the benchmark scenario, we assume that the bank would not be able to sell any uninsured liabilities and so the entries in column 2 and 3 will be zero. In subsequent scenarios, the managers of the bank may wish to take a less pessimistic view and attempt to estimate the amount of insured liabilities they expect the bank would be able to sell even if the bank's creditworthiness is subject to question. This is the most difficult part of the exercise, but it is also potentially the most rewarding in terms of insights it provides regarding options to enhance the bank's liquidity.

Table 3–1
An Accounting Framework for a Liquidity Shock Scenario

Day	1. Net Cash Flow with No Roll-over	2. New Issues of Liabilities	3. Loss from New Issues of Liabilities	4. Sales of Assets	5. Loss from Sales of Assets	6. Loss of Income from Decline in Assets	7. Cumulative Loss
1							
2							
3							
…							
N							

The estimates in column 2 require a careful assessment of customers for the bank's liabilities. Which customers are likely to withdraw their credit lines to the bank and decline to roll over maturing liabilities? Which customers are likely to reduce placements, shorten maturities, or switch instruments? Which customers may be induced to increase their outstandings with the bank? Such assessments are crucial to prudent liability management, yet some banks have not even made the initial step of carefully inventorying the existing customers for their liabilities, much less projecting the behavior of customers in the event of a shock.

Alternative estimates can also be developed to meet varying assumptions regarding the magnitude of the shock, varying degrees of optimism and pessimism regarding how creditors respond, or both. This approach is a reflection of the underlying premise of all strategic planning, that the firm can to a degree control its own destiny. The estimates in column 2 can be affected by the policies the bank follows, both before a crisis hits and afterward. We will consider this strategic aspect of the problem after we survey the rest of the framework.

The bank will meet the cash flow requirement in column 1 with the combination of new issues of liabilities and sales of assets that generates the smallest total loss for that period. Column 3 shows the estimated loss from new issues of liabilities during the liquidity crisis. The loss is the difference between the cost of the new issues and the cost of raising the same amount of funds if the liquidity shock had not occurred. For analytical clarity, it is important that the average duration of liabilities be held constant, which implies that liabilities should be priced at the average duration.[14] The loss in column 3 may reflect a higher risk premium on the same mix of liability instruments it would otherwise have employed or a change in mix that increases the proportion of instruments such as Eurodeposits that bear a higher yield.

Column 4 lists the amounts of funds that will be raised through sales of assets. This is a residual in the sense that the cash requirements shown in column 1 that are not met by the new liability issues in column 2 must be met by asset sales. In the benchmark scenario, the amount in column 4 must equal column 1. In less extreme scenarios, however, the bank will have some discretion over liability sales, so that the sale of assets will be determined jointly with the sale of liabilities in order to minimize costs. On the margin, the loss in raising an additional amount of funds through issuing new liabilities will be equal to the loss in raising the same amount of funds through asset sales.

The cost of asset sales has two components. The first, shown in column 5, is the difference between the true market value of the asset sold and the value that can be realized upon sale at short notice. In determining the loss, assets would be ranked by marketability with the most marketable assets sold first. The marketability of a bank's assets may vary from short-term government instruments which have virtually perfect marketability to real estate or subsidiaries which may require lengthy preparations for sale in order to realize the maximum market value. Although it is easy to ascertain the market price of assets that are actively traded on secondary markets, it is difficult to estimate the amount of funds that can be realized from selling less marketable assets such as participations in corporate loans, restructured country debt, or the corporate headquarters building. Nonetheless, such estimates are a necessary component of an evaluation of the bank's liquidity.

Once the ranking is accomplished, the bank would sell the most marketable assets first, being careful (as in the case of new issues of liabilities) to maintain the average duration of the bank's assets so that the bank does not inadvertently increase its exposure to an interest rate shock. Another complication may arise if some highly marketable assets must be held to fulfill regulatory requirements or if they are already being used to provide funds through repurchase agreements.

Column 6 shows the second component of the cost of asset sales, the loss in spread income when the bank reduces its assets rather than rolling over its liabilities. Even if an asset has perfect marketability so that no loss appears in column 5, the bank nonetheless sustains an opportunity cost loss when it repays a maturing liability with the proceeds from the sale of an asset that yields a higher return. The loss in spread income should be cumulated throughout the scenario beginning on the day in which the decrease in assets occurred. An approximation of the cumulative loss through any day in the scenario can be made by multiplying the amount by which assets have declined since the occurrence of the shock by the average spread—the yield the bank earned on assets of average duration minus the yield the bank paid on liabilities of average duration just before the shock.

Column 7 lists the cumulative loss the bank incurs to manage the liquidity crisis. It is the sum of the losses on new issues of liabilities and on sales of assets including loss of spread income cumulated from the first day of the crisis. The scenario ends when the cumulative loss is equal to the market value of the bank's equity just before the shock occurred.[15]

This exercise provides a straightforward measure of the bank's vulnerability to a bank-specific liquidity crisis—the number of days it can continue operations before it exhausts the market value of its equity. Of course, it is only a snapshot—a measure of the bank's exposure at a particular moment. Nonetheless, it provides crucial information for developing operating constraints to keep exposure within policy-determined guidelines. In principle, the exercise need be repeated only when there are important changes in the underlying assumptions that may have a significant impact on the bank's exposure. In practice, an annual review may be useful, if only to sensitize decision-makers to the dimensions of the problem.

Liquidity Crisis Management

The process of constructing the scenario is helpful in identifying methods of enhancing liquidity, pinpointing information the bank may need but does not have, and stimulating thinking about how the bank can respond quickly and effectively when trouble occurs.[16] The essence of a bank-specific liquidity crisis is asymmetric information: in the wake of the shock, outsiders have a much more pessimistic view of the bank's prospects than insiders. Thus, a critical problem in managing a liquidity crisis is to transmit accurate information regarding the bank's condition in order to convert at least some outsiders into insiders. This is a difficult challenge, partly because outsiders are likely to take a skeptical view of self-serving pronouncements from a bank in distress. With the bank's credibility at stake, it is important that the information provided include forthright acknowledgement of any difficulties while demonstrating that these difficulties do not impair the bank's solvency.

Another difficulty that must be overcome is that outsiders are unlikely to make use of information that is costly to evaluate. The expected benefit of making a more careful assessment of the bank's prospects must outweigh the relatively trivial cost of switching out of the bank's liabilities into a substitute asset.

Relationships may ease this information transmission problem. If a bank's liability managers have personal relationships with the customer and there are strong institutional ties between the bank and the customer, information can be transmitted at much lower cost. This raises the issue of whether it may be useful for a bank to avoid brokers and place its liabilities directly with customers in order to maintain a better flow of information about who the bank's customers are and what their preferences are. This may even involve developing a market-making capacity in short-term money market instruments in order to be able to satisfy customer requests when the bank prefers not to issue its own liabilities at the maturity or in the instrument desired. Knowing the customer also involves knowing the constraints on the customer's action. Even a persuaded customer may lack the discretion to act on favorable information. For example, a corporate treasurer may be convinced that the bank is safe but be unable at reasonable cost to persuade the corporation's unsophisticated board of directors. Managers of money market mutual funds are tightly constrained by the perceptions of thousands of badly informed individual investors. Even though relationships may ease the information transmission problem, it is also important to understand the constraints on customers' asset placement decisions. The upshot of these considerations is that some customers are more valuable than others because they are less likely to run in the event of a liquidity shock. It may be worthwhile to identify and cultivate such customers for the bank's liabilities even if it requires new organizational structures or information systems.

When a bank's prospects are uncertain and information is costly to evaluate, it may be useful to try to make "insiders" of influential third parties. The central bank or supervisory agencies may be valuable in this regard. Even if direct financial assistance would undermine confidence in the bank, an official's discreet assurance that the bank is sound may substantially improve the bank's access to funds. The rating agencies or bank security analysts may also be useful allies. Any money market brokers may play a helpful role in dampening rumors and identifying customers for the bank's liabilities. The bank may attempt to gain the trust of such third parties by forewarning them when there is unfavorable news about the bank and by making a special effort to persuade them that the bank is fundamentally sound.[17]

When information is costly and uncertain, potential customers may place special reliance on market indicators of a bank's creditworthiness, such as the rate it is willing to pay on its liabilities. In a liquidity crisis, it may be counterproductive for the bank to offer an unusually high spread over prevailing money market rates since potential customers for the bank's liabilities may interpret the premium as a signal that the bank is desperate or that it intends to use the funds in an extraordinarily risky way.[18] Moreover, once a bank pays a higher spread, it must continue paying "up-market" until it can convince potential customers that it is sounder than banks that previously were considered its peers. Thus, permitting a large risk premium to develop may jeopardize profitability over the medium term.

Just as some customers are more valuable than others, some liability instruments may be worth more to a bank than others because they are less costly to manage in a liquidity crisis. A bank can exercise some control over the risk premium it pays by limiting new issues of liabilities, but liabilities that are negotiable instruments, such as certificates of deposit or floating-rate notes, present a special problem. If the volume of secondary market activity is thin (as it is likely to be in the event of a liquidity crisis), interest rates on the bank's liabilities may rise to a substantial premium. In order to avoid the damaging impact of such premiums on confidence in the bank and on the interest rates it may pay on new issues, the bank may find it worthwhile to buy its own obligations, despite the fact that supporting the secondary market would exacerbate its short-term cash flow problem. Anticipated secondary market support should be netted against the estimate of new issues.

This section has highlighted several speculative considerations which are crucial inputs into the strategic planning exercise. Much of the information is highly subjective; inevitably the estimates will be subject to substantial error. But the questions posed are issues that must be confronted in order to manage a bank's vulnerability to a liquidity crisis. Moreover, the principal value of the procedure is not so much to arrive at a precise quantitative estimate of the bank's exposure as to identify sources of vulnerability and spur strategic thinking about the ways that vulnerability can be reduced. The procedure provides a systematic framework for asking questions about how a bank can enhance control over its exposure to a funding shock. The answers it elicits will not only help decision-makers control exposure at a level they deem acceptable, but also will strengthen their ability to act effectively if a shock should occur.

Concluding Comment

Martin Shubik (1983, p. 136) has observed that, "A key task of good corporate strategic planning is to avoid major disasters." The low-frequency, high-downside hazards we have discussed may jeopardize the survival of the bank. The scenario approach we have described is a mechanism for evaluating the bank's vulnerability to such hazards. Moreover, the approach is also helpful in identifying active, anticipatory measures the bank can take to reduce its exposure to such hazards rather than simply reacting after trouble has occurred. But the approach leaves at least one important question unanswered: is the reduction in vulnerability worth the cost of protective actions? This depends on a judgment concerning the likelihood that the shock will occur, a judgment that we have argued is necessarily subjective. This judgment is properly the prerogative of senior management. Our procedure is designed to bring the issue onto the agenda of senior managers and to present them with the best information for dealing with it.

Notes

1. Perfect certainty implies not only that we have the utmost confidence in the accuracy of our knowledge but also that we know that p_i is either zero or one.

2. It should be noted, however, that the experimental evidence to be referred to here is based on behavior with regard to low-probability risk that the experimenters assume is applicable to uncertainty.

3. Some uncertainty remains in connection with unpredictable events such as war or a major depression.

4. For an interesting illustration of the issue, see the debate between the authors of this chapter and a senior officer of a major bank, "Is a Global Debt Crisis Looming" (*ABA Banking Journal,* June 1981).

5. A recent IMF report (Brau et al., 1983) notes that, "Of the non-oil developing countries that either have restructured or were in the process of restructuring their bank debt between 1978 and the third quarter of 1983, all experienced a period of very rapid increase in international bank loans prior to the development of debt service difficulties." Although some of this increase in outstanding exposure was due to the borrowers having drawn on previously established commitments, a considerable amount of the increase was attributable to new short-term lending just before the crisis. Moreover, the Country Exposure Lending Survey for U.S. banks indicates

that from December 1981 to June 1982, the period just before the crisis, commitments to Venezuela and Brazil increased and those to Mexico were virtually unchanged.

6. Ackerlof and Dickens (1982) have recently made an application of the concept of cognitive dissonance to economic decisions.

7. For alternative hypotheses about why banks assume excessive exposures, see Kindleberger (1978) and Minsky (1977).

8. The qualification is necessary because bank shareholders are no longer liable to make good any losses of the bank on liquidation. Hence, if there is any significant probability that true net worth is less than zero, the market value of equity will exceed true net worth.

9. We acknowledge the assistance of Russell L. Ackoff in facilitating our understanding of the dialectic process. For further details regarding the dialectic approach, see Mason (1969) and Mitroff et al. (1977). See Cossier (1978) for evidence favoring an alternative "devil's advocate" technique.

10. Woods (1966) has described several instances in which corporate control systems inhibit the transmission of information concerning risks upward through the corporate hierarchy.

11. Simon (1978) views this as the key challenge to procedural rationality. He argues that the scarcest resource for dealing with many problems is not information, but the decision-maker's attention.

12. For a further discussion of these points, see Guttentag and Herring (1983).

13. Commitments that may be drawn at the discretion of the counterparty present a more complicated problem, however. As with other columns, the planner must enlist the assistance of various operational departments of the bank to determine how the bank's customers are likely to react to the shock. For example, will customers draw on commitments in advance of their need for funds as a precaution against the prospect that the bank may be unable to fulfill the commitment in the future? Will customers that have used the bank's credit to back up their own issues of money market instruments be forced to draw on those standby credits when confidence in the bank is undermined? Complications will also arise if the liquidity shock affects another bank or if it occurs in combination with a credit shock since some amortization and interest schedules will not be met and some customers will be forced to draw on commitments.

14. In the face of a liquidity shock, there may be a great temptation to shorten the duration of liabilities, both because short-term interest rates will be less than longer-term interest rates when the yield curve assumes a normal positive slope and because potential creditors may charge a higher default premium or may be unwilling to lend at longer maturities. Although shortening the duration of liabilities may reduce the measured funding cost, it does so only at the price of increasing the bank's exposure to interest rate risk. In a more general treatment, this cost of greater exposure to interest rate risk could be explicitly treated, but for purposes of this illustration, we will hold interest rate risk exposure constant.

15. It is arguable that this exercise should incorporate another column reflecting the bank's net cash flows from other, non–funds-related activities. This would enhance the realism of the approach, but would also involve further complexities. The cash flow from other activities may also be adversely affected if counterparties lose confidence in the bank.

16. De Leon (1975) notes the the process of constructing a scenario can act as an "educational ... perhaps sensitizing ... [device] for actual or potential decisionmakers."

17. Laws against insider trading may severely limit the scope for this sort of approach.

18. See Guttentag and Herring (1984) for an analysis of credit rationing in response to perceptions of moral hazard.

References

Ackerlof, George, & William T. Dickens. "The Economic Consequences of Cognitive Dissonance." *American Economic Review* (June 1982), pp. 307–19.

Brau, E., & R. C. Williams with P. M. Keller & M. Nowak. "Recent Multilateral Debt Restructurings with Official and Bank Creditors." Occasional Paper 25. International Monetary Fund, Washington, D.C. (December 1983).

Cossier, R. A. "The Effects of Three Potential Aids for Making Strategic Decisions on Prediction Accuracy." *Organizational Behavior and Human Performance* (1978), pp. 295–306.

de Leon, Peter. "Scenario Designs: An Overview." *Simulation and Games* (March 1975), pp. 39–60.

Guenther, Jack D. "Is Global Debt Crisis Zooming?" *ABA Banking Journal* (June 1981).

Guttentag, Jack. "Defensive and Dynamic Open Market Operations and the Federal Reserve System Crisis-Prevention Responsibilities." *Journal of Finance* (May 1969).

Guttentag, Jack, & Richard Herring. *The Lender-of-Last-Resort Function in an International Context.* Essays in International Finance, no. 151. Princeton, N.J. Princeton University (May 1983).

———. "Credit Rationing and Financial Disorder." *Journal of Finance* (December 1984).

Kindleberger, Charles P. *Manias, Panics and Crashes.* New York: Basic Books (1978).

Mason, R. O. "Dialectical Approach to Strategic Planning." *Management Science* (1969), B403–B414.

Minsky, Hyman. "A Theory of Systematic Fragility." In E. A. Altman & A. W. Sametz (eds.), *Financial Crises.* New York: Wiley Interscience (1977).

Mitroff, I. I., V. P. Barabba, & R. H. Kilmann. "The Application of Behavioral and Philosophical Technologies to Strategic Planning: A Case Study of a Large Federal Agency." *Management Science* (1977), pp. 44–58.

Pollock, Alex J. "Why Most Strategic Financial Plans are Useless." *Long Range Planning* (April 1984).

Prussia, Leland S. "Structural Change and Innovation in International Banking." Paper presented at the meeting of the American Finance Association, New York City (December 1983).

Shubik, Martin. "Political Risk: Analysis, Process and Purpose." In R. Herring (ed.), *Managing International Risk*. New York: Cambridge University Press (1983), pp. 109–138.

Simon, Herbert A. "Rationality as Process and as Product of Thought." *American Economic Review* (May 1978), pp. 1–16.

Tversky, Amos, & David Kahneman. "Availability: A Heuristic for Judging Frequency and Probability." *Cognitive Psychology* vol. 5, no. 2 (September 1973), pp. 207–232. Slovic & Tversky (eds.), *Judgment under Uncertainty: Heuristics and Biases*. New York: Cambridge University Press (1982), pp. 163–178.

Woods, Donald H. "Improving Estimates that Involve Uncertainty." *Harvard Business Review* (July-August 1966), pp. 91–98.

4
Exchange Rate–Related Exposures in a Macroeconomic Perspective

Lars Oxelheim
Clas Wihlborg

ABSTRACT

Exposure to exchange rates cannot be considered independently of exposures to related macroeconomic variables such as price levels, interest rates, and relative prices. We discuss whether a regression approach to measuring exposure should use these market price variables or underlying macroeconomic disturbances such as money supplies and fiscal policy measures. The choice depends on the stability of regression coefficients which in turn depends on the stability of policy authorities' behavior. We discuss also the role of the firm's time perspective for the determination of relevant exposure measures and a rational hedging strategy.

It is widely perceived that the degree of uncertainty in the business environment increased during the 1970s as a result of the shift to flexible exchange rates. Many observers would argue, however, that increased uncertainty about exchange rates, inflation rates, interest rates, and other macroeconomic variables was not a result of the new exchange rate regime, but a consequence of macroeconomic developments, oil price uncertainty, and central bank behavior in the late 1960s and the 1970s.

There are many channels through which macroeconomic uncertainty in general and exchange rate uncertainty in particular may affect the general level of welfare and business activity as well as more specific variables such as exports or the stock market value of an individual firm. Willett (1986) discusses at length several such channels. One important issue is the extent to which uncertainty influences firms' behavior through their choices of exposure measures, exposure management strategies, investment strategies, and so forth.

The authors are grateful for comments by Richard M. Levich and other seminar participants in the International Business Workshop at New York University.

This chapter concerns the basic issue of developing measures of exposure to changes in macroeconomic variables such as exchange rates, interest rates, and inflation rates. We emphasize exchange rate exposure since it has received the most attention during the past decade. A major point of our analysis is that managing exchange rate exposure per se is not clearly meaningful without considering the interdependence between the exchange rate and other variables related to the exchange rate in a general equilibrium system such as inflation rates and interest rates. We discuss alternative formulations of exposure taking such interdependence into account. A particular problem is how to account for political risk (the uncertainty about the legal/regulatory environment and the behavior of policy-making authorities).

A measure of exposure to changes in the exchange rate and related variables form the firm's point of view should have at least two characteristics. First, it should be *separable* from exposure to other variables; that is, the measure should not be sensitive to variables causing exposure that may be managed elsewhere in a firm. Second, it should be *operational* in the sense that it provides relevant guidelines for hedging and other adjustments if so desired.

In the next section, we discuss why exposure is of interest and compare different exchange rate exposure measures which have been used in academically and practically oriented writings. We choose an economic view of exposure for further analysis. In the following section, we analyze the drawbacks of viewing exchange rate exposure in isolation and discuss two ways in which related variables can be taken into consideration. The relative advantage of each is discussed from the points of view referred to above.

The next major section, "Decomposing Cash Flows," discusses how cash flows may be disaggregated for the purpose of exposure analysis. In the subsequent section, we discuss the importance of the firm's time perspective for defining exposure. The final section contains a summary.

Exposure Measures

Exposure often has the connotation of sensitivity to changes in different variables. There are reasons to distinguish between exposure to anticipated and unanticipated changes in, for example, the exchange rate. The firm can incorporate the former in its budget and planning process, while exposure to unanticipated changes constitutes the firm's risk exposure. A risk-neutral firm is by definition only concerned with exposure to anticipated changes. If an anticipated change is favorable, the firm may wish to maximize its exposure. The risk-averse firm, on the other hand, is willing to incur a cost to decrease its exposure to unanticipated changes. We emphasize exposure to unanticipated changes for risk-averse firms, but the analysis is to a large extent rele-

vant for risk-neutral firms as well, since the techniques for measuring exposure to anticipated and unanticipated changes are similar.

It should be observed that firms which according to finance theory would
be risk-neutral when shareholders are able to diversity macroeconomic risk
on their own may have economic as well as internal behavioral reasons to
behave in a risk-averse fashion. Default risk combined with *costs of default*
is often mentioned (Dufey and Srinivasulu, 1983) as a reason for risk-aver-
sion. Furthermore, when there are costs of *changing* output or sales in different markets, increased uncertainty about the firm's optimal production or
sales volume reduces expected profits for the risk-neutral firms. Therefore,
the firm may behave in a risk-averse way with respect to variables causing
output or sales uncertainty. (See also Shapiro and Titman, 1984.)

Conventional practically oriented exchange-rate exposure measures are
translation and transaction exposures. (See, for example, Evans, Folks, and
Jilling, 1978; and Oxelheim, 1984.) Translation exposure is an accounting-
based exposure measure and would be a valid concern from the stockholders'
point of view if book value were equal to or at least the best available measure of economic value. However, if a firm knows that there are better measures of economic exposure than accounting exposure, then there is no economic reason for the firm to manage on purely accounting-based exposure.

Transaction exposure measures are typically limited to future cash flows
contractually fixed in different currencies. Thus, they are often short-term as
well as partial in nature since the exposure of a large share of most firms'
expected cash flows is disregarded.

In this chapter, we assume that the firm has an economic objective. Such
an objective may be defined in terms of the net present value of future expected cash flows as in Lessard (1979) or in terms of near-term cash flows or
profits. Economic exposure would be defined correspondingly as the sensitivity of net present value, cash flows, or profits with respect to, for example,
exchange rate changes. According to Oxelheim (1984), many firms desire
exposure measures closely related to sensitivities of this kind. For example,
some firms worry about fluctuations over time in market value, others about
the magnitude of fluctuations in profits or cash flows.

We adopt the view that exposure can be seen as the sensitivity of cash
flows to changes in different macroeconomic variables, thereby extending approaches by Hodder (1982), Adler and Dumas (1983), and Garner and Shapiro (1984). Since the net present value depends on future expected cash
flows, it is simple—at least conceptually—to take the additional step of defining exposure as sensitivity of net present value of cash flows in many periods. Practical difficulties of measuring net present value exposure have been
pointed out by Adler and Dumas (1980) and will be discussed further in the
final section.

One way of measuring exchange rate exposure as cash flow sensitivity has been used in Garner and Shapiro (1984) and other studies referred to above. Their measure is expressed as:

$$\frac{\text{cov}[CF_t, e_t]}{\text{var }[CF_t]}, \tag{4.1}$$

that is, the covariance between cash flows and the exchange rate in period t relative to the variance of all cash flows. This measure tells us the contribution of the exchange rate to the variance of all cash flows. It could be obtained by regressing cash flows on the exchange rate. We turn next to a discussion of drawbacks of this exposure measure and extend the analysis to incorporate additional macroeconomic variables.

Measuring Exchange Rate and Related Exposures

The exposure measure described in the previous section has at least two serious drawbacks:

1. It is not separable from exposures to variables related to the exchange rate such as interest rates and inflation rates.
2. It may not be stable over time. Exposure coefficients obtained from historical data may not provide good guidance for the future.

The first drawback can be understood by considering other exposures of a firm. For example, it exchange rate exposure is defined as above, the firm would in a consistent manner measure interest rate exposure by estimating

$$\frac{\text{cov}[CF_t, i_t]}{\text{var }[CF_t]}, $$

where i_t is the interest rate in period t. Since the exchange rate and the interest rate are correlated according to most macroeconomic models, the two exposures would be partly overlapping. Similarly, if the firm measures inflation risk, and inflation and exchange rates are correlated, inflation exposure and exchange rate exposure would be overlapping. To resolve this overlap problem, the exposure coefficients should be partial correlation coefficients such that covariances are estimated holding all other variables constant. A multiple regression analysis of cash flows on the exchange rate and variables that may be suspected to be correlated in a general equilibrium system with this variable would accordingly resolve the problem of overlap.

The second problem concerning stability is due to the fact that an exchange rate change may be real or it may correspond to inflation in one country.[1] The frequency and magnitude of each kind of exchange rate change vary over time. One would not, therefore, suspect a stable relationship over time between the exchange rate and nominal cash flows. Depending on the nature of underlying real and monetary disturbances, difference relative price and demand effects accompany exchange rate changes over time. A second stability problem with the above exposure measure occurs if the degree to which exchange rate changes are anticipated varies over time.

We suggest now two methods for obtaining improved exposure measures by analyzing historical data. The first method—presented under "Exposure in Terms of Market Price Variables"—clarifies the distinction between real and nominal variables, while the second model—presented in the subsequent subsection—expresses cash flows as a function of underlying macroeconomic disturbances. In the following subsection, we argue that the advantage of one method over the other depends largely on uncertainty about the behavior of government authorities, that is, on political risk.

Exposure in Terms of Market Price Variables

The firm trying to evaluate its exposure may run the following regression:

$$\frac{CF_t^\$}{P_t^{US}} = E_{t-1}\left(\frac{CF_t^\$}{P_t^{US}}\right) + a_1\,[P_t^{US} - E_{t-1}\,(P_t^{US})] + a_2\,[P_t^F - E_{t-1}\,(P_t^F)]$$
$$+ a_3\,[u_t - E_{t-1}\,(u_t)] + a_4\,[i_t - E_{t-1}\,(i_t)] + a_5\,[i_t^F - E_{t-1}\,(i_t^F)] \quad (4.2)$$
$$+ a_6\,[r_t - E_{t-1}\,(r_t)] + \varepsilon_t$$

where:

$CF_t^\$$ = total cash flows in dollars
P_t^{US} = price level in the United States (shareholders' habitat)
E_{t-1} = expectations operator in period $t - 1$
P_t^F = foreign price level
u_t = real exchange rate (deviations from purchasing power parity, PPP)
i_t = interest rate in home market
i_t^F = foreign interest rate
r_t = relative price(s) of relevance for firm's profitability
ε_t = error term

The dependent variable in equation 4.2 is the real value of cash flow from the shareholders' perspective. The first variable on the right-hand side is the expected cash flows as of period $t - 1$. The other independent variables capture real cash flow effects of unanticipated changes in the domestic price level, the foreign price level(s), the real exchange rate(s), the domestic and the foreign interest rate(s), and relative prices in the firm's commodity markets. Expected cash flows would depend on expected levels of the different variables and the cash flow sensitivity to expected changes in them. These sensitivities may or may not differ from coefficients a_1 through a_6 for unanticipated changes.

The length of one period in equation 4.2 would depend on the time period over which the firm forms expectations of cash flows and the speed with which it may wish to take action in the form of hedging and so forth. For realism, we may envision all variables as quarterly averages.

By definition, exchange rate changes may correspond to either country's inflation rate or to deviations from PPP, in which case there are *real* exchange rate changes.[2] The cash flow effects of these different exchange rate changes are bound to be different. They would depend on which relative prices and which demand and cost effects are associated with domestic inflation, foreign inflation, and real exchange rate changes, respectively. (See, for example, Cornell, 1980.)[3] It is important also to distinguish between the impact of those relative price changes that are independent of exchange rates and inflation, and those relative price changes that occur in the macroeconomic adjustment process. The former impact is captured by coefficient a_6 and the latter by a_1, a_2, and a_3.

Each a-coefficient is a sensitivity measure in the form of a covariance between real cash flows and each variable holding other variables constant, relative to the total variance of real cash flows. The coefficient in front of expected cash flows should be equal to one and the error term should be randomly distributed. If not, additional variables may have to be introduced in the equation, for example, by distinguishing between different foreign currencies.

Exposure in Terms of Macroeconomic Disturbances

Real exchange rate changes occur for a number of reasons. An unanticipated monetary disturbance such as a money supply increase would, according to many macroeconomic models, lead to an immediate real depreciation, a fall in the interest rate, and an increase in the demand for goods. A fiscal contraction, on the other hand, could lead to a real depreciation, a fall in the interest rate, and a decrease in the demand for goods. Clearly, the magnitude of the demand effect associated with a particular real exchange rate change would depend on the source of the disturbance. Accordingly, the coefficient a_3 in equation 4.2 may not be stable over time but instead may depend on the relative frequency and magnitude of monetary and fiscal policy changes.

These considerations suggest that exposure could be defined in terms of underlying macroeconomic disturbances. We may, for example, define exposure based on coefficients in the following expression:

$$\frac{CF_t^\$}{P_t^{US}} = E_{t-1}\left(\frac{CF_t^\$}{P_t^{US}}\right) + b_1\,[M_t^{US} - E_{t-1}\,(M_t^{US})] + b_2\,[M_t^F$$
$$- E_{t-1}\,(M_t^F)] + b_3\,[D_t^{US} - E_{t-1}\,(D_t^{US})] + b_4\,[D_t^F - E_{t-1}\,(D_t^F)] \quad (4.3)$$
$$+ b_5\,[r_t - E_{t-1}\,(r_t)] + \pi_t$$

where:

M^{US}, M^F = the money supplies of the United States and foreign country(ies), respectively

D^{US}, D^F = the budget deficit of the United States and foreign country(ies), respectively

π = error term.

Equation 4.3 can naturally be extended to include other macroeconomic variables such as productivity growth and oil price shocks until the error term obtains desired properties. The sensitivity coefficients represent as above the covariances between real cash flows and each exogenous disturbance holding other variables constant relative to the total cash flow variance.

Comparing the Exposure Measures and Political Risk

We argued above that the *a*-coefficients in equation 4.2 may not be stable over time since their magnitudes depend on the source of underlying disturbances. Can we expect the *b*-coefficients in equation 4.3 to be stable? As Lucas (1976) has pointed out, shifts in the behavior of policy authorities influence coefficients in regressions like equation 4.3. Assume, for example, that the central bank first behaves according to a rule such as $M_t = \bar{M} + v_t$, where $\bar{M}$ is a constant and v_t is a random disturbance. The authority then shifts to another rule such as $M_t = cM_{t-1} + v'_t$ where c is a correlation coefficient and v'_t is the new random disturbance term. If cash flows in period t depend on the expected future money supply for period $t + 1$, then the relationship between cash flows and the money supply in period t in a reduced form such as equation 4.3 would be influenced by the above policy rule shift. In other words, the coefficient b_1 in the reduced form equation is influenced by policy rules. Similar arguments can be made for coefficients b_2, b_3, and b_4. The stability of each of these coefficients depends on the stability of policy rules for domestic and foreign fiscal policy and foreign monetary policy, respectively.

Uncertainty about policy rules is an element of *political risk*. The above analysis implies that political risk causes *uncertainty about coefficients* of sensitivity of cash flows to macroeconomic disturbances. Another source of political risk is caused by the potential imposition of exchange controls and credit controls. Such controls could influence structural relationships among, for example, real exchange rates, interest rates, and money supplies. Direct regulatory policy measures may have direct cash flow effects as well (see Dooley and Isard, 1980), but to the extent they are not forecast, their most important effects would be structural. (See, for example, Wihlborg, 1980.)

An important effect of uncertainty about policy rules is that it creates uncertainty for each economic agent about the expectation formation of other agents. Rational expectations models generally presume that each agent knows how other agents form expectations based on known structural relationships and policy rules. However, after each policy rule shift, it takes time for all agents to learn the new rule. In the meantime, the relationship between the current level of a policy variable and average expectations of future levels will be changing.[4] During this learning process, the exchange rate and other price variables are changing or fluctuating even at constant money supplies and fiscal policies.

This discussion indicates that when there is uncertainty about policy rules and average perceptions of these rules are changing, there occur exchange rate changes, inflation, and interest rate changes that cannot be explained by exogenous disturbances in a simple regression such as equation 4.3. Another way of expressing the same phenomenon is that the *b*-coefficients in regression 4.3 are changing during the learning process. Meese and Rogoff (1983) confirm this discussion by showing, using alternative models of the exchange rate, that a large share of the exchange rate variance cannot be explained by "fundamental" variables and that coefficients tend to be unstable.

We would expect that periods during which learning processes occur are characterized by a large amount of speculative activity since individual and average expectations differ. Therefore, periods of substantial speculative activity should be characterized by relatively large exchange rate changes without simultaneous changes in "fundamental" factors such as the money supply or the budget deficit.

Comparing equations 4.2 and 4.3 as ways of measuring exposure with historical data, the discussion implies that the more political risk there is, the more stable is equation 4.2 relative to 4.3. The reason is that with higher political risk, the instability of coefficients in equation 4.3 increases, and the exchange rate and other price variables tend to change and fluctuate even at constant levels of policy variables. The larger the proportion of the variance in the price variables in 4.2 that cannot be explained by shifts in policy variables, the more likely it is that *a*-coefficients in 4.2 are stable. In other words, real exchange rate changes, interest rate changes, and so on may be viewed as purely exogenous disturbances in themselves. On the other hand, with relative certainty about policy rules, coefficients in equation 4.2 could be unstable since they depend on the nature of underlying disturbances.

Decomposing Cash Flows

Coefficients of the type described in equations 4.2 and 4.3 are economic measures of exposure, and they provide a guide for hedging or adjusting business activity. Their estimation enables the manager to judge how sensitive the firm is to macroeconomic disturbances without having to estimate a complete macroeconomic model. Thus, the estimation of such coefficients would be an important objective of exposure analysis. We turn now to a discussion of the difficulties associated with an implementation of this kind of exposure analysis. A more extensive analysis of these difficulties can be found in Oxelheim and Wihlborg (1986).

We mentioned that it is desirable to distinguish between anticipated and unanticipated changes in variables influencing cash flows. Anticipated changes are obtained by forecasting. The firm's budget can be seen as a forecast of cash flows based on forecasts of exchange rates, prices, and so on. To fulfill this role, the budget must truly reflect market price forecasts rather than be based on current prices.[5]

When implementing the exposure analysis, a decision must be made regarding the level of aggregation of cash flows on which the analysis should be performed. Total cash flows may consist of flows from a number of products as well as from several subsidiaries in different countries. The total real after-tax value of cash flows for product i in country j in dollar terms ($CF^{ij\$}/P^{US}$) can be written as:

$$\frac{CF^{ij\$}}{P^{US}} = \frac{CF^{ij} \cdot e^j}{P^{US}} \tag{4.4}$$

where CF^{ij} is cash flows in j-currency and e^j is dollars per j-currency unit. these cash flows can be broken down further. After defining

$$e^j \equiv \frac{P^{US}}{P^j} \cdot u^j \tag{4.5}$$

we can express cash flows for product i in subsidiary j in the following way:

$$\frac{CF^{ij} \cdot u^j}{P^j} = u^j q^{ij} \left(\frac{OP^{ij}}{P^j} - \frac{IP^{ij}}{P^j} - \frac{W^{ij}}{P^j} \right) (1 - t^j) + \frac{t^j DEP^{ij} \cdot u^j}{P^j}$$

$$- \frac{u^j}{P^j} (1 - t^j) [i^j D^{ij} - (1 - \beta^j) \cdot \dot{p}^j \cdot D^{ij}] \quad (4.6)$$

where

$$u^j/p^j \equiv e^j/P^{\text{US}},$$

and

u^j = the real exchange rate between the dollar and *j*'s currency,
q^{ij} = quantity sold of product *i* in country *j*,
OP^{ij} = *i*-output price in country *j*,
IP^{ij} = input price per unit of *i*-output in country *j*,
W^{ij} = wages per unit of *i*-output in country *j*,
t^j = tax rate for subsidiary in country *j*,
DEP^{ij} = depreciation in country *j* for product *i*,
i^j = interest rate for subsidiary in *j*,
D^{ij} = nominal debt in *j*-currency associated with production of product *i*,
β^j = degree of indexation of debt in country *j*,
$P^j (\dot{P}^j)$ = price level (inflation) in country *j*.

Equation 4.6 decomposes cash flows for a particular product in a particular country into a "business operation component" (as a function of relative prices), a depreciation tax shield component, and a financial cost component. All terms on the right-hand side are expressed as *real* cash flows in terms of country *j*'s currency multiplied by the real exchange rate between the home currency (dollars) and country *j*'s currency. We can see in the first term on the right-hand side how real cash flows from business operations are influenced by volume and relative price effects. The second term is the depreciation tax shield evaluated in real foreign currency terms and multiplied by the real exchange rate.

The third term captures financial costs after tax. We include this term under the assumption that the firm is concerned with cash flows available for distribution to shareholders. D^{ij} refers to the debt capacity from the project and is expressed in the foreign currency. Financial costs consist of interest costs and real capital gains from inflation. If $\beta^j = 1$, there is perfect indexation of foreign currency debts and the inflation gain is zero.[6]

Equation 4.6 shows the main categories of cash flows on which exchange rates, interest rates, and price levels have an impact. Clearly, these variables may influence each category in a different way. Equation 4.6 also demonstrates how exposure may depend on capital intensity (through depreciation) and capital structure (through debt capacity).

Total cash flows for a firm is the summation of cash flows (as in equation 4.6) over products (i) and countries (j). Thus, the estimation of a cash flow exposure by means of equations 4.2 or 4.3 on an aggregate level presumes that the share of product i and country j in cash flows is constant, and that depreciation tax shields as well as financial cash flows remain constant shares of each subsidiary's cash flows.

Recognizing the possible variability in the structure of cash flows in equation 4.6 as well as in macroeconomic relationships underlying exposure coefficients in equations 4.2 and 4.3, there are substantial informational advantages to decomposing cash flows for purposes of exposure analysis. Cash flows may be broken down by:

country,

product, and

variable cash flows from business operations as opposed to depreciation and financial cash flows.

After decomposition, exposure coefficients of the type described equations 4.2 and 4.3 may be estimated for each cash flow component. Further decomposition into cash flows that are adjustable and nonadjustable in terms of currency denomination is desirable if there are opportunities to influence exposure by adjusting currency denomination of loans, currency of invoice, and so forth. After decomposition of cash flows, dispersed judgmental information can be used to complement regression analysis of exposure coefficients for different parts of the firm. In times of political uncertainty and uncertainty about the validity of regression coefficients, this kind of judgmental information may be particularly valuable.

Assume now that exposure coefficients as in equation 4.2 have been obtained for cash flows for specific products in each country. The *decentralized* firm may be satisfied with such exposure measures, although overlapping hedging transactions may be performed. On the other hand, if hedging decisions are made at a centralized level for a multinational corporation, all exposure coefficients can be combined into a comprehensive exposure measure. There are gains in terms of transaction costs from such centralization, since offsetting hedging transactions can be avoided and exposures of different flows can be matched against each other. Needless to say, the centralization of exposure management and the estimation of a comprehensive exposure measure demand a substantial data base and effective internal information systems.

The Role of the Firm's Time Perspective

The section "Exposure Measures" mentioned that the stockholders' concern is with the net present value of future cash flows. Whether exposure of cash flows as expressed in equations 4.2 and 4.3 actually affects stockholders' valuation of a firm depends on four factors. First, intertemporal covariances among macroeconomic variables causing exposure in specific periods influence the degree to which cash flow exposure translates into net present value exposure. (See, for example, Lessard, 1979.) Second, the cost of capital at which future cash flows are discounted influences the relative weights of near-term and distant cash flows in the net present value. Third, the extent to which stockholders can diversify macroeconomic risk influences the firm's response to exposure. When macroeconomic risk is diversifiable, stockholders will not claim compensation for absorbing such risk. Fourth, if cash flow variability causes outright costs in terms of increased probability of costly default or costs of adjustment in output and sales, then high cash flow variability reduces stockholders' valuation of the firm. (See the section "Decomposing Cash Flows.")

In this section we focus on the first and the second factors. The time perspective of the firm is directly reflected in the second factor—the discount rate. The importance of the first factor—the intertemporal pattern of cash flows—increases with the length of the firm's perspective. As an illustration of the role of the discount rate, we may consider a firm with quarterly cash flows of X units of foreign currency. Assume that the firm has the choice of always leaving these X units uncovered, or of covering in every quarter the next quarter's cash flow by selling X units of foreign currency in the three-month forward market.

The present value of a stream of X units of foreign currency uncovered is:

$$PV_{uc} = E\left[\frac{X \cdot e_1}{(1 + d/4)} + \ldots + \frac{X \cdot e_n}{(1 + d/4)^n}\right] \qquad (4.7)$$

where d is the discount rate and e_2 through e_n are exchange rates.

If the firm consecutively covers on a quarterly basis its present value becomes:

$$PV_c = E\left[\frac{X \cdot f_0}{(1 + d/4)} + \ldots \frac{X \cdot f_{n-1}}{(1 + d/4)^n}\right] \qquad (4.8)$$

where f_0 is *today's* forward rate for three-month delivery, and f_{n-1} is the forward rate in period $n - 1$ for delivery in period n.

Variances of PV_{uc} and PV_c can be written in the following way:

$$V[PV_{uc}] = X \cdot V\left[\frac{e_1}{(1 + d/4)} + \cdots + \frac{e_n}{(1 + d/4)^n}\right], \qquad (4.9)$$

$$V[PV_c] = \frac{X}{(1 + d/4)^2} \cdot V\left[\frac{f_1}{(1 + d/4)} + \cdots + \frac{f_{n-1}}{(1 + d/4)^n}\right], \quad (4.10)$$

where $V[\ldots]$ is a variance of the expression within brackets.

If n is large, the last term in 4.9 is negligible, in which case the relative variance of 4.9 and 4.10 depends on the discount rate, d, and the variance of spot and forward rates, respectively.[7] It has been noted by Levich (1979), Mussa (1982), Shapiro (1982), and Oxelheim (1985) that the forward rate tends to follow the spot rate, that is, $V[e_t] \equiv V[f_t]$. Then, the gain from consecutive covering depends only on the discount rate, d, or more properly on $(1 + d/4)^2$, which for most firms is likely to be close to one. The "ineffectiveness" in terms of variance reduction of consecutive covering arises due to the discrepancy between the firm's long time perspective as reflected in the discount rate and its short "action horizon."

The importance of intertemporal covariances can also be seen in equations 4.9 and 4.10. If the exchange rate in 4.9 is mean-reverting, the variance of PV_{uc} tends to *decrease* with a longer time perspective (a lower discount rate). In the theoretical macroeconomic literature, the *real* exchange rate has this property although it has not been definitely confirmed in the empirical literature. (See, for example, Roll, 1979; and Pigott and Sweeney, 1985.) The price level does not have this property, however, with the consequence that inflation uncertainty tends to become the dominant reason for exchange rate uncertainty in the long run. Since the forward rate, f, tends to follow the nominal exchange rate, which depends on both inflation and real exchange rate changes, the forward market becomes a more inefficient hedge of real exchange rate risk the more distant are cash flows.

Without going further into hedging policy, we conclude that although exposure of cash flows is an essential component of measuring the exposure of present values, a hedging policy for present value should take into consideration complementary judgment about intertemporal relationships as well.

Summary

Traditional exposure measures are either partial, accounting-based, or both. Partiality reveals itself in two ways. First, exposure measures are often restricted to a limited share of cash flows (such as transactions exposure). Second, they usually refer to exposure to exchange rate changes neglecting variables that may be related to these exchange rates in a general equilibrium system. Since changes in these related variables also cause exposure, management of exchange rate and related exposures should be coordinated.

Exposure may be defined in terms of market price variables or in terms of underlying macroeconomic disturbances. The advantage of one approach over the other would depend on the relative stability over time on estimated exposure coefficients. We argue that in times of high uncertainty about the behavior pattern of policy authorities, exposure should be defined in terms of market price variables. Then, a large share of the exchange rate variability will be independent of variability in exogenous macroeconomic variables.

We suggest that before estimating exposure coefficients, cash flows should be disaggregated by, for example, product, subsidiary, and type of cash flow (such as commercial versus financial). The advantage of such disaggregation is that changes in the composition of the firm's cash flows are easily recognized.

Finally, we discussed the link between cash flow exposure and net present value exposure. Intertemporal covariances between different variables and the firm's discount rate determine whether cash flow exposures tend to cancel over time. If a variable is mean-reverting, as is often assumed for the real exchange rate, then the exposure of the firm's value may be negligible in comparison with the cash flow exposure for one period.

The analysis has strong implications for firms' exposure management strategies. For example, if the discount rate of the firm is not very high, there may be little gain in terms of decreased value variances of consecutively covering accounts receivables and payables. Another implication is that the relevant exposure to, for example, an exchange rate should take into account that is may be overlapping with exposures to interest rates, inflation rates, and the commercial exposure of the firm.

Notes

1. In our terminology, a real exchange rate change is a deviation from relative purchasing power parity. Relative purchasing power parity holds when the rate of change of the exchange rate offsets the inflation differential between two countries. Therefore, a real exchange rate change implies that there is a change in the relative price between countries of a bundle of goods. (See also note 2.)

An exchange rate change may have real effects even if relative purchasing power parity holds if there are, i.e., relative prices among goods that are affected by the exchange rate adjustment process.

In this chapter, we are not interested in defining the exact conditions under which exposure of different kinds arise. We limit the analysis to the more general problem of how exposure can be measured independently of the nature of underlying price adjustment processes. The role of these for exposure has been discussed extensively by, for example, Shapiro (1983) and Wihlborg (1980).

2. Formally, $e_t/e_{t-1} \equiv [(P_t^{US}/P_{t-1}^{US}) / (P_t^F/P_{t-1}^F)] (u_t/u_{t-1})$, where e_t is dollars per unit of foreign currency. Changes in the relative price, r, in equation 4.2 may be correlated with either the relative inflation term or the real exchange rate change in the adjustment process to macroeconomic disturbances.

3. The nominal exchange rate may be used instead of the real exchange rate in equation 4.2 since coefficient a_3 measures exchange rate effects holding price levels constant.

4. Frydman (1982) demonstrates the importance of average expectations in macro models with rational expectations.

5. Lessard and Lorange (1977) discuss alternative exchange rates in firms' budget and evaluation systems.

6. The inflation gain is a positive cash flow under the assumption that the debt-equity ratio is held constant. This assumption enables discounting of future cash flows at a constant rate.

7. We assume that conditions for obtaining finite variances are fulfilled.

References

Adler, M., & B. Dumas, in B. Antl (ed.), *Currency Risk and the Corporation*. London: Euromoney (1980), 145–58.

———, "International Portfolio Choice and Corporation Finance: A Synthesis," *Journal of Finance*, 38 (June 1983), 925—84.

Cornell, B., "Inflation, Relative Prices and Exchange Risk," *Financial Management*, 9 (Autumn 1980), 30–34.

Dooley, M., & P. Isard, "Capital Controls, Political Risks and Deviations from Interest-Rate Parity," *Journal of Political Economy*, 88 (April 1980), 370–84.

Dufey, G., & S. L. Srinvasulu, "The Case for Corporate Management of Foreign Exchange Risk," *Financial Management* (Winter 1983).

Evans, P., M. Folks, Jr., & M. Jilling, *The Impact of Statement of Financial Standards No. 8 on the Foreign Risk Management Practices of American Multinationals*. Financial Accounting Standards Board, Stamford, Conn. (1978).

Fama, E., "Forward and Spot Exchange Rates," *Journal of Monetary Economics*, 14 (April 1984), 319–38.

Frenkel, J., & R. M. Levich, "Covered Interest Arbitrage: Unexploitable Profits?" *Journal of Political Economy*, 83 (April 1975), 325–38.

Frydman, R., "Towards an Understanding of Market Processes: Individual Expectations, Learning and Convergence to Rational Expectations Equilibrium," *American Economic Review*, 72 (September 1982), 652–68.

Garner, K., & A. Shapiro, "A Practical Method of Assessing Foreign Exchange Risk," *Midland Corporate Finance Journal* (Fall 1984), 6–17.

Hodder, J. E., "Exposure to Exchange Rate Movements," *Journal of International Economics* (November 1982), 375–86.

Lessard, D. R., "Financial Management of International Operations: Introduction," in *International Financial Management, Theory and Application.* Boston; Warren, Gorham & Lamont (1979).

Lessard, D. R., & P. Lorange, "Currency Changes and Management Control: Resolving the Centralization/Decentralization Dilemma," *Accounting Review* (July 1977), 628–37.

Levich, R. M., *The International Money Market.* New York: JAI Press, 1979.

Lucas, R. E., "Econometric Policy Evaluation: A Critique," in K. Brunner & A. H. Meltzer (eds.), *Carnegie-Mellon Conference Series on Public Policy,* vol. 1. Amsterdam: North Holland (1976).

Meese, R. A., & K. Rogoff, "Empirical Exchange Rate Models of the Seventies—Do They Fit Out of Sample?" *Journal of International Economics,* 14 (January 1983), 3–24.

Mussa, M., "A Model of Exchange Rate Dynamics," *Journal of Political Economy,* 90 (February 1982), 74–104.

Oxelheim, L., *Foreign Exchange Risk Management in the Modern Company—A Total Perspective.* Stockholm: Scandinavian Institute for Foreign Exchange Research (June 1984).

———, *International Financial Market Fluctuations.* Chichester, England: John Wiley & Sons (1985).

Oxelheim, L., & C. Wihlborg, "Exchange Rate and Related Economic Exposures—A Theory for Management Strategy and Information Needs." Working paper. Claremont, Calif.: Claremont Center for Economic Policy Studies, Department of Economics, The Claremont Graduate School (1986).

Pigott, C., & R. J. Sweeney, "Purchasing Power Parity and Exchange Rate Dynamics: Some Empirical Results," in S. W. Arndt, R. J. Sweeney & T. D. Willett (eds.), *Exchange Rates, Trade and the U.S. Economy.* Cambridge, Mass.: Ballinger (1985).

Roll, R., "Violations of Purchasing Power Parity and Their Implications for Efficient International Commodity Markets," in M. Sarnat & G. P. Szego (eds.), *International Finance and Trade.* Cambridge, Mass.: Ballinger (1979).

Shapiro, A., *Multinational Financial Management.* Boston: Allyn & Bacon, (1982).

———, "What Does Purchasing Power Parity Really Mean?" *Journal of International Money and Finance,* 2 (December 1983); reprinted in D. Lessard (ed.), *International Financial Management Theory and Application.* Wiley (1984).

Shapiro, A., & S. Titman, "An Integrated View of Risk Management," *Working Paper.* Los Angeles: University of Southern California (December 1984).

Wihlborg, C., "Currency Exposure—Taxonomy and Theory," in R. M. Levich & C. Wihlborg (eds.), *Exchange Risk and Exposure.* Lexington, Mass.: Lexington Books (1980).

———, "The Effectiveness of Exchange Controls on Financial Capital Flows," *Columbia Journal of World Business* (Winter 1980).

Willett, T. D., "Exchange Rate Volatility, International Trade, and Resource Allocation: A Perspective on Recent Research," *Journal of International Money and Finance,* 5, supplement (March 1986), 101–12.

5

A New Way to Cover Foreign Currency Bonds

William R. Folks, Jr.
Chuck C. Y. Kwok

ABSTRACT

The authors develop a methodology, aggregate iterative covering, for covering the discounted value of the cash flow of a specific foreign currency debt service stream. The methodology provides for a series of one-period forward purchases of the discounted value of future debt service outflows, adjusted for the expected series of forward discounts prevailing in the marketplace. To demonstrate the efficacy of this methodology, a simulation model is constructed. An eight-year bullet maturity bond that is denominated in German marks and carries 6 percent annual coupon is taken as an example. Using empirically developed estimates of the variance of year-to-year rate changes and forward premiums for the German mark, the authors show that the variance of the discounted value of bond servicing flows can be reduced by 95.34 percent under the new covering methodology.

Recent developments in global financial markets have created a wide range of funding alternatives for borrowers with international credit standing. Two developments in particular, the growth of liability swaps and the enhanced availability of long-dated forwards, allow borrowers to access funds in currencies where they have unutilized or underutilized borrowing capacity and still manage the resulting currency risk. Firms either may swap the liability created by the funding for a liability position in the desired currency or may cover the currency risk on the funding through long-dated forwards that match in amount and maturity the interest payment and principal repayment of the debt.

Long-dated forwards have evidently grown significantly in availability and price competitiveness over the past decade. Nonetheless, these contracts are typically based on negotiated rather than market-determined prices.

The authors would like to express their appreciation to Professor Michael Oliff for his technical advice.

This chapter develops an iterative covering method which eliminates most of the uncertainty associated with foreign currency funding through a series of one-year forward contracts. Unlike the works of Folks (1980) and Eaker and Grant (1985), whose methods revolve around the use of forward contracts to hedge two-period cash flows, the methodology utilized in this chapter is for hedging the more common case of multiperiod cash flows.

The chapter is divided into four parts, corresponding to the four major components of the logical approach needed to establish the method's validity. In the first part, we demonstrate the surprising fact that uncertainty in the domestic-currency–discounted value of a bond denominated in foreign currency can be completely eliminated by a series of forward sales, provided only that the forward premiums from year to year are known for certain. Put another way, by covering from year to year, using a series of carefully constructed hedges, the issues can fix the discounted value of a foreign currency debt obligation, as long as the issuer knows the size of the forward premiums that will prevail over the life of the loan.

Of course, there is always some uncertainty in the forward premiums, but, empirically, that uncertainty tends to be significantly lower (measured by its standard deviation) than the uncertainty in year-to-year exchange rate changes. The authors hypothesize that the type of hedges that completely eliminate uncertainty in the case where the forward premiums are known for certain can, if constructed using the expected forward premiums, result in substantial reduction in the standard deviation of the discounted value of bond servicing flows. In part 2 of the chapter, we develop the formulae for construction of these hedges on an expectations basis.

To demonstrate the efficacy of the methodology, we show the results of a simulation model constructed to demonstrate the uncertainty-reducing characteristics of the new covering technique. Using empirically developed estimates of the variance of year-to-year rate changes and forward premiums for the German mark, we show that the variance of the discounted value of bond servicing flows on a 6 percent annual coupon eight-year bullet maturity bond denominated in German marks can be reduced by 95.34 percent under the new covering methodology.

The final portion of the chapter summarizes our findings and identifies other areas where the new covering methodology might have validity.

Covering a Bond When the Forward Premiums Are Known

We are considering the situation of the issuer of an n-year maturity foreign currency bond with foreign currency face amount F and annual interest payment C. To ease exposition, we assume that the entire principal amount is due at maturity.

At time O, when the bond is issued, the direct exchange rate is x_o; at any year t, the exchange rate is x_t, a random variable. We define the annual currency appreciation from time $t - 1$ to time t as

$$\tilde{\delta}_t = \frac{\tilde{x}_{t-1}}{\tilde{x}_t - \tilde{x}_{t-1}}. \tag{5.1}$$

There exists a forward market with a one-year maturity. At time t, the one-year forward rate is y_t; we define the forward rate premiums at time t,

$$\tilde{\Delta}_t = \frac{\tilde{y}_t - \tilde{x}_t}{\tilde{x}_t}. \tag{5.2}$$

The primary assumption of this section is that Δ_t is known for certain. The implication is that there is a direct functional relationship between $\tilde{y}_t$ and $\tilde{x}_t$; rewriting 5.2, we find that

$$\tilde{y}_t = \tilde{x}_t (1 + \Delta_t). \tag{5.3}$$

We hypothesize that a company issues a foreign currency bond which pays C units of foreign currency in interest at the end of each year, for years 1 to n, and repays the face amount F at maturity year. The technique can be applied to any known amortization schedule of the debt, but we have chosen a bullet issue for simplicity.

Assuming a discount rate d, the discounted domestic currency value (designated V) of the foreign currency outflows needed to service this debt is

$$V = \sum_{t=1}^{n-1} \frac{C\tilde{x}_t}{(1 + d)^t} + \frac{(C + F)\tilde{x}_n}{(1 + d)^n}. \tag{5.4}$$

V is thus a linear function of the ending exchange rates $\tilde{x}_1, \ldots \tilde{x}_n$.

The basic approach of the technique is to use the forward market at time $t - 1$ and the fact that Δ_{t-1} is known for certain to remove the functional dependency on $\tilde{x}_t$. At time $n - 1$, one period before the maturity of the bond, the issuer buys the principal F and the interest C in the forward market at the rate $\tilde{y}_{t-1}$. At time n, the profit from the transaction is

$$(C + F) (\tilde{x}_n - \tilde{y}_{n-1}), \tag{5.5}$$

which is discounted by the n-period discount factor $(1 + d)^n$. If we subtract the discounted value of the profit from the forward contract (a cash inflow)

from the discounted cash outflows required to service the debt, we find that
the discounted value is

$$\sum_{t=1}^{n-1} \frac{C\,\tilde{x}_t}{(1+d)^t} + \frac{(C+F)}{(1+d)^n}(\tilde{x}_n) - \frac{(C+F)}{(1+d)^n}(\tilde{x}_n - \tilde{y}_{n-1}) \qquad (5.6)$$

$$= \sum_{t=1}^{n-1} \frac{C\tilde{x}_t}{(1+d)^t} + \frac{(C+F)}{(1+d)^n}(\tilde{y}_{n-1}). \qquad (5.7)$$

Since $\tilde{y}_{n-1} = \tilde{x}_{n-1}(1+\Delta_{n-1})$, the expression of discounted value 5.2 can be
rewritten to show dependence only on exchange rates $\tilde{x}_1, \ldots \tilde{x}_{n-1}$. We designate by V_{n-1} the discounted value obtained by completing the forward operation to remove dependency on $\tilde{x}_n$, and, in general, V_{t-1}, the discounted
value obtained by removing dependency on $\tilde{x}_t, \ldots \tilde{x}_n$. Thus,

$$V_{n-1} = \sum_{t=1}^{n-2} \frac{C\tilde{x}_t}{(1+d)^t} + \left[C + \frac{(C+F)(1+\Delta_{n-1})}{(1+d)} \right] \frac{\tilde{x}_{n-1}}{(1+d)^{n-1}}. \qquad (5.8)$$

In Equation 5.8 we have collected all terms dependent on $\tilde{x}_{n-1}$.

The difference in discounted value, $V - V_{n-1}$, is the discounted profit
on the forward contract 5.5; rewriting 5.5 in terms of Δ_{n-1} and $\tilde{\delta}_n$, rate of
appreciation from time $n-1$ to n, we find the profit is

$$(C+F)\,\tilde{x}_{n-1}\,[1 + \tilde{\delta}_n - (1+\Delta_{n-1})]$$
$$= (C+F)\,\tilde{x}_{n-1}\,(\tilde{\delta}_n - \Delta_{n-1}). \qquad (5.9)$$

On the two assumptions that $\tilde{\delta}_n$ is independent of $\tilde{x}_{n-1}$ and that $E(\tilde{\delta}_n) = \Delta_{n-1}$,
the expected profit from the forward contract is zero and there is no differ-
ence between $E(V)$ and $E(V_{n-1})$. The first assumption is that the current level
of the exchange rate does not interact with the level of exchange rate change
over the next period; the second is that the forward premium is an unbiased
predictor of the rate of change in the spot. Both these assumptions, while not
completely verified empirically, are generally accepted as a logical point of
departure. Should they not hold, the discounted value of the fully covered
bond stream will be different from the expected discounted value of the uncovered stream.

By inspection of equation 5.8, we can see how to eliminate the functional
dependence on x_{n-1}. A forward market purchase at time $n-2$ should be
taken in the amount

$$C + \frac{(C+F)(1+\Delta_{n-1})}{(1+d)}; \qquad (5.10)$$

the profits from this forward contract are discounted back $n - 1$ periods. Thus,

$$
\begin{aligned}
V_{n-2} &= \sum_{t=1}^{n-2} \frac{C\tilde{x}_t}{(1 + d)^t} + \left[C + \frac{(C + F)(1 + \Delta_{n-1})}{(1 + d)} \right] \frac{\tilde{y}_{n-2}}{(1 + d)^{n-1}} \\
&= \sum_{t=1}^{n-3} \frac{C\tilde{x}_t}{(1 + d)^t} + \left[C + \frac{C(1 + \Delta_{n-2})}{(1 + d)} \right. \\
&\quad + \left. \frac{(C + F)(1 + \Delta_{n-1})(1 + \Delta_{n-2})}{(1 + d)^2} \right] \frac{\tilde{x}_{n-2}}{(1 + d)^{n-2}}.
\end{aligned} \tag{5.11}
$$

By continued elimination of the dependence on $\tilde{x}_t$ by forward operations using the same pattern, we find

$$
\begin{aligned}
V_{n-3} &= \sum_{t=1}^{n-4} \frac{C\tilde{x}_t}{(1 + d)^t} + \left[C + \frac{C(1 + \Delta_{n-3})}{(1 + d)} + \frac{C(1 + \Delta_{n-2})(1 + \Delta_{n-3})}{(1 + d)^2} \right. \\
&\quad + \left. \frac{(C + F)(1 + \Delta_{n-1})(1 + \Delta_{n-2})(1 + \Delta_{n-3})}{(1 + d)^3} \right] \frac{\tilde{x}_{n-3}}{(1 + d)^{n-3}}.
\end{aligned} \tag{5.12}
$$

In general,

$$
\begin{aligned}
V_{n-k} &= \sum_{t=1}^{n-k-1} \frac{C\tilde{x}_t}{(1 + d)^t} + \left[C + \sum_{t=1}^{k-1} C \left(\frac{\prod_{l=n-k}^{(n-k)+(t-1)} (1 \right.\right. \\
&\quad \left.\left. + \Delta_l)}{(1 + d)^t} \right) + \frac{(C + F) \prod_{l=n-k}^{n-1} (1 + \Delta_l)}{(1 + d)^k} \right] \frac{\tilde{x}_{n-k}}{(1 + d)^{n-k}}.
\end{aligned} \tag{5.13}
$$

At time $n - k - 1$, the covering purchase is

$$
\left\{ C + \sum_{t=1}^{k-1} C \left[\frac{\prod_{l=n-k}^{(n-k)+(t-1)} (1 + \Delta_l)}{(1 + d)^t} \right] + \frac{(C + F) \prod_{l=n-k}^{n-1} (1 + \Delta_l)}{(1 + d)^k} \right\} \tag{5.14}
$$

When $k = n - 1$,

$$V_{n-(n-1)} = V_1 = \left\{ C + \sum_{t=1}^{n-2} C \left[\frac{\prod_{l=1}^{t} (1 + \Delta_l)}{(1 + d)^t} \right] \right.$$

$$\left. + \frac{(C + F) \prod_{l=1}^{n-1} (1 + \Delta_l)}{(1 + d)^{n-1}} \right\} \frac{\tilde{x}_1}{(1 + d)}. \quad (5.15)$$

At time O, the initial covering forward purchase is

$$\left\{ C + \sum_{t=1}^{n-2} C \left[\frac{\prod_{l=1}^{t} (1 + \Delta_l)}{(1 + d)^t} \right] + \frac{(C + F) \prod_{l=1}^{n-1} (1 + \Delta_l)}{(1 + d)^{n-1}} \right\}. \quad (5.16)$$

The final value, taking into account covering operations from time O to time $n - 1$,

$$V_O = \left\{ \sum_{t=0}^{n-2} C \left[\frac{\prod_{l=0}^{t} (1 + \Delta_l)}{(1 + d)^{t+1}} \right] + \frac{(C + F) \prod_{l=0}^{n-1} (1 + \Delta_l)}{(1 + d)^n} \right\} x_o.$$

Since all Δ_t are known for certain, V_O is known for certain; under the assumption that $E(V_t) - E(V_{t-1}) = 0$ for all t, as developed by the same arguments that used to show that $E(V) = E(V_{n-1})$, we see that $E(V_O) = E(V_1) = \ldots E(V_{n-1}) = E(V)$. Thus, we have developed a methodology that

1. completely eliminates uncertainty in the discounted value of bond service cash flows, and
2. has the same expected value as V.

It must be noted that the methodology does not guarantee that the per period cash flows from pursuing this iterative covering approach are fixed for certain. Each individual period's cash flow depends on the exchange rate. However, what the method does guarantee is that the discounted value of these flows is fixed, and that, under certain generally discussed foreign exchange market conditions, it is fixed without sacrifice of expected value. Thus, the aggregate iterative covering technique (the name which we give to the technique of covering forward a discounted aggregate value of future cash flows) is clearly superior to leaving the flows uncovered, in any mean-variance framework of analysis.

Covering a Bond When the Forward Premiums Are Uncertain

Analysis of the case where the forward premiums $\tilde{\Delta}_t$ are uncertain does not yet lead to a closed-form demonstration that aggregate iterative covering is a superior technique. Indeed, uncertainty in the forward premiums may totally eliminate the uncertainty reduction characteristics of the technique. However, according to Frenkel (1981), the forward premiums in the marketplace are characterized by lower historical variance than the year-to-year changes in spot exchange rates. Should this phenomenon be general, use of the aggregate iterative hedging technique may lead to a significant reduction in variance for the discounted value of the foreign bond. An empirical estimate of the historical variance of Deutsche mark annual forward premiums compared to year-to-year rate movements demonstrates that in recent years the forward premiums had substantially less variance.

The approach to aggregate iterative covering when $\tilde{\Delta}_t$ are uncertain makes it impossible to eliminate uncertainty completely. Inspection of expressions 5.14 and 5.16, which show the forward purchases required at time $n - k - 1$ and time O, respectively, reveal that these expressions depend on exact knowledge of $\Delta_{n-k-1}, \ldots \Delta_{n-1}$; at time $n - k - 1$, only Δ_{n-k-1} is known for certain. The approach is modified by estimating Δ_t by $E(\Delta_t)$. Thus, at time $n - k - 1$, the appropriate covering purchase is

$$\left\{ C + \sum_{t=1}^{k-1} C \left[\frac{\prod_{l=n-k}^{(n-k)+(t-1)} [1 + E(\Delta_l)]}{(1 + d)^t} \right] + \frac{(C + F) \prod_{l=n-k}^{n-1} [1 + E(\Delta_l)]}{(1 + d)^k} \right\}. \quad (5.17)$$

While the general formulae developed above and the general result do not depend on this assumption, to simplify the formulation of their simulation model, the authors have assumed that each forward premium $\tilde{\Delta}_t$ has the same expectation $\bar{\Delta}$ and the same variance, which is estimated using historical data.

The appropriate covering operation at time $n - k - 1$ can be simplified from expression 5.17 to

$$\left[C + \sum_{t=1}^{k-1} C \left(\frac{1 + \bar{\Delta}}{1 + d} \right)^t + (C + F) \left(\frac{1 + \bar{\Delta}}{1 + d} \right)^k \right];$$ (5.18)

the initial covering operation at time O is

$$\left[\sum_{t=0}^{n-2} C \left(\frac{1 + \bar{\Delta}}{1 + d} \right)^t + (C + F) \left(\frac{1 + \bar{\Delta}}{1 + d} \right)^{n-1} \right].$$ (5.19)

If Δ is known for certain and constant from year to year,

$$V_O = X_o \left[\sum_{t=1}^{n-1} C \left(\frac{1 + \Delta}{1 + d} \right)^t + (C + F) \left(\frac{1 + \Delta}{1 + d} \right)^n \right].$$ (5.20)

If the expected forward premium $E(\Delta_{t-1}) = E(\delta_t)$, the expected movement in exchange rate from time $t - 1$ to time t, and if Δ_t and δ_t are independent, there should be no expected gain or loss from forward market operations. These assumptions would suggest that $E(V_O) = E(V)$, even when the $\tilde{\Delta}_t$ are random.

Thus, our simulation model attempts to demonstrate that

1. Var (V_O) < Var (V), if Var (Δ_{t-1}) < Var (δ_t), for all t, and
2. $E(V_O) = E(V)$, if $E(\Delta_{t-1}) = E(\delta_t)$, for all t.

Simulation

Our simulation model uses an eight-year bullet maturity bond as an example. The bond carries a 6 percent annual coupon rate and is issued with a face value of DM 100 million. The discount rate of the firm is taken to be 10 percent. It is also assumed that the spot rate at the initial period is $.4000/DM and that both the annual changes of spot rates and the forward premiums are independent and normally distributed with $E(\delta_t) = E(\Delta_{t-1}) = 4$ percent. Expressed in the notations used above:

F = DM 100 million,

C = DM 6 million (based on 6 percent coupon rate),

x_o = $.4000/DM,

d = 10 percent,

$E(\tilde{\delta}_t) = E(\tilde{\Delta}_t) = 4$ percent,

$\text{Var}(\tilde{\delta}_t) = 187.4$ percent,

$\text{Var}(\tilde{\Delta}_t) = 8.35$ percent

Although both $\tilde{\delta}_t$ and $\tilde{\Delta}_t$ have the same expected values, their variances which are estimated with historical data differ substantially. In fact, the variance of $\tilde{\delta}_t$ is twenty-two times of the variance of $\tilde{\Delta}_t$. Table 5–1 lists the midyear spot and forward rates between the Deutsche marks and the dollars over the twelve years 1974–85. The midyear rates are used instead of the year-end rates to avoid end-of-year effects. Furthermore, since the *Wall Street Journal* does not list one-year forward rates, we used the six-month forward rates instead. The six-month forward premiums are calculated and annualized to serve as the approximations of one-year forward premiums. However, the differences in the variances of six-month and one-year forward premiums are expected to be small when both are expressed on per annum basis.

Given the expected values and variances, two sets of normally distributed random numbers are generated. One set has an expected value of 4 percent and variance of 187.4 percent which provide the values for $\tilde{\delta}_t$, the annual spot rate change. The other set has the same expected value of 4 percent but with a variance of 8.35 percent. This latter set provides the values for $\tilde{\Delta}_t$, the one-year forward premium.

Table 5–1
Spot and Forward Rates between Deutsche Marks and U.S. Dollars, Midyear 1974–85

	Spot Rates $(\tilde{\chi}_t)$	6-Month Forward Rates	Percent Change of Spot Rates $(\tilde{\delta}_t)$	Percent Forward Premiums per Annum $(\tilde{\Delta}_t)$
June 30, 1974	\$.3927/DM			
1975	.4242	.4290	8.021%	2.263%
1976	.3885	.3926	−8.416	2.111
1977	.4271	.4316	9.936	2.107
1978	.4276	.4321	0.117	2.105
1979	.5443	.5553	27.292	4.042
1980	.5673	.5713	4.226	1.410
1981	.4180	.4279	−26.318	4.737
1982	.4060	.4198	−2.871	6.798
1983	.3931	.4018	−3.177	4.426
1984	.3596	.3720	−8.522	6.897
1985	.3299	.3340	−8.259	2.486
Variances:			187.4%	8.74%

Sources: *Wall Street Journal*, various issues.

The simulation model is iterated five hundred times. In each run, the simulation computes the present values of cash flows under the two different strategies of no hedging and aggregate iterative hedging. For examples, table 5–2 shows the results of the first three runs. At the conclusion of the simulation, the means and variances of these present values over the five hundred runs are calculated. The results are shown in table 5–3.

Table 5–3 shows that the expected present values of the two strategies are very similar. The difference is not even significant at the .10 level. On the contrary, the difference between the two variances are highly significant (p < .005). In fact, the aggregate iterative technique provides a reduction of 95.34 percent of the original variance. These results strongly support what we hypothesized earlier:

$$\text{Var}\ (V_O) < \text{Var}\ (V), \text{ if Var}(\Delta_{t-1}) < \text{Var}(\delta_t), \text{ for all } t;\text{ and}$$

$$E(V_O) = E(V), \text{ if } E(\Delta_{t-1}) = E(\delta_t), \text{ for all } t.$$

Summary, Applications, and Extensions

The simulation results of the previous section indicate clearly that the aggregate iterative covering technique has enormous potential for reducing the uncertainty associated with medium- to long-term foreign currency borrowing. Unlike long forward contracts or swaps, which totally eliminate exchange risk, the aggregate iterative covering technique does leave some residual uncertainty, caused primarily by uncertainty in the year-to-year forward premiums.

Perhaps the most useful application of the approach would be to the individual purchaser of foreign currency bonds who seeks a way of reducing exchange-rate–induced uncertainty. Small investors would not typically have access to swaps or buy-dated forwards, except at prices that would reflect the significant expense of putting together a sophisticated financing package on a very small scale. Aggregate iterative covering utilizes existing forward or futures markets where the average deal size would be much lower.

Since contract commitments are at most year-to-year in nature, aggregate iterative covering allows for selective covering. An investor or issuer, utilizing a momentum or other forecasting model that gives signals as to currency direction and desired position (long or short), can readily unwind a forward position with a maturity of one year or less, where it might be more difficult to unwind a long forward or swap position. Selective hedging does, of course, materially enhance the risk which the covering operation is designed to eliminate.

The technique can be extended to any stream of foreign currency cash

Table 5–2
Simulation Results

Time Period	t	1st	2nd	3rd	4th	5th	6th	7th	8th
Number of run: 1									
Initial exchange rate	x_0	$.4000/DM							
Spot rate changes %	$\bar{\delta}_t$	1.62900	8.41600	0.69300	−15.31100	4.10200	2.69800	9.52800	16.92700
Spot rates $/DM	$\bar{x}_t$	0.40652	0.44073	0.44378	0.37583	0.39125	0.40181	0.44009	0.51458
Forward premiums %	$\bar{A}_{t-1}$	3.48800	4.95400	3.28600	−0.17100	4.02200	3.71900	5.19400	6.79200
Forward rates $/DM	$\bar{y}_{t-1}$	0.43195	0.42665	0.45521	0.44302	0.39095	0.40580	0.42268	0.46998
1st strategy—no hedging									
Cash flows (in $ millions)		2.43885	2.64384	2.66189	2.25410	2.34633	2.40939	2.63869	54.50229
Present values ($D = 10\%$)		2.21714	2.18499	1.99992	1.53958	1.45689	1.36004	1.35407	25.42574
Total present value		37.53835							
2nd strategy—aggregate iterative hedging									
Cash flows (in $ millions)		3.23619	1.13698	3.88358	9.42474	2.31429	2.83419	0.79046	49.77814
Present values ($D = 10\%$)		2.94199	0.93966	2.91779	6.43723	1.43699	1.59983	0.40563	23.22188
Total present value		39.90099							
Number of run: 2									
Initial exchange rate	x_0	$.4000/DM							
Spot rate changes %	$\bar{\delta}_t$	3.14300	−9.95800	12.67800	14.40900	9.86500	22.85001	−9.12300	33.38800
Spot rates $/DM	$\bar{x}_t$	0.41257	0.37149	0.41858	0.47890	0.52614	0.64636	0.58740	0.78352
Forward premiums %	$\bar{A}_{t-1}$	3.81500	0.98600	5.87400	6.24800	5.26700	8.07100	1.16600	10.34700
Forward rates $/DM	$\bar{y}_{t-1}$	0.41526	0.41664	0.39331	0.44474	0.50412	0.56861	0.65390	0.64817

Table 5–2 continued

Time Period	t	x_0	1st	2nd	3rd	4th	5th	6th	7th	8th
1st strategy—no hedging										
Cash flows (in $ millions)			2.47518	2.22848	2.51075	2.87224	3.15527	3.87586	3.52191	82.98625
Present values ($D = 10\%$)			2.25016	1.84172	1.88637	1.96178	1.95917	2.18782	1.80730	38.71371
Total present value			52.60803							
2nd strategy—aggregate iterative hedging										
Cash flows (in $ millions)			2.76343	7.06279	-0.19127	-0.77351	0.80931	-4.39305	10.58026	68.65149
Present values ($D = 10\%$)			2.51221	5.83702	-0.14371	-0.52832	0.50252	-2.47976	5.42935	32.02644
Total present value			43.15575							
Number of run: 3										
Initial exchange rate		$.4000/DM								
	$\bar{\delta}_t$		15.69600	10.61300	28.40199	28.28000	6.07500	-6.24900	11.85300	2.28100
Spot rate changes %										
Spot rates $/DM	$\bar{x}_t$		0.46278	0.51190	0.65729	0.84317	0.89439	0.83850	0.93789	0.95928
Forward premiums %	$\bar{\Delta}_{t-1}$		6.52600	5.42800	9.27000	9.24400	4.44800	1.78700	5.69600	3.62900
Forward rates $/DM	$\bar{y}_{t-1}$		0.42610	0.48790	0.55935	0.71805	0.88067	0.91037	0.88626	0.97192
1st strategy—no hedging										
Cash flows (in $ millions)			2.77642	3.07078	3.94254	5.05699	5.36366	5.02798	5.62339	101.60233
Present values ($D = 10\%$)			2.52402	2.53783	2.96209	3.45399	3.33041	2.83817	2.88569	47.39825
Total present value			67.93044							
2nd strategy—aggregate iterative hedging										
Cash flows (in $ millions)			-1.15668	0.50161	-6.52693	-8.29647	3.90208	12.67106	0.14406	102.94128
Present values ($D = 10\%$)			-1.05153	0.41455	-4.90378	-5.66660	2.42289	7.15248	0.07392	48.02289
Total present value			46.46481							

Table 5–3
Means and Variances of the Present Values
($ millions)

	No Hedging	*Aggregate Iterative Hedging*
Means of Present Values[a]	40.399	40.517
Variances of Present Values[b]	169.630	7.912

[a]Difference of the means are insignificant at .10 level.
[b]Difference of the variances are significant at .005 level.

flows. Thus, bonds with fixed amortization schedules or other features that allow the calculation of exact cash flow levels can be covered using the technique. Further research will be needed to determine the model's comparative sensitivity to bond features such as callability or extendability which impact the timing of servicing cash flows. However, any other covering methodology that eliminates uncertainty in foreign currency cash value must also be unwound in the event of a change in the timing of cash flows.

Thus, aggregate iterative covering is a technique that, using readily available short-term forward contracts, eliminates most of the uncertainty in the discounted value of a stream of cash flows. In some cases, it offers the borrower or investor a more flexible mechanism for managing exchange risk. As long as the period-to-period swings in exchange rates are more variable than changes in the forward premium, the technique places a powerful exchange risk management tool at the disposal of global financial managers.

References

Eaker, Mark R., & Dwight Grant, "Optimal Hedging of Uncertain and Long-Term Foreign Exchange Exposure," *Journal of Banking and Finance,* 9(1985), pp. 221–31.

Folks, William R., Jr., "Evaluating Foreign Currency Denominated Debt: An Uncertain Absorption Approach," paper presented at the Academy of International Business Extraordinary Meeting, Alexandria, Egypt, December 1976.

———, "Using Forward Exchange Rates in Currency of Denomination Decisions," paper presented at the Institute of Management Science Meeting, New York, May 1980.

Frenkel, Jacob, A., "Flexible Exchange Rates, Prices and the Role of 'News': Lessons from the 1970s," *Journal of Political Economy,* 89, no. 4 (1981), pp. 665–705.

Giddy, Ian, & Gunter Dufey, "The Random Behavior of Flexible Exchange Rates: Implications for Forecasting," *Journal of International Business Studies,* 6, no. 1 (Spring 1975), pp. 1–31.

Logue, Dennis E., & George S. Oldfield, "Managing Foreign Assets When Foreign Exchange Markets Are Efficient," *Financial Management*, 6, no. 2 (Summer 1977), pp. 16–22.

Shapiro, Alan C., & David P. Rutenberg, "Managing Exchange Risks in a Floating Rate World," *Financial Management*, 5, no. 2 (Summer, 1976), pp. 48–58.

6

The Performance of a Class of Long-Term Currency Hedges

Michael R. Granito
Michael Kelley

ABSTRACT

This chapter is a technical note that examines the performance of certain long-term currency hedges that may be substitutes for long-term forward contracts. We start by reviewing the mathematics of the hedge. This turns out to be closely related to the mathematics of bond immunization. We then test the theory using the data from four countries over the period 1974–83. Conclusions are drawn for the use of these methods as an alternative to the use of long-term forward contracts.

One of the factors that has inhibited the international flow of capital is the inadequacy of long-term forward markets. Such markets would enable an investor to take positions that could produce distant payoffs in a foreign currency, but hedge the exchange rate so that the currency risk would be diminished. For instance, a Japanese or European investor could wish to purchase a U.S. bond portfolio that would have a known payoff pattern over a given horizon. Indeed, Japanese investors, for instance, do own large portions of many long U.S. treasury bond issues. But a sequence of long-term forward contracts would often be desired to hedge the currency risk. While long-term contracts can be arranged, these generally lack liquidity and entail large transaction costs making them unsuitable in many cases.

In recent years, an apparently unrelated development has been the theoretical evolution and the practice of bond immunization. This is a technique of management in which one identifies an investment horizon, and over that period manages a coupon bond portfolio according to certain rules. The objective is to achieve the target compound return that is stated at the outset of the period, despite the impact of uncertain interest rate shifts during the period. Generally, we wish to achieve the return profile of a long-term zero-coupon bond: we wish to invest a fixed sum now, add or withdraw nothing during the period, but have precisely the amount at the end of the horizon that we predicted at the outset on the basis of market yields. The primary rule for accomplishing this result is to keep the duration of the portfolio equal to the time remaining until the end of the horizon, where duration is a present-value weighted measure of maturity. This equality is maintained through periodic rebalancing.

The awareness that immunization performs well in the bond market suggests the possibility that an analogous process could work in the currency market. Here the objective would be to lock in an exchange rate that would apply to a distant payoff in a foreign currency. This theoretical question has been investigated by Granito (1984). Under certain simplified assumptions, Granito develops a generalized immunization formula that naturally applies in the case of currencies, thus proving that currency immunization is a meaningful notion. The precise value of the exchange rate achieved depends upon the relationship of the spot currency rate to the short-term forward rate through time. Specifically, the realized rate equals the initial rate less the cumulative impact of the short-term premium or discount of the forward rate versus the spot. In a world of certainty, this realized rate would exactly equal the long-term forward rate if that market in fact existed. The import of this work is not the discovery of the rate this method locks in, since this is understood. The impact is the framework for analyzing the construction and maintenance of the hedge—an important question considering that most actual traders use far less accurate methods in practice.

The purpose of this chapter is mainly to test the performance of the hedging technique discussed above. First, we test the basic theory in a multicountry framework over the ten-year period 1974–83. Second, we interpret the practical role of this approach as compared with the approach of using long-term forward contracts when these are available. Finally, the relationship of the general technique to other recent findings in the theory of hedging is explored.

The following three sections provide a brief review of the theory. The next section presents the test methodology and results. The final section concludes the analysis with a discussion of the role of this approach and its relations to other findings.

Comparing Immunization and Currency Hedging: A Review of the Theory

The analytical approach employed in bond immunization involves the fact that over a short period of time, the rate of return on a bond portfolio consists of a contribution due to the level of yields (and the change in time itself) plus a contribution due to the change in yields. Specifically, let $y(t)$ denote portfolio yield at time t, let dt denote the change in time, let $D(t)$ denote portfolio duration at time t, and let $dy(t)$ denote the change in portfolio yield over the change in time dt. Then

$$\text{instantaneous portfolio rate of return} = y(t) \times dt - D(t) \times dy(t) \quad (6.1)$$

If yields decline, there will be a capital gain, but the contribution from yield to *future* returns is reduced. If, on the other hand, yields increase, there is a capital loss, but the contribution from yield to future return is increased. The key insight in immunization is that if duration equals the remaining time to the end of the horizon, then these effects are precisely offsetting regardless of the direction of the change in yields. This fact is demonstrated mathematically by setting the duration term, $D(t)$, in expression 6.1 equal to the remaining horizon and then summing this expression over all the short intervals that comprise the total horizon. The resulting sum, which will be the continuously compounded total return, is independent of the time path of yield and is equal to the *initial* yield, $y(0)$, times the horizon length. Consequently, the continuously compounded rate of return is the initial yield, $y(0)$.[1]

In the case of currency exposure, the intuition runs as follows: suppose that a U.S. resident is long a level flow of 1mm DM (Deutsche marks) per unit time over the next T years. Thus, the total DM to be exchange is Tmm. If $f(t)$ is the $/DM exchange rate in effect at time t, then the value of the *exchanged* flow over the interval $(t, t + dt)$ is

$$f(t) \times (1\text{mm DM}) \times dt \quad (6.2)$$

Suppose, however, that in the interest of reducing uncertainty from the impact of changes in the exchange rate, the individual puts on a short position in DM at the same time. Intuitively, he is long DM to be paid in the future; therefore, DM should be shorted (for dollars) to reduce the exchange risk. Denote the size of the short position by $S(t)$. We will suppose that this position is put on at time t and reversed at time $t + dt$. We will also assume, at the outset, that this short position fully hedges the change in the exchange rate, $df(t)$, over the interval. This is equivalent to the assumption that DM can be shorted (in the forward market, say) at the spot rate, with the position expiring or being reversed at the spot rate at the end of the period. Our profit (loss) on the hedge is therefore

$$- S(t) \times df(t) \quad (6.3)$$

If we now combine expressions 6.2 and 6.3, we arrive at the total dollar flow over the interval $(t, t + dt)$.

$$f(t) \times 1\text{mm} \times dt - S(t) \times df \qquad (6.4)$$

The analogy of our situation to bond immunization can now be seen clearly. Expression 6.4 for currency is nearly identical in appearance to expression 6.1 for bonds. In the bond case, we carefully select the duration term, $D(t)$, sot that the *sum* of all the individual instantaneous returns gives us a result that is independent of movement in $y(t)$, but depends only on its starting value $y(0)$. Similarly, by selecting the short position to be maintained, $S(t)$, at each point in time, we can produce the result that the flow into dollars (made up of the sum of all the individual flows given by expression 6.4) does not depend on changes in $f(t)$, but only on the initial value $f(0)$. In the present case, there is a constant flow of 1mm DM per period over the total period of T years. If we set $S(t)$ equal to the remaining DM to be transferred, then $S(t) = (T - t) \times 1\text{mm}$. Substituting this into expression 6.4 gives

$$f(t) \times 1\text{mm} \times dt - (T - t) \times 1\text{mm} \times df(t) \qquad (6.5)$$

or

$$1\text{mm} \times [f(t) \times dt - (T - t) \times df(t)] \qquad (6.6)$$

The right-hand side of expression 6.6 has exactly the same form as in the bond immunization case where we set duration, $D(t)$, equal to the remaining time until the end of the horizon, $T - t$. Hence, the sum of all the flows given by 6.6 must equal 1mm $\times$ $f(0)$ $\times$ T or $(T\text{mm}) \times f(0)$. Recalling that $T\text{mm}$ is the total DM to be exchanged, the realized average exchange rate is $f(0)$—that is, $[(T\text{mm}) \times f(0)]/T\text{mm}$—regardless of fluctuations in $F(t)$ during the period.

Extension of the Theory: Hedging Future Values, Nonlevel Flows, and Shorting at Nonspot Rates

The discussion in the previous section illustrated the basic argument of why currency immunization is possible. The specific example used, however, only demonstrated that the total volume of a level flow could be exchanged at an average exchange rate equal to the initial rate, $f(0)$. Moreover, this assumed an ability to short DM at the spot rate. None of these conditions is plausible.

In particular, we are more concerned with locking in the future value of a potentially uneven flow of currency, rather than the average exchange rate; and we should only assume that we can short currency at the forward rate rather than at the spot rate.

As demonstrated in Granito (1984), it turns out that locking in the future value of an uneven flow requires only a simple modification to the hedge rule: maintain at each point a short position equal to the present value of the currency yet to be exchanged. This is proven through the demonstration of a *generalized immunization theorem*.[2] The intuition behind this result is easily seen in the context of the following simple example.

Suppose that we have 1mm DM due in T years, that the U.S. interest rate is r percent, and that the \$/DM exchange rate, f, will change just once over the next instant of time from f_0 to f_1, and stay at f_1 for the balance of the T years. The future value of our position consists of 1mm DM exchanged at f_1 plus the gain (loss) on our short position, $S(t)$, reinvested for T years at the U.S. rate. This latter amount is

$$- S(t) \times e^{r \times T} \times (f_1 - f_0) \qquad (6.7)$$

and the total future value is thus

$$1\text{mm DM} \times f_1 - S(t) \times e^{r \times T} \times (f_1 - f_0) \qquad (6.8)$$

Setting $S(t)$ equal to the present value of 1mm DM, that is,

$$S(t) = e^{-r \times T} \times 1\text{mm DM}$$

we may write expression 6.8 as

$$(1\text{mm DM} \times f_1) - e^{-r \times T} \times 1\text{mm DM}$$
$$\times e^{r \times T} \times (f_1 - f_0) = 1\text{mm DM} \times f_0 \qquad (6.9)$$

Consequently, the future value of the payment is locked in at the initial exchange rate f_0. It is now simple to extend this to a flow of currency since any flow is conceptually just an infinitely fine sequence of lump sum payments. The possibility of continuous movements in $f(t)$ is accounted for by the fact that, as long as we are hedged against each infinitely close and successive *one-time* move, we are hedged against the continuum of moves. We must, of course, continuously revise the short position, $S(t)$, to remain hedged.[3]

These arguments illustrate how to lock in the future value of an uneven flow when we can short currency at the spot rate. In fact, we can only short currency at the forward rate. Consequently, we proceed as follows. We seek a vehicle for going short that has maximal correlation with the exchange rate itself. Thus, we shall focus on the short-term forward rate and assume that all short sales are executed through this market. Assuming that the one-month forward market is used, compute at the start of each month the present value of the future currency exposure using the domestic interest rate appropriate for that horizon. Using our previous example, we compute the present value (in DM) of 1mm DM due in, say, five years, at the U.S. five-year rate. Then sell short this volume of DM in the forward market. At the end of the month, buy DM at the spot rate to cover the short. The profit (or loss) is realized in dollars and is reinvested (borrowed) through to the horizon at the U.S. five-year (four-year, eleven-month) rate. Next, compute the present value of 1mm DM due in four years and eleven months, and short this volume at the new one-month forward rate. At the end of this month, cover the short and reinvest the proceeds. Proceed in this way until the end of the horizon.

Granito has shown that this process will lock in the initial spot rate less the cumulative influence of the forward discount or premium. This premium emerges because we are constantly selling currency at the forward rate and covering at the spot rate. The (one-month) forward premium is determined by the (one-month) interest rate differential between the respective countries. In particular, the one-month forward rate equates the one-month interest rates earned domestically with rates in the foreign market. It is important to note that, although we cannot predict what the total impact of the forward premium will be, it is clear that the realized exchange rate obtained (initial spot plus cumulative one-month premiums) often suffers from less variation than the movements in the spot itself. Thus, we can immunize against all variations in the exchange rate except those that are "anticipated" by interest rate differentials.

The intuition for why the forward premium correction is necessary is simple: we are invested in DM and hedge our position. If the interest rate were higher in Germany, we should give this up on our forward cover. Since we choose to roll a one-month hedge, we give up the one-month rate differential whose cumulative value cannot be anticipated. To develop these results in the context of our simple one-period example (expression 6.9), the gain (loss) on our short position reinvested to the horizon is now

$$- S(t) \times e^{r \times T} \times [f_1 - (f_0 + p_0)] \qquad (6.10)$$

where $(f_0 + p_0)$ is the initial forward rate (spot, f_0, plus one-month forward premium, p_0). That is, we are not concerned with the difference $f_1 - f_0$, or the change in the spot rates. Instead, we are concerned with the difference between the ending spot rate f_1 and the initial forward since these are the rates at which we transact. Carrying through the calculations, our total future value is

$$(1\text{mm DM} \times f_1) - e^{-r \times T} \times 1\text{mm DM} \times e^{r \times T}$$
$$\times [f_1 - (f_0 + p_0)] = 1\text{mm DM} \times (f_0 + p_0). \quad (6.11)$$

In order to formulate this as a dynamic strategy, we now suppose that this transaction takes place over the first month but that during the second month, the exchange rate could change again. Consequently, we again take a short position at the start of the second month. Repeating all calculations, at the end of the second month, the estimated *terminal* value of our position is

$$1\text{mm DM} \times (f_0 + p_0 + p_1) \quad (6.12)$$

where p_1 is the one-month forward premium at the start of the second month. Carrying this on to the end of the horizon, sixty months, produces the following expression for terminal value:

$$1\text{mm DM} \times (f_0 + p_0 + p_1 + \ldots + p_{59}) \quad (6.13)$$

where p_i, $i = 0, \ldots 59$ are the one-month forward premiums in effect at the start of each of the 60 months. Thus, the realized exchange rate would equal expression 6.13 divided by 1mm DM, or the initial spot rate plus the sum of the one-month forward premiums.

Extension of the Theory: Stochastic Interest Rates

Up to now, we have assumed that the interest rate is a constant. It is simple to adjust this to assume stochastic interest rates and thus a possible correlation of interest rate and exchange rate changes. To illustrate, we use a continuous time analysis in which T is the terminal date on which 1mm DM is received, $P(t)$ is the price (at time t) of a discount bond maturing at time T, $p(t)$ is the instantaneous rate of forward premium, and all other definitions are as before. Then the future value of our position, at time T, is computed as follows. The expression $f_1 - (f_0 + p_0)$ in 6.11 now becomes $df - p(t)\, dt$, and the expression $e^{-rt} \times e^{rt}$ becomes $P(t) \times \dfrac{1}{P(t + dt)}$ or $P(t) \left[\dfrac{1}{P(t)} + d\, \dfrac{1}{P(t)} \right]$. Integrating this result gives

$$[1\text{mm DM} \times f(T) - 1\text{mm DM} \int_0^T P(t) \left[\frac{1}{P(t)} + d\, \frac{1}{P(t)} \right] [df - p(t)\, dt]$$
$$= (1\text{mm DM}) \times [f(0) - \int_0^T p(t)\, dt] - (1\text{mm DM}) \left(\int_0^T \frac{dp(t)}{P(t)} \cdot df \right).$$
$$(6.14)$$

The first term on the right-hand side is exactly the same as before where we now have the integral of p(t) instead of the sum $p_0 + p_1 + p_2 \ldots$ The second term on the right-hand side is new and reflects the cumulative instantaneous correlation of bond returns and exchange rate changes. If this correlation were zero, the realized rate would be identical to the nonstochastic case. The correlation, however, could be positive or negative depending on, among other things, the correlation of the difference of international rates with the levels. The import of this result is that it shows that in a stochastic world, the theoretical performance of the hedge is not simply the short rate differential, as it would be if the correlation term were zero. That is, the cumulative premium should reflect the cumulative short rate differential. In a certain world, this is what we give up (gain) by investing abroad but rolling over a short hedge. In a stochastic world, this is no longer the case since the correlation term is also present.

Testing the Theory

The theoretical developments of the previous three sections demonstrate the simple concept that a long-term hedge can be constructed out of a sequence of short hedges. The parallel with immunization theory helps rigorously identify the appropriate technical rule for constructing the short-term hedges. The corresponding perspective from forward rate theory is that instead of locking in a single long-term forward rate (spot plus a long-term premium), the impact of rolling short hedges is to construct an effective forward rate equal to the spot plus the sum of the short-term forward premiums plus a term relating to the correlation of interest and exchange rate changes.

These results are intuitive against the backdrop of general exchange rate theory. Less obvious is the performance of this method as a practical vehicle for hedging. In order to test this method, we collected interest rate and exchange rate data from four countries—Britain, Germany, Japan, and the United States—covering the period July 1974 through December 1983. Our test methodology was to assume that a resident of Britain, Japan, or Germany had a known dollar exposure in five years. In each of these nations, we tested fifty-four five-year periods from July 1974 through December 1978. Within each five-year period and from the point of view of each nation, we simulated the rolling monthly hedge described in the section "Extension of the Theory" using the actual exchange rates and interest rates that would have confronted investors at that time.

To review the hedge procedure, assume the case of a British investor on July 1, 1974 with a 1mm dollar exposure as of July 1, 1979. At the start of each month, the present value of the 1mm is computed using the appropriate British government rate. This volume of dollars was shorted at the one-month forward rate. At the end of the month, the short position was covered at the spot rate and a new short position established. Gains or losses on the short positions were assumed to be realized in sterling and reinvested through July 1, 1979 (the horizon for the five-year period commencing July 1, 1974) at the appropriate British spot rate. Transaction costs were assessed for both bond and currency transactions.[4] This process is continued monthly until July 1, 1979, when the total dollar exposure is exchanged to sterling at the spot rate. The total sterling position at July 1, 1979 consists of the final conversion of dollars plus the cumulative reinvested gain or loss on the sixty monthly short positions.

The performance of the hedge in this hypothetical test from July 1, 1974 through July 1, 1979 is illustrated in three ways. First, we compare the realized terminal sterling position on July 1, 1979 to a measure of what "should" have been realized. This latter amount is taken to be the dollar exposure times an estimate of the exchange rate that the hedge should have produced: the initial spot rate plus the sum of the one-month forward premiums.[5] Any difference between actual and "theoretical" is expressed as an annualized transaction cost in basis points. This definition of theoretical is what the hedge should have done under certainty and, in effect, defines as a transaction cost anything that causes the hedge to give up (gain) anything other than the average short rate differential. The second illustration of the performance of the hedge is simply to compare the sum of the monthly forward premiums (as a percentage of initial spot) to the total loss (gain) from the hedge, again as a percentage of initial spot. Finally, we show the actual transaction cost as a percentage of the cumulative theoretical premium.

Figures 6–1 through 6–9 contain the test results. Figures 6–1 through 6–3 show for Britain, Germany, and Japan, respectively, the annualized transaction costs (in basis points) associated with the hedge. Figures 6–4 through 6–6 show the cumulative forward premium or discount versus the cumulative gain or loss from the hedge. Figures 6–7 through 6–9 show the transaction cost as a percentage of premium for the respective countries.

Overall, the hedge performance is quite good. Annualized transaction costs vary from just a few basis points (bp) to as high as 40–45 bp. As expected, transaction costs are correlated with the magnitude of the cumulative premium. That is, as the cumulative premium increases, so does the volume of transactions, and hence, so do the transaction costs. The correlations of transaction costs and cumulative premium are 97.68, 63,62, and 95.90 for Britain, Germany, and Japan, respectively. This relationship is also seen in the form of the relative stability in the ratio of transaction cost to cumulative premium shown in Figures 6–7 through 6–9. The ratio tends to be larger when the cumulative premium is smaller in absolute amount. The reason is that even a negligible premium would still entail transactions because it would normally be composed of positives and negatives that cancel. Hence, the ratio of transaction cost to the premium would be large.

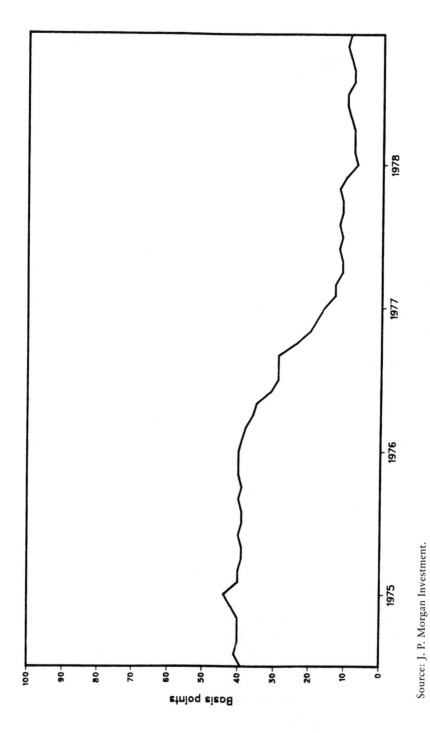

Source: J. P. Morgan Investment.

Figure 6–1. Hedging from Great Britain: Transaction Costs per Year in Basis Points, July 1, 1974 to July 1, 1979

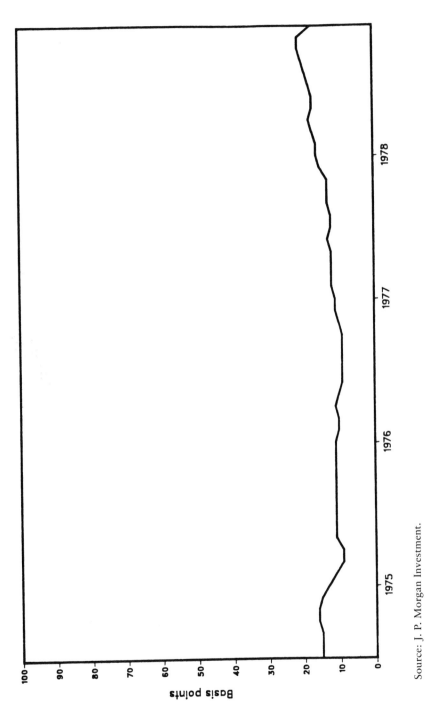

Figure 6–2. Hedging from Germany: Transaction Costs per Year in Basis Points, July 1, 1974 to July 1, 1979

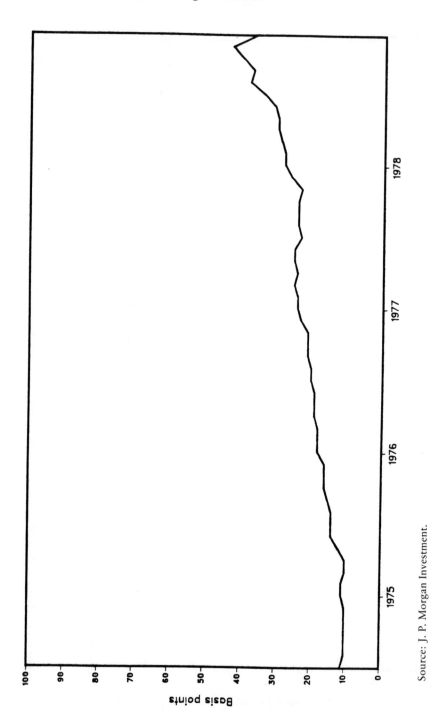

Source: J. P. Morgan Investment.

Figure 6–3. Hedging from Japan: Transaction Costs per Year in Basis Points, July 1, 1974 to July 1, 1979

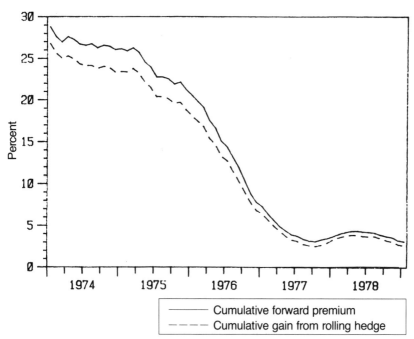

Figure 6–4. Performance of One-Month Rolling Hedge: Short Sterling One-Month Forward versus the U.S. Dollar, July 1, 1974 to July 1, 1979

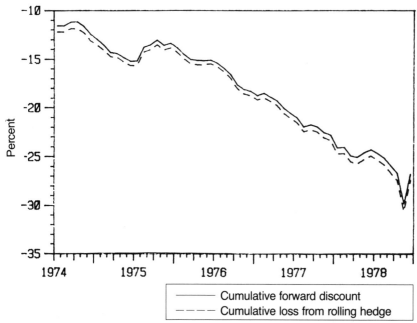

Figure 6–5. Performance of One-Month Rolling Hedge: Short Deutsche Mark One-Month Forward versus the U.S. Dollar, July 1, 1974 to July 1, 1979

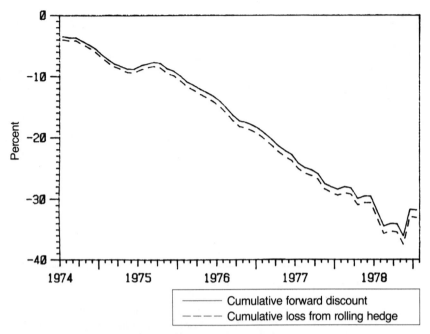

Figure 6–6. Performance of One-Month Rolling Hedge: Short Yen One-Month Forward versus the U.S. Dollar, July 1, 1974 to July 1, 1979

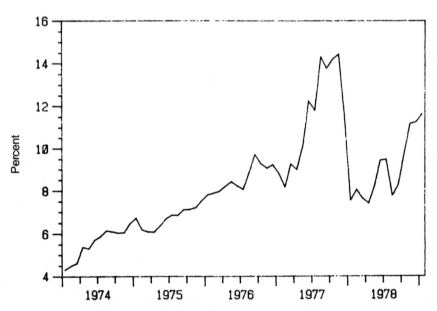

Figure 6–7. Hedging from Great Britain: Transaction Costs as a Percentage of Cumulative Premiums, July 1, 1974 to July 1, 1979

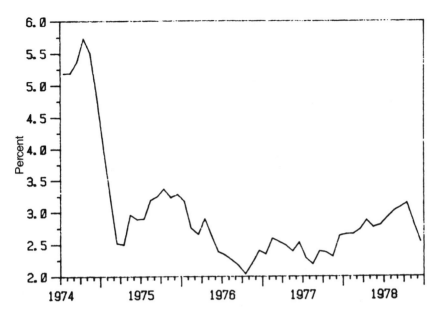

Figure 6–8. Hedging from West Germany: Transaction Costs as a
Percentage of Cumulative Premiums, July 1, 1974 to July 1,
1979

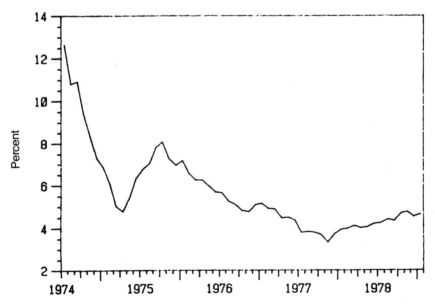

Figure 6–9. Hedging from Japan: Transaction Costs as a Percentage of
Cumulative Premiums, July 1, 1974 to July 1, 1979

Interpretation and Conclusions

Our results confirm the hypothesis that the short-term hedging technique discussed represents a reasonable alternative to long-term forward contracts. Transaction costs implicit in the method tested range from 7 to 44 basis points over the period studied and averaged 24.74, 13.09, and 21.33 in Britain, Germany, and Japan, respectively. Of course, the results in the future will depend on the cumulative premium that is realized and the instantaneous correlation of interest rates and exchange rates. It is useful to compare these levels, however, to transaction costs that are implicit in long-term contracts. While precise data are unavailable, market-makers in these contracts indicate that 35 to 75 basis points per year is a typical range, over and above the impact of whatever formula is used to compute the contract price itself.

The disadvantage of the short hedge method is that, while much of the uncertainty in the exchange rate is removed, variation remains—largely in the cumulative forward premium that reflects the cumulative short rate interest differential. This fact helps illustrate the relationship of this technique to the long-term contract. We can use a bond market analogy. Over a five-year investment period, one could buy a five-year zero-coupon bond or roll short-term instruments. The decision would depend on one's interest rate outlook. In the case of currency, the long contract "should" equate long-term spot rates in the respective countries, just as the short forward rate equates short-term rates. *One can therefore choose the long hedge or the short hedge depending upon expectations about the future average short interest rate differential compared with the current long rate differential.* Of course, it is difficult to implement this choice at present because, while performance of the short hedge clearly reflects the short rate differential, the pricing of the long contracts may not closely reflect long interest rate differentials due, for instance, to transaction costs imposed by the market-makers. This may represent an advantage to the short hedge, since in theory, pricing without high transactions costs at the long end should equate demand for the respective approaches.

It is useful to compare this work to the recent work of Stulz (June 1984, August 1984). Stulz develops a stochastic model of the international economy and arrives at the optimal exchange position for a representative individual. Under certain conditions, he finds that the risk-reducing position for an investor with exposure such as we have considered is to be short the present value of the future long position, exactly the rule developed here. In the stochastic case, he believes that this rule may have to be modified in order to reflect complexities that we have not dealt with, such as the instantaneous correlation of exchange rates and interest rates. In either case, the presence of a stochastic environment also implies that the hedge may differ from that expressed here—the initial spot plus cumulative instantaneous premiums. It should also be understood that the development of a similar rule in the work of Stulz does not imply that the individual he identifies actually "immunizes" as we have discussed here. This is because the treatment of gains and losses on the short position in that model can differ from the way they are handled here, although a close relationship can exist.

Beyond its general contribution, the interesting element in Stulz's work from our immediate perspective is the confirmation of the present value rule as the appropriate device to reduce risk in a very general stochastic model. Moreover, we have demonstrated that the present value rule is essentially an immunization rule. Thus, concepts of immunization appear to be central to risk reduction in both the bond and currency markets.

Notes

1. The mathematical demonstration of this fact is found by setting $D(t) = T - t$ and then integrating expression 6.1 under the assumption that $y(t)$ is continuous.

2. This theorem states that if $f(t)$ and $c(t)$ are continuous and if

$$C(b) = \int_0^b c(t) \, dt$$

then

$$\int_0^T f(t) \, c(t) \, dt - \int_0^T [C(T) - C(t)] \, df(t) = f(0) \, C(T)$$

3. These statements are rigorously demonstrated by the generalized immunization theorem stated in note 2 and proven in Granito (1984).

4. For bonds in Britain and Germany, a sliding scale was used ranging from $\frac{1}{16}$ of a point on three-month instruments to $\frac{1}{2}$ of a point for long bonds. For Japan, $\frac{1}{4}$ of a point was used throughout. For currencies, the transactions costs are quite small since market-makers do not generally charge for rolling over a forward position. Consequently, the full transaction cost is realized just once on the total amount. This is negligible on a five-year annualized basis.

5. This requires qualification. The theory developed in Granito (1984) assumes certainty and continuous trading. In this case, the theoretical exchange rate equals the initial spot plus the cumulative sum (integral) of the instantaneous forward premiums. Our present analysis is an approximation based on monthly trading that should be of practical interest. Potential problems with the approximation involve fluctuations in interest rates that occur within the month so as to upset the equality of the rate for taking the present value of the exposure and the reinvestment rate. One potential concern is that changes in interest rates themselves can induce changes in exchange rates and hence profit or loss on the short position.

References

Granito, Michael R., *Bond Portfolio Immunization*. Lexington, Mass.: Lexington Books, 1984.

Stulz, Rene, "Optimal Hedging Policies," *Journal of Financial and Quantitative Analysis*, June 1984, pp. 127–39.

———, "Currency Preferences, Purchasing Power Risks, and the Determination of Exchange Rates in an Optimizing Model," *Journal of Money Credit and Banking*, August 1984, pp. 302–316.

7
International Diversification under Estimation Risk: Actual versus Potential Gains

Cheol S. Eun
Bruce G. Resnick

ABSTRACT

In this chapter, we evaluate the out-of-sample performance of internationally diversified portfolios vis-à-vis purely domestic portfolios under flexible exchange rates. We also examine the actual and potential gains from international diversification from the viewpoint of each of fifteen national investors. Despite the adverse effect of fluctuating exchange rates, every national investor can "potentially" benefit from international diversification. The actual gains accruing from a particular investment strategy, however, tend to be lower than the potential gains and, in some cases, negative. This divergence of actual from potential gains reflects estimation risk or parameter uncertainty, which, in turn, may contribute to the "home-bias" in portfolio holdings.

Since the pioneering work of Grubel (1968) appeared, the case for international portfolio diversification has been convincingly argued in the framework of mean-variance analysis by a number of researchers, such as Lessard (1974), Levy and Sarnat (1970), and Solnik (1974).[1] Most of the previous studies constructed optimal international portfolios using "historical" return data and showed that internationally diversified portfolios dominated purely domestic portfolios in terms of mean-variance efficiency. These studies thus implicitly assumed that investors know the true probability distribution of stock market returns. This, of course, is not the case in reality, especially concerning international investment.

It is well known that to construct an optimal portfolio using modern portfolio theory, one has to estimate such parameters as the expected returns, standard deviations, and the correlation coefficients. Estimation of these parameters is, in general, subject to errors. Compounded by such factors as government control of the capital and foreign exchange markets, disparate accounting standards, language barriers and, more recently, gyrating exchange rates, estimation of the parameters is particularly difficult at the international level. By relying on the ex post mean-variance analysis, previous studies of international diversification ignored the problem of estimation risk and, consequently, may have overestimated the possible gains from international diversification.

Therefore, even if there are currently large "potential" gains from international diversification, the existence of estimation risk (parameter uncertainty due to estimation) brings into question whether and to what extent it is possible to capture these gains. The "actual" gains associated with a particular investment strategy may well diverge from the potential gains under estimation risk.[2] Furthermore, to the extent that investors are concerned with the returns in terms of their national currencies, both potential and actual gains from international diversification will vary across national investors under flexible exchange rates.

In this chapter, our purpose is to determine the potential gains from international diversification for each of fifteen national investors and compare them with the actual gains associated with each of three alternative (ex ante) strategies for implementing modern portfolio theory. The three portfolio strategies are:

1. Naive diversification strategy,
2. Historical diversification strategy, and
3. Jobson-Korkie diversification strategy.

Unlike most of the previous studies, we will examine the out-of-sample performance of internationally diversified portfolios vis-à-vis domestic portfolios from the viewpoint of each national investor.

The rest of the chapter is organized as follows. The next section briefly examines the risk-return characteristics of fifteen major stock markets. The following section describes the three international diversification strategies and presents their compositions. The subsequent section evaluates the performance of international and domestic portfolios and compares the actual gains with the potential gains from international diversification. The final section offers concluding remarks.

Risk and Return in International Stock Markets

Let us first examine the ex post risk–return characteristics for each of fifteen major stock market indices, which represent the fifteen largest stock markets in the world in terms of capitalization value. For each stock market index, we examine the mean return (mean), the standard deviation (SD) of return as a measure of total risk (beta or β), and the Sharpe performance measure (SHP). Betas were calculated using a world index, and they represent the systematic or nondiversifiable risk inherent in each national stock market index. The Sharpe performance measure, which is the mean excess return per standard deviation, was calculated using the (annualized) risk-free rate of 5 percent. We also calculated the correlation matrix among the fifteen stock markets. These parameters were calculated from 120 monthly returns during the period January 1973–December 1982, a period characterized by flexible exchange rates. The data were gathered from monthly issues of *Capital International Perspective (CIP)* (published in Geneva, Switzerland), which has become the standard source of international stock market data. The *CIP* stock market indices and world index are value-weighted.

Table 7–1 provides the numerical values of the parameters in terms of U.S. dollars. As can be seen from table 7–1, the pairwise correlation varies widely—from .15 for Singapore/Spain and the United States/Spain to .78 for the Netherlands/Switzerland. It is noted that Spain and Italy generally have low correlations with other countries. It is also noted that the correlations among three European countries (Germany, the Netherlands, and Switzerland) are very high, in fact, .70 or higher. This may partly reflect a high degree of economic integration as well as close coordination of monetary policies among these countries. As can be expected, United States/Canada exhibits a high correlation, .68.

It is evident from table 7–1 that the national stock markets displayed rather disparate risk–return characteristics. Measured in the U.S. dollar, for example, the mean returns ranged from -.46 percent for Spain to 1.18 percent for Sweden. The standard deviations, on the other hand, ranged from 4.84 percent for the United States to 14.54 percent for Hong Kong, while betas ranged from .45 for Spain to 1.54 for Singapore. Roughly speaking, Hong Kong, Singapore, and the U.K. stock markets are characterized by high risk and high return. In contrast, the U.S. market is characterized by low risk and low return. Both the German and the Japanese markets yield medium returns at low risk levels. It is noteworthy that the Swedish market yields the highest return at a very low risk level. Thus, it is not surprising that Sweden turns out to be the best performing market with SHP value of .130. Other high-performance countries include the Netherlands, Germany, and Japan, followed by Singapore, Britain, and Belgium. Countries such as Spain, Australia, France, and the United States registered rather lackluster performances.

Lastly, we briefly examine the distributional properties of international stock market returns from the viewpoint of the U.S. investors. Specifically, we calculated the autocorrelations at the lags of one month through twelve months to ascertain if there exists any intertemporal dependence in the stock market returns. We also calculated such parameters as the studentized range,

Table 7–1
Summary Statistics of the Monthly Returns for Fifteen Major Stock Markets, 1973–82
($ U.S.)

Stock Market	Correlation Coefficient														Mean	SD	β	SHP
	AU	BE	CA	FR	GE	HK	IT	JA	NE	SG	SP	SD	SW	UK				
Australia (AU)															.63	7.97	1.25	.027
Belgium (BE)	.36														.80	5.92	.84	.065
Canada (CA)	.62	.36													.78	6.52	1.16	.056
France (FR)	.46	.61	.46												.67	8.04	1.16	.032
Germany (GE)	.33	.65	.31	.52											.83	5.44	.73	.076
Hong Kong (HK)	.34	.36	.27	.30	.33										1.10	14.54	1.52	.047
Italy (IT)	.29	.36	.28	.39	.28	.21									.27	8.47	.74	.017
Japan (JA)	.34	.43	.29	.40	.49	.45	.37								.85	5.77	.78	.075
Netherlands (NE)	.43	.69	.53	.59	.70	.45	.30	.44							1.01	5.80	1.06	.102
Singapore (SG)	.46	.40	.41	.38	.38	.48	.23	.43	.54						1.08	10.20	1.54	.065
Spain (SP)	.28	.28	.24	.26	.28	.20	.25	.32	.31	.15					-.46	6.12	.45	-.143
Sweden (SD)	.30	.44	.28	.29	.42	.24	.16	.35	.46	.34	.23				1.18	5.89	.66	.130
Switzerland (SW)	.48	.72	.46	.60	.75	.38	.38	.46	.78	.53	.25	.52			.77	6.01	1.00	.059
U.K. (UK)	.46	.50	.48	.53	.40	.36	.38	.32	.63	.58	.22	.32	.54		1.02	9.27	1.47	.065
U.S. (US)	.53	.37	.68	.41	.32	.24	.16	.27	.58	.48	.15	.36	.49	.46	.57	4.84	1.03	.032

Source: Data were obtained from various monthly issues of *Capital International Perspective*, Geneva, Switzerland.
Note: Means and standard deviations are given in terms of percentage.

skewness, and kurtosis to ascertain if the stock market returns conform to normality. The numerical values of these parameters are provided in table 7–2. Table 7–2 shows that with the exception of two autocorrelations for Singapore, all the other autocorrelations are not statistically significantly different from zero. This result is consistent with the notion of the stock market efficiency in its weak form. Table 7–2 also shows that for the majority of foreign markets, the rate of returns in terms of U.S. dollar seems to deviate from normal distributions.[3]

Alternative Strategies of International Diversification

Currently, there exists a considerable amount of empirical evidence showing that there are "potential" gains from international portfolio diversification. However, the extent to which investors can actually realize these potential gains depends on the particular investment strategies they adopt. In this section, we examine three alternative strategies of international portfolio diversification: naive diversification, historical diversification, and the Jobson-Korkie variant of historical diversification. These strategies are alternative methods of finding the ex ante optimal portfolio investment weights that are necessary to implement modern portfolio theory.

The naive diversification strategy is the simplest strategy. It calls for equal investment in each national market. The historical diversification strategy, on the other hand, determines the optimal portfolio investment weights by using as inputs into the portfolio problem the historical mean returns of each stock market and the covariance matrix calculated from an estimation period. The Jobson-Korkie diversification strategy (which uses a James-Stein estimator) is based on the assumption that the best estimate of a stock's expected return is the grand mean of the historical mean returns on all the stocks being considered for investment. Recently, Jobson and Korkie (1980, 1981) found that the grand mean approach resulted in the most efficient portfolio in the domestic setting. For the purpose at hand, the Jobson-Korkie diversification strategy determines the optimal portfolio weights by using as inputs the grand mean of all the international stock market's mean returns and the historical covariance matrix. In what follows, we construct international portfolios using the historical return data on the fifteen major stock markets during the seven-year estimation period of 1973–79. The 1980–82 period represents the holding period. We assume that investors can lend and borrow at the risk-free rate of 5 percent, and that no short sales of risky assets are allowed.[4]

Table 7–3 presents the compositions of both the historical international portfolio and the Jobson-Korkie international portfolio for each of the fifteen national investors. Table 7–4, on the other hand, presents the compositions of the ex post optimal international portfolios obtained from the true mean

Table 7–2
Autocorrelations, Studentized Range, Skewness, and Kurtosis of the Monthly Returns for Fifteen Major Stock Markets in U.S. Dollars

Stock Market	ρ_1	ρ_2	ρ_3	ρ_4	ρ_5	ρ_6	ρ_7	ρ_8	ρ_9	ρ_{10}	ρ_{11}	ρ_{12}	Studentized Range	Skewness	Kurtosis[a]
Australia	.013	−.051	.005	.033	.083	−.063	−.076	.040	.124	.042	.017	−.005	7.03c	−.660d	5.79
Belgium	.070	−.008	.138	.012	−.102	−.106	−.044	−.055	.039	.095	−.037	.087	5.97	−.132	4.36
Canada	−.048	−.109	.135	−.043	.162	.020	−.135	.021	.106	−.067	.016	.015	6.31c	−.435d	4.34
France	.109	−.053	.153	−.003	.038	.010	−.145	−.127	.096	.075	−.054	−.066	6.21c	−.234	4.06
Germany	−.015	−.058	.091	−.066	−.106	−.159	.064	−.046	.033	.162	.034	−.052	5.76	−.417d	4.07
Hong Kong	.111	−.130	−.031	−.050	.044	−.060	.035	.119	.012	−.013	.126	.069	8.48c	.090	7.30
Italy	.073	−.113	.078	.032	−.116	.155	.101	−.077	.057	.006	.051	.033	5.44	−.208	3.16
Japan	.079	−.042	.046	.068	−.056	−.131	.032	.119	−.022	−.060	.141	.041	5.56	.044	3.29
Netherlands	.068	−.024	.031	−.097	−.022	−.123	−.128	−.171	.152	.103	.059	.076	7.31c	−.318	5.35
Singapore	.076	−.043	−.085	.039	−.021	−.203b	−.036	.138	.062	.018	.144	.210b	6.90c	.286	5.21
Spain	−.001	.043	−.011	−.038	−.047	.149	.015	.016	.052	.085	−.002	−.052	7.24c	−.962d	6.81
Sweden	−.041	−.074	.163	.001	−.120	−.124	−.036	−.090	−.044	.128	−.008	.061	5.47	−.096	2.92
Switzerland	.071	−.168	.118	.005	−.131	−.090	−.015	−.116	.056	.108	−.000	.063	6.54c	−.173	4.48
U.K.	.132	−.081	.097	.010	−.141	−.035	−.045	−.033	.082	−.001	−.008	.049	7.35c	.924d	7.68
U.S.	.012	−.046	.080	.071	.057	−.132	−.065	.016	.001	.052	−.081	.131	5.91	.196	3.75
World	.116	−.084	.116	.019	.011	−.114	−.122	.003	.084	.057	−.035	.120	6.54c	−.319	4.37

Note: Return data are continuously compounded and obtained from *Capital International Perspective*.

[a] Long, thick tail relative to a normal distribution is evident in distribution when a value of the kurtosis measure exceeds 3.00: M_4/M_2^2; $M_i = \Sigma(R - \bar{R})^i/n$, $i = 2, 4$.

[b] Autocorrelation (ρ_τ, $\tau = 1, \ldots, 12$) exceeds two standard deviations from a hypothesized value of zero.

[c] Studentized range value exceeds what would be expected in 95 percent of the cases if the samples were drawn from a normal distribution.

[d] Significant at the 10 percent level in a two-tailed test of the skewness measure: $M_3/M_2^{3/2}$; $M_i = \Sigma(R - \bar{R})^i/n$, $i = 2, 3$, $\bar{R}$

Table 7-3
Compositions of Ex Ante International Portfolios by Country

$R_f = 5\%$

Habitats of Investors

	LC[a]	AU	BE	CA	FR	GE	HK	IT	JA	NE	SG	SP	SD	SW	UK	US
Jobson-Korkie International Portfolios																
Australia		.1463														
Belgium	.1481				.1695	.0417	.0178		.0158		.0981	.0052	.1069	.3075	.0874	
Canada	.0812	.3006		.2564			.1150	.0710	.0649		.0438		.0716		.1290	.1237
France			.3546		.0953	.3861								.2439		
Germany	.2183	.1306	.3261	.1395	.3656	.2138	.1827	.1761	.1104	.3504	.1635	.0529	.2189	.1838	.2470	.1409
Hong Kong			.3194		.3697	.3585				.3331				.2648		
Italy	.2611			.0053			.0398	.2387	.0408		.0320	.0372	.0037		.1136	.0367
Japan	.1355			.1596			.1928	.1591	.4576		.2266	.2063	.1581		.1506	.1581
Spain				.1487			.1429	.1230	.1480		.1440	.4166	.0909		.0929	.1560
Sweden	.1558	.0341		.1011			.1111	.1112	.1383		.1053	.0934	.2776		.1603	.1120
U.S.				.1895			.1979	.1208	.0243	.3166	.1866	.1884	.0723		.0193	.2726
Historical International Portfolios																
Australia	.1092	.0917												N/A		
Belgium		.3001	.5465	.3106	.4445		.4650	.4226	.4384	.1879	.5071	.5162	.5447	N/A	.4960	.4084
Canada	.8100	.1593		.2635				.0516			.0221	.0218		N/A	.0439	.1009
France		.0365	.0062		.0942	.3508	.0136	.0365	.0505	.2252				N/A	.0092	
Germany		.3742	.4033	.4259	.4001		.4120	.4381	.4464	.3771	.4233	.3709	.4225	N/A	.4509	.4331
Hong Kong	.0808	.0381	.0441		.0612	.6492	.0331		.0646	.2097	.0343	.0359	.0009	N/A		
Netherlands							.0762				.0132	.0552	.0319	N/A		.0576
Switzerland[b]								.0512						N/A		

Note: N/A = not available.

[a]LC = Lichtenstein.

[b]It was impossible for the Swiss investor to construct the historical international portfolio whose mean return is higher than the risk-free rate.

Table 7–4
Compositions of Ex Post Optimal International Portfolios by Country
$R_f = 5\%$

								Habitats of Investors								
	LC	AU	BE	CA	FR	GE	HK	IT	JA	NE	SG	SP	SD	SW	UK	US
Belgium	.1782		.1151		.0707	.1005		.1513		.0699						
France					.0194									.0605		
Germany					.0407			.0454								
Hong Kong													.0236			
Italy	.1506	.0545		.0921	.0315		.0513	.0414	.0435		.0525	.0360	.0734		.0982	.0559
Japan		.2046	.2615	.0306	.1844	.1154	.1423	.1387	.4400	.1027	.0820	.1328	.1769	.1856	.0677	
Netherlands														.0576		
Singapore		.0534	.0105	.0818	.0078	.0094	.0663		.0405		.1167	.0369			.0506	.0663
Spain	.0646											.0223				
Sweden	.4958	.4872	.3171	.5519	.4088	.4902	.5476	.3851	.4759	.4614	.6088	.3362	.5323	.4499	.3402	.6930
U.K.	.1108		.0131	.0428	.0094	.0233	.0855	.0029		.0608		.1380	.1937	.1221	.2171	
U.S.		.2002	.2828	.2007	.2272	.2611	.1070	.2352		.3053	.1399	.2979		.1244	.2262	.1847

returns and covariance matrix calculated over the three-year holding period.[5] The true values of these parameters are, of course, unobservable ex ante. Tables 7–3 and 7–4 also present the compositions of international portfolios in terms of the local currency (LC) without incorporating the exchange rate changes. These portfolios represent the hypothetical portfolios that would have been held by every national investor, had there been no changes in the exchange rates.

It is evident from table 7–3 that the alternative strategies produce markedly different portfolio weights, and that national investors hold substantially different portfolios as a result of the fluctuating exchange rates. It is also evident from comparing tables 7–3 and 7–4 that the portfolio weights of each of the three strategies substantially deviate from those of the ex post optimal international portfolio. From the viewpoint of the U.S. investor, for example, the Jobson-Korkie international portfolio is composed of the Canadian fund (12.37%), German (14.09%), Italian (3.67%), Japanese (15.81%), Spanish (15.60%), Swedish (11.20%), and United States (27.26%). The historical international portfolio, on the other hand, is composed of the Belgian fund (40.84%), Canadian (10.09%), German (43.31%), and Dutch (5.76%). As is shown in table 7–4, the U.S. investor should have invested in the Italian fund (5.59%), Singaporean (6.63%), Swedish (69.30%), and the United States (18.47%) to fully realize the potential gains from international diversification.

Actual and Potential Gains from International Diversification

In this section, for each national investor we examine the ex post performance of each of the three ex ante international portfolios under the assumption that the portfolio weights determined ex ante were used to construct portfolios to be held over the three-year holding period. The international portfolio results are compared with the respective performance from investment solely in the domestic portfolio. Let SHP (*IP*) denote the Sharpe performance measure's value of an international portfolio and let SHP(*DP*) denote the SHP value of the investor's domestic portfolio. Then the actual gains from international diversification can be measured by the SHP differential:

$$\Delta SHP = SHP(IP) - SHP(DP). \tag{7.1}$$

The ΔSHP is interpreted as the actual excess mean return differential per unit of standard deviation which accrues from holding the international portfolio in lieu of the domestic portfolio. A corresponding calculation for the ex post optimal portfolio—SHP*(*IP*)—results in ΔSHP^*, which represents the potential gains from international diversification.

Table 7–5 presents the SHP values together with the means and standard deviations for the domestic and international portfolios. Table 7–5 also presents the ΔSHP value for each international portfolio. Corresponding values for the ex post optimal portfolio (denoted by *) are also presented.

First, note that ΔSHP* is positive for each of the fifteen national investors. This, of course, implies that every national investor could potentially benefit from international diversification during the holding period. The magnitude of potential gains, however, varies across countries. The potential gains are relatively large for the Australian, Belgian, French, German, Hong Kong, Italian, Spanish, and Swiss investors, whereas they are rather modest for the Japanese, Singaporean, Swedish, U.K., and U.S. investors.

Second, for every national investor, the actual gains (ΔSHP) associated with each of the three strategies are substantially smaller than the potential gains. Among the three international portfolios, the historical international portfolio performed most poorly. For every national investor, the historical diversification strategy was dominated by either the naive or the Jobson-Korkie diversification strategy. In fact, the historical international portfolio resulted in a negative ΔSHP value for ten out of the total of fifteen national investors.[6] This implies that these investors would have been better off if they had held their domestic portfolios instead of the historical international portfolios. Given that the historical international portfolio is, in fact, the ex post optimal international portfolio for the estimation period, the poor performance of the portfolio suggests that the composition of the ex post optimal international portfolio is rather unstable over time.

Third, as for the naive international portfolio and the Jobson-Korkie international portfolio, the latter outperformed the former for nine national investors, while the opposite is true for six national investors. This result implies that the historical covariance matrix contains useful information only for some national investors.

Fourth, for four national investors (Japan, Singapore, Sweden, and the United States, none of the three diversification strategies was able to outperform their respective domestic portfolios. In other words, the ΔSHP value for each of the three strategies is negative for these four national investors. It is interesting to note that the magnitude of potential gains from international diversification (the ΔSHP* value) is smallest for these four national investors.

Fifth, the exchange rate changes tend to mitigate both the actual and potential gains from international diversification. In the absence of the exchange rate changes, for example, the ex post optimal international portfolio has the SHP* value of .737. Once the exchange rate changes are incorporated, the SHP* value declines for eleven out of the fifteen national investors. For the U.S. investor, for example, the SHP* value declines to .352.

Table 7-5
Actual and Potential Gains from International Diversification by Country
$R_f = 5\%$

Investor Habitats	Domestic Portfolio			Naive International Portfolio				Historical International Portfolio				Jobson-Korkie International Portfolio				Ex Post Optimal International Portfolio			
	Mean	SD	SHP	Mean	SD	SHP	ΔSHP	Mean	SD	SHP	ΔSHP	Mean	SD	SHP	ΔSHP	Mean[a]	SD[a]	SHP[a]	ΔSHP[a]
Australia	.35	7.33	-.009	.89	3.93	.120	.129	.32	4.65	-.021	-.012	.82	4.48	.089	.098	2.17	3.56	.491	.500
Belgium	1.14	5.32	.136	1.97	3.79	.410	.274	1.21	3.88	.205	.069	1.11	4.90	.142	.006	2.89	3.45	.717	.581
Canada	.74	7.58	.043	.68	3.90	.069	.026	.19	4.53	-.051	-.094	.90	3.69	.131	.088	2.07	4.16	.398	.355
France	.55	5.95	.023	1.99	3.68	.427	.404	1.18	3.53	.217	.194	1.30	4.97	.178	.155	2.98	3.34	.768	.745
Germany	.74	3.20	.100	1.45	3.86	.269	.169	.69	8.12	.034	-.066	.57	5.17	.030	-.070	2.59	3.44	.633	.533
Hong Kong	.77	11.00	.032	1.33	4.09	.223	.191	.66	4.66	.051	.019	1.58	3.77	.307	.275	2.68	3.85	.587	.555
Italy	2.62	9.21	.240	2.02	3.69	.435	.195	1.27	3.28	.261	.021	2.34	3.69	.522	.282	2.90	3.10	.800	.560
Japan	1.01	3.63	.163	.50	4.11	.020	-.143	-.22	4.88	-.130	-.293	.82	2.86	.142	-.021	1.70	3.47	.371	.208
Netherlands	1.41	5.09	.196	1.46	3.79	.275	.079	.63	3.76	.056	-.140	.59	4.70	.037	-.159	2.61	3.52	.622	.426
Singapore	1.55	8.13	.139	.47	3.75	.013	-.126	-.26	4.41	-.153	-.292	.64	2.97	.076	-.063	1.93	4.11	.368	.229
Spain	1.37	4.96	.193	2.36	4.16	.466	.273	1.65	4.82	.255	.062	2.39	3.59	.550	.357	3.44	4.01	.753	.560
Sweden	4.07	6.18	.592	2.14	4.44	.389	-.203	1.42	4.98	.202	-.390	2.53	4.15	.509	-.083	3.41	4.28	.699	.107
Switzerland	.72	3.20	.095	1.60	3.42	.345	.250	N/A	N/A	N/A	N/A	.76	4.10	.084	-.011	2.68	2.78	.813	.718
U.K.	1.96	5.44	.283	1.44	3.75	.274	-.009	.77	5.03	.071	-.212	1.63	3.90	.311	.028	2.55	3.91	.545	.262
U.S.	1.29	4.72	.185	.58	4.78	.034	-.151	-.01	5.32	-.080	-.265	.87	3.96	.113	-.072	2.11	4.82	.352	.167
Lichtenstein	N/A	N/A	N/A	1.35	3.33	.281	N/A	.70	7.07	.040	N/A	1.47	2.56	.413	N/A	2.92	3.40	.737	N/A

[a]Ex post.

Concluding Remarks

In this chapter, we have evaluated the out-of-sample performance of the domestic and international portfolios under flexible exchange rates. We also examined the actual and potential gains from international diversification. In spite of the adverse effect of the fluctuating exchange rates, every national investor can potentially benefit from international diversification. The actual gains associated with a particular investment strategy, however, tend to be substantially lower than the potential gains and, in some cases, they turned out to be negative. This is a result of parameter uncertainty or estimation risk. Unless investors know the "true" probability distributions of future stock market returns, they will be prevented from fully realizing the potential gains. This result underlines the importance of improving the accuracy with which input parameters are estimated. In fact, the existence of estimation risk may be responsible, at least in part, for the so-called "home-bias" in portfolio holdings. The current state of the art of implementing modern portfolio theory, however, allows the majority of international investors (though not all) to realize enough of the potential gains to make international diversification beneficial.

Notes

1. Other notable works include Agmon (1972), McDonald (1973), and Subrahmanyam (1975). It is beyond the scope of this chapter to provide a detailed survey of the existing literature. Readers are referred to Adler and Dumas (1983) for such a survey.

2. For a detailed discussion of estimation risk, readers are referred to Jobson and Korkie (1980 and 1981). In this chapter, the concept of potential gains involves the gains investors can realize when they know the true probability distribution of stock market returns. On the other hand, actual gains refer to the gains investors can realize while they bear estimation risk.

3. Though much of the distributional properties of both stock market returns in terms of local currencies and the exchange rate changes are known, little is known so far about the distributional properties of the stock market returns measured in a foreign currency. Though this issue is important enough in its own right to deserve further scrutiny, it goes beyond the scope of this chapter.

Evidence of departure from normality is somewhat incongruous with the mean-variance analysis. Since the focus of this chapter is not on the distributional property, we simply assume either that normality is a good approximation or that investors have quadratic utility functions.

4. We have deliberately assumed no short selling in the portfolio construction because of our desire to present our findings in a realistic perspective. The assumption of unrestricted short selling frequently results in one or more assets being held in a negative quantity equal to several times the budget constraint. This result is unrealistic, especially when foreign assets are required to be sold short. In his presidential

address, Markowitz (1959) argues that the assumption of unrestricted short selling is unrealistic and has been rejected by institutions that use modern portfolio theory to guide their investment decisions. It is also pointed out that short sales of securities are illegal in some foreign countries.

5. The compositions of both the historical international portfolio and the ex post optimal international portfolio are dependent on the particular risk-free interest rate assumed. Results obtained from the alternative risk-free rates are available from the authors. Note, however, that due to the grand mean approach, the composition of the Jobson-Korkie international portfolio is independent of the risk-free rate assumed.

6. For the Swiss investor, we also constructed the historical international portfolio at the risk-free rate of 4 percent. The resulting portfolio has the SHP value of .066 which is compared with .122 for the Swiss domestic portfolio.

References

Adler, Michael, & Bernard Dumas. "International Portfolio Choice and Corporation Finance: A Synthesis." *Journal of Finance,* 38 (June 1983), 925–84.

Agmon, Tamir. "The Relations among Equity Markets in the United States, United Kingdom, Germany and Japan." *Journal of Finance,* 27 (September 1972), 839–56.

Grubel, Herbert. "Internationally Diversified Portfolios: Welfare Gains and Capital Flows." *American Economic Review* 58 (December 1968), 1299–1314.

Jobson, J. D., & Bob Korkie. "Improved Estimation and Selection Rules for Markowitz Portfolios." Paper presented at the Western Finance Association meeting (June 1980).

———. "Putting Markowitz Theory to Work." *Journal of Portfolio Management,* 7 (Summer 1981), 70–74.

Lessard, Donald. "World, National and Industry Factors in Equity Returns." *Journal of Finance,* 29 (May 1974), 379–391.

———. "World, Country and Industry Relationships in Equity Returns: Implications for Risk Reduction through International Diversification." *Financial Analysts Journal* (January/February 1976), 2–8.

Levy, Haim, & Marshall Sarnat. "International Diversification of Investment Portfolios." *American Economic Review,* 60 (September 1970), 668–75.

Markowitz, Harry. *Portfolio Selection: Efficient Diversification of Investments.* New York: John Wiley & Sons, 1959.

———. "Nonnegative or Not Nonnegative: A Question about CAPMs." *Journal of Finance,* 38 (May 1983), 283–95.

McDonald, John. "French Mutual Fund Performance: Evaluation of Internationally Diversified Portfolios." *Journal of Finance,* 28 (December 1973), 1161–80.

Solnik, Bruno. "Why Not Diversify Internationally?" *Financial Analyst Journal,* 20 (July/August 1974), 48–54.

Subrahmanyam, Marti. "On the Optimality of International Capital Market Integration." *Journal of Financial Economics,* 2 (March 1975), 3–28.

Tobin, James. "Liquidity Preference as Behavior toward Risk." *Review of Economic Studies,* 25 (February 1958), 65–86.

8

Lead–Lag Relationships among National Equity Markets: An Empirical Investigation

Hans Schollhammer
Ole Christian Sand

ABSTRACT

This chapter examines the interdependencies or comovements among stock price indices of thirteen major industrialized countries and identifies the magnitude of lead–lag relationships. As a data base the chapter uses daily observations of the national stock price indices from January 1, 1981 through June 30, 1983. The data series was examined for the existence of national patterns of stock price movements; to the extent that these movements did not reflect random walk processes, the data series was prewhitened and the residuals cross-correlated at various lags of up to three months on a pair-wise basis using the Box-Jenkins autoreggressive integrated moving average (ARIMA) method. Contrary to previous analyses this chapter provides evidence of significant and positive correlations between inter- as well as intracontinental equity market indices. The stock markets of only three countries—Italy, France, and Sweden—are largely unaffected by stock market developments in other countries. For most of the investigated countries, stock price developments show various degrees of interdependencies. However, the correlation coefficients are generally low, suggesting that national markets are still relatively segmented. As expected, the U.S. equity market generally leads other national markets. Most of the documented lead–lag relationships are of one trading day or less and thus not inconsistent with the efficient market hypothesis. However, this chapter also provides evidence of the existence of unexploited arbitrage opportunities and market imperfections. The chapter concludes with a recognition of some limitations of the analysis and indicates areas of further research.

The remarkable expansion of national equity markets, the increasing interdependence among these markets, the emergence of a huge offshore market in stocks, and the general awareness of the benefits to be derived from an internationally diversified investment portfolio are some of the developments that stimulate an interest in reinvestigating the comovement of national equity markets and related lead–lag relationships. Intuitively, it seems plausible to argue that the growing economic interdependence among countries as reflected in trade and capital flows leads to a high degree of synchronization of other economic conditions and developments among countries. Since stock market indices can be viewed as indicators of the expected, economically relevant developments in a country, one can hypothesize that a high degree of economic interdependence among countries will manifest itself in the synchronization of stock price developments across national equity markets.

Rationale and Objective of This Chapter

In an efficient equity market, stock prices adjust instantaneously in accordance with the flow of incoming information so that, at any point in time, the price of stock reflects all relevant information that affects it. One possible source of information affecting stock prices in one country is the movement of stock prices in other markets around the world. There are several theoretical explanations of why we should expect national equity markets to be correlated. Ripley (1973) gives three main reasons: (1) Common movements in national income and expectations among countries may indirectly link these countries' stock prices. (2) Through international capital flow, real interest rates will tend to equalize across countries (through what is called the international Fisher relation), thereby stimulating covariation in equity prices. (3) The rising dominance of multinational companies, whose stocks are traded in several national markets, will directly contribute to comovements among equity markets. Additional reasons are the increasing speed and efficiency of information flow worldwide, a heightened investor sensitivity to relevant information and a greater facilitates the sophistication in its interpretation. Furthermore, investor's sensitivity to such information has heightened and greater sophistication is applied in this information's interpretation. Thus, we may expect the short-run correlation in stock price movements across countries to be an increasing function of time.

The purpose of this chapter is to examine patterns of stock price movements in the major stock markets around the world and to analyze the extent to which a change in one country's stock price index exerts an influence on stock prices of other countries. The consistent and significant interdependence among national equity markets could be reflected in lead or lag relationships which could signal unexploited arbitrage and profit opportunities and, thus, inefficiencies in the international equity markets. This chapter focuses on the stock price developments of thirteen countries shown in table 8–1, which account for over 90 percent of the total global market value of stocks. The growing proportion of foreign stocks in many investment portfolios has given rise to the establishment of a global stock index that incorporates stock price developments of almost 1,300 companies which together account for nearly three-quarters of the worldwide market capitalization of stocks. The weighting of the stock markets of the thirteen countries included in this chapter for the purpose of the global stock index is also shown in table 8–1.

Prior Research

Empirical investigations of the interdependence among national stock markets and stock price movements have frequently focused on the merits of an international diversification of security portfolios. The more segmented the

Table 8–1
Capitalization and Weighting of the World's Largest Stock Markets Included in Chapter 8
($ billion, U.S.)

	Total Capitalization	Euromoney/First Boston Stock Index (percentage weighting)
North America		
United States	1,955.0	53.03%
Canada	147.0	2.87
Europe		
France	79.0	1.54
Germany	179.0	4.84
Italy	65.0	1.57
Netherlands	52.0	1.67
Norway	9.8	0.22
Sweden	30.0	0.27
Switzerland	90.0	1.37
United Kingdom	328.0	7.32
Asia and Oceania		
Australia	63.0	0.95
Japan	909.0	22.01
Singapore	20.0	0.28
	3,926.8	97.94
Other	95.0	2.06
Global market value of stocks	4,021.8	100

Source: *Capital International* and *Euromoney*, May 1986.

markets are, the greater the rationale for diversification. In contrast, a high degree of comovement among national equity markets undermines the benefits to be derived from a geographically diversified equity portfolio. Existing empirical studies have come overwhelmingly to the conclusion that the correlation between national equity markets is low (Agmon, 1974; Branch, 1974; Lessard, 1976; Levy and Sarnat, 1970). In particular, little or no correlation is found on an intercontinental basis (Hilliard, 1979). This segmentation and absence of a synchronization of stock price movements among national equity markets is explained by barriers to free trade and capital flows as well as by dissonances in sovereign government policies.

In a study of stock indices for ten major industrialized countries using spectral analysis on daily data from July 7, 1973 to April 30, 1974, Hilliard (7) found that "most intracontinental prices move simultaneously, even in the context of hourly fluctuations." With the exception of a strong correlation between the New York and Amsterdam exchanges, Hilliard found no close relationship between intercontinental prices and concluded therefore that the question of leads and lags is irrelevant. In an otherwise similar study using weekly observations from August 9, 1961 to September 2, 1964, Granger and Morgenstern (1970) found no relationship between national equity indices and, hence, no leads or lags. The same conclusion was reached by Agmon (1974), who hypothesized that the world's various equity markets behaved like an integrated, multiregional national model. Agmon found, however, no significant leads or lags among common stocks of Germany, Japan, the United Kingdom, and the United States using monthly data. Except for Hilliard's work, these studies compare equity prices based on weekly or monthly observations. If the purpose is to analyze how local stock markets react to incoming information from abroad, including information about movements in stock prices in other countries, such infrequent observations are inadequate. Conclusions based on these studies should be in terms of medium- and long-term adjustments in equity prices across countries.

Since more than a decade has passed since the data were generated for any of the above studies, we feel a new and more comprehensive empirical study is justified. There are strong reasons to believe that stock markets have become more correlated in today's integrated and interdependent world, reinforcing the importance of studying lead–lag relationships.

Expected Lead–Lag Relationships

Although existing studies have come to the conclusion that the interdependence between national equity markets is low, there is evidence that the markets are not totally uncorrelated even in the short run. A relevant question is thus whether lead–lag relations exist between these markets. If the global equity market is efficient, no lead—lag relationship should be large enough to provide unexploited arbitrage opportunities.

An important and complicating factor is that stock markets are located in different time zones with different opening and closing times. If stock markets are affected by the same worldwide news, we should expect stock prices to adjust simultaneously in real time. In fact, stock markets with different opening and closing times may both lead and lag each other. At the closing of market *X*, this market will have the most current information. Hence, it should lead all other markets that open later. Similarly, market *X* should lag those markets that close between its closing time and its reopening the next day. A lag of up to one day may therefore be consistent with an efficient market since the opening prices in the market found to be lagging may have already incorporated the new information from the markets. Note here that a significant correlation at day zero may be interpreted as a lag of one day since we have not broken down the frequency of our observations beyond calendar days. For example, the U.S. and Canadian markets are the last to close each calendar day and should therefore be expected to lead other markets by one day. However, these two markets are also the last to open each trading day, so they will lag all other markets (as the latter have opened earlier). Thus, a two-way lead–lag structure is to be expected.

It is difficult to empirically distinguish between actual lags and real time comovements of markets with different opening and closing times and periods when both markets are open. However, under no circumstances should we expect to find significant lags of two days or more. This would indicate that unexploited arbitrage opportunities exist and contradict the efficient market hypothesis.

It would be naive to think that each stock exchange is equally important internationally so that any existing lead–lag structure is determined by the differences in opening and closing times only. Clearly, changes in the underlying conditions determining prices on the New York Stock Exchange are likely to have a stronger impact internationally than new developments on the Oslo Bors, for example. However, if important events occur while the U.S. market is closed, these will first show up in other markets. A potentially fruitful approach would be to identify major international events (such as wars, trade embargoes, political turmoil, or major changes in economic policies) and analyze the process in which their effects are transmitted from market to market. Since we have used daily observations for two-and-one-half years, we assume that no systematic bias occurs due to particular events. Still, relevant information is more likely to be generated in some countries than others. Because of its size and international importance, we expect the U.S. market to lead other markets on the average. The general acceptance of the U.S. economy as the locomotive for the world economy should reinforce this situation.

The Data

Daily closing prices of major industrial or composite indices on thirteen world exchanges were used in the analysis. The data were extracted from *Financial Times* of London and cover the period from January 1, 1981 to June 30, 1983. The length of each series is therefore 650 observations. No adjustment was made for changes in the foreign exchange rates since our objective is to analyze how local stock markets react to information from foreign equity markets (that is, we have taken the point of view of the local investor). If the purpose had been to identify international arbitrage opportunities, it would have been appropriate to convert all prices to a common numeraire.

In cases of missing data (due to national holidays, for example), the price was set equal to the last closing price recorded. Table 8–2 gives a list of the indices included in this chapter. The approximate differences between closing times of the exchanges included are also given.

Methodology

Box-Jenkins (1970) ARIMA time-series analysis was used to study the relationship between the indices. The advantage of this method is that it is simple, yet statistically powerful and conceptually sound.

Rather than using the original data, we took the first difference for all series. This was necessary in order to make the series stationary, a requirement for the application of ARIMA model building. Since we had little a priori information about the direction of any potential causality (indeed, it would be no surprise to find a two-way causality), we first prewhitened all series and then cross-correlated the residuals at various lags on a pairwise basis. For comparison, the cross-correlations were also calculated before prewhitening the series; these results are reported in Tables 8–6 and 8–7.

As shown by Granger and Newbold (1970) and others, correlations of the original data are likely to be spurious. A "double" prewhitening (meaning that the trend is taken out of both series before they are cross-correlated) is therefore preferred unless the level of a priori information enables the researcher to identify the input series and the output series. An analysis of the interrelationships among national stock market indices using prewhitened data series leads to results that are not contaminated by existing national patterns of stock price movements or trends. In previous empirical studies, no trend has been removed from the data before cross-correlation.

The prewhitened series were obtained through the usual interactive and stepwise process of (1) identification of the ARIMA model, (2) estimation of the model, and (3) diagnostic checking to ensure that the residuals are white

Table 8–2
Stock Indices Included in Chapter 8

Country	Index	Hours Ahead of N.Y. Close
Australia	All Ord.	15.50 hours
Canada	TSE Composite 300	0.00
France	Industrial Tendance	7.00
Germany	FAZ Aktien	8.00
Italy	Banca Comm. Italy	7.75
Japan	Tokyo SE New	14.50
Netherlands	AND DBS, Industrial	8.25
Norway	Industriindexen	8.50
Singapore	Straights Times	13.00
Sweden	Jacobsen & P.	7.00
Switzerland	Swiss Bank OPH	8.75
United Kingdom	Financial Times, Ind.	5.00
United States	Dow Jones, Industrial	—

noise. With thirteen countries included in our analysis, seventy-eight possible pairs of countries were cross-correlated $[N^* (N - 1)/2]$. The cross-correlations were calculated for lags of up to sixty days in each direction.

Findings

Country-Specific Patterns of Stock Price Movements

The analysis of stock price developments of thirteen countries is given in table 8–3. It shows that the stock price movements for only five of the thirteen countries resemble random walk processes. (Aggregate stock price changes in France, Germany, Switzerland, the United Kingdom, and Japan do not reflect any discernible patterns and a random walk model gives the best fit of the data.) This implies that our estimated cross-correlations, to be discussed in the next section, are not likely to be different from what they would have been without initial prewhitening of the data series. A comparison of tables 8–4 through 8–7 shows that this is indeed the case.

The largest deviations from the random walk model were detected for stock price movements in the smaller countries, notably Norway, Sweden, Italy, Australia, and the Netherlands. Stock price movements of these countries can be characterized as autoregressive, which means that changes in the stock price index have discernible and predictable after-effects. As an example, table 8–3 shows that for Norway, the coefficient for the first-order au-

Table 8–3
Univariate Models for Thirteen Stock Indices

Country	Process	Order	Coefficient(s)	t-value(s)
Australia	AR	(1)	.123	2.90
Canada	MA	(1,9)	−.250, .116	−6.08, 2.81
France	Random walk			
Germany	Random walk			
Italy	AR	(1,2,7)	.151, −.120, −.090	3.5, −2.80, −2.11
Japan	Random walk			
Netherlands	AR	(1)	−.113	−2.66
Norway	AR	(1,10)	.292, .119	7.15, 2.80
Singapore	MA	(1,10)	−.143, −.135	−3.40, −3.22
Sweden	AR	(16)	.193	4.11
Switzerland	Random walk			
U.K.	Random walk			
U.S.	MA	(5)	.112	2.62

Note: AR = autoregressive, MA = moving average.

tocorrelation is as high as .292, implying that successive changes in Norway's stock price index are positively correlated. If Norway's stock price index goes up by one point one day, it will contribute to a rise the following day (coefficient .292) as well as ten days later (coefficient .119). Aggregate stock price developments in Italy are also autoregressive but reflect a more complicated pattern. As table 8–3 shows, a change in Italy's stock price index tends to be associated with a change in the index in the same direction the following day (coefficient .151), but a change in the opposite direction the second day (coefficient −.120) and a further change in the opposite direction on the seventh day (coefficient −.090). A possible explanation for this situation is the existence of different groups of investors reacting with different speeds to stock market developments in a relatively closed and small market. One group of investors may set upper price limits for their buy orders and floor prices for their sell orders without following stock price developments on a daily or even more frequent basis. Other investors and institutions may follow stock price developments much more closely. If the stock prices rise, the latter group may want to benefit from a trend, triggering more buy orders the following day, thus contributing to a further rise of the stock price index the following day. As stock prices rise, more sell orders from the first group of investors become effective; together with profit taking, this leads then to a relative decline in stock prices on the second day with an after-ripple on the seventh day.

Table 8–3 also documents a pattern of stock price developments for Canada, Singapore, and the United States. For example, Canadian stock prices show a strong first-order (day) moving-average process with a negative coefficient of −.250 and a ninth-order (day) positive coefficient of .116. This means that a rise in the Canadian stock price index one day contributes to a decline in the index the following day (possibly on account of profit taking), but a rise on the ninth day. Our analyses also show a pattern of stock price movements for the United States: a change in the Dow Jones index on one day is associated with a change in the same direction five trading days later. This effect is, however, relatively weak (coefficient .112) and has low statistical significance (*t*-value of 2.62). The U.S. pattern is difficult to explain; we believe it is caused by different levels of stock-trading activities on various days of the week, thus giving rise to the observed weekly (five–trading-day) pattern.

The findings presented in table 8–3 provide evidence of the necessity to prewhiten the data series for those countries whose stock price movements do not resemble random walk processes in order to investigate lead–lag relationships among national stock price movements free from distortions brought about by country-specific patterns. The findings also signal the existence of market inefficiencies and exploitable arbitrage opportunities for those countries whose stock price movements do not resemble random walk processes. In general, the higher-order processes (those of two days and more) are only marginally significant. Roll (1981) and Scholes and Williams (1977) have shown that the existence of long autocorrelation structures in indices (an extreme example is the sixteenth-day autoregressive process detected for the Swedish stock price index) may be due to infrequent trading of stocks included in the indices. According to these studies, the small deviations from pure random walk processes as shown in table 8–3 may not necessarily constitute sufficient evidence of market inefficiencies.

The Interdependence among National Stock Price Movements

Due to the large number of correlations estimated, we expected to find some anomalous significant coefficients just by chance. To alleviate this problem we applied strict significance criteria: only correlations significant at the 99 percent confidence level are reported. Furthermore, we divided the period studied into two subperiods of equal length (first quarter 1981 through second quarter 1982 and second quarter 1982 through fourth quarter 1983) to see whether lead–lag relationships reappear in consecutive periods. To the extent that the findings for the subperiods are similar and consistent, one can conclude that the interrelationships among national equity markets are stable over time. Comparing the findings from the subperiods may also reveal changes in the degree of interdependence among stock markets.

Before we compare the results for the two subperiods, a few comments about the overall findings are in order. As Tables 8–4 and 8–5 show, we found significant and consistent inter- as well as intracontinental correlations between stock market indices on a daily basis. Thus, our findings contradict previous analyses that found little or no comovement in intercontinental stock prices. We believe that this result is in part due to a more comprehensive data base and the use of daily observations of stock price movements over a relatively long period of time. But more important, the findings of this investigation provide evidence of noticeable change during the past decade toward a much more integrated, global equity market. Yet, the correlation coefficients between the national stock markets are still relatively low, meaning that most countries have little systematic risk relative to a worldwide market factor.

A surprising finding is the low correlations among stock price movements of European countries. As tables 8–4 and 8–5 show, short-term stock price developments in France and Italy are not affected by stock market conditions in any of the other European countries that were analyzed. This is an unexpected finding given the high degree of economic integration and cooperation to which both countries are committed as members of the European Economic Community. In fact, the European exchanges in general show stronger or equally strong correlations with the exchanges in the United States, Canada, and Japan than with each other.

With the exception of one of the correlation coefficients found significant, all have the expected positive sign implying that stock prices in different countries tend to move in the same direction in terms of daily fluctuations. The only negative correlation occurs in the second subperiod, when the U.K. lags the United States by two days. Note that the U.K. index is strongly positively correlated with the Dow Jones the two days previous to the negative correlation. Our explanation for this anomalous negative correlation is that a reaction occurs in the U.K. market after a strong positive impulse from abroad.

The results emphasize the importance of the New York exchange as a leading market. Of the twelve indices, nine lag the U.S. index by one day in the first subperiod and by eleven days in the second subperiod. The average coefficients for these one-day lagged correlations are .23 and .32, respectively, for the two subperiods, which is high considering the daily data. This is largely due to the high correlation between the U.S. and the Canadian stock markets. The close links between the New York and Toronto exchanges with the same opening and closing times and the same stocks traded are well known. Their correlation coefficients of .66 and .55 for the two periods are the highest found in our sample.

When comparing the results for the two subperiods, we first note that the comovements in national stock prices were stronger in the second period.

Table 8–4
Lead–Lag Structure between Stock Indices, January 1, 1981 to March 31, 1982

	AUS	CAN	FRA	GER	ITA	JAP	NET	NOR	SIN	SWE	SWI	UK	US
Australia (AUS)													
Canada (CAN)	.31+1 .17+2												
France (FRA)	*	*											
Germany (GER)	.19 .25+1	.34−1	*										
Italy (ITA)	*	*	*	*									
Japan (JAP)	*	.22−1	*	.26	*								
Netherlands (NET)	*	.34−1	*	.23	*	.20							
Norway (NOR)	*	.17−1	*	*	*	*	*						
Singapore (SIN)	*	*	*	*	*	.17	*	*					
Sweden (SWE)	*	.19−1	*	*	*	*	*	*	*				
Switzerland (SWI)	*	.21−1	*	.25	*	.28	*	*	*	.19			
U.K. (UK)	.30+1	.18 .27−1	*	.30	*	.20	.28 .17+1	*	*	*	.17		
U.S. (US)	.25+1	.66	.20+1	.33+1	*	*	.32+1	.19+1 .18+7	.19+1	.17+1	.20 .17+1	.17 .23+1	

Notes: * indicates no significant cross-correlation at any lag (99% level). +1 after two-decimal correlation coefficient indicates lead of one day. −1 after two-decimal correlation coefficient indicates lag of one day.

Table 8–5
Lead–Lag Structure between Stock Indices, April 1, 1982 to June 30, 1983

	AUS	CAN	FRA	GER	ITA	JAP	NET	NOR	SIN	SWE	SWI	UK	US
Australia (AUS)													
Canada (CAN)	.33+1	*											
France (FRA)	.19	*	*										
Germany (GER)	*	.22−1	*	*									
Italy (ITA)	*	*	*	*	*								
Japan (JAP)	.29	.22 .26−1	*	.26	*								
Netherlands (NET)	.24	.38−1	.25	.35	*	.27							
Norway (NOR)	*	.33−1	.22	.22	*	*	.26						
Singapore (SIN)	.17	.24−1	*	.20	*	.20	*	.23					
Sweden (SWE)	*	*	*	*	*	*	*	*	*				
Switzerland (SWI)	.18	.17 .21−1	*	.34	*	.23	.20	.22	*	*			
U.K. (UK)	.18 .20+1	.26	*	.22	*	.31+1	.23 .27+1	*	.22+1	*	.20		
U.S. (US)	.36+1	.55 .21+1	.26+1	.37+1	*	.40+1 .24+2	.48+1	.35+1	.31+1	.20+1	.26+1	.22 .29+1 −.20+2	

Notes: * indicates no significant cross-correlation at any lag (99% level). +1 after two-decimal correlation coefficient indicates lead of one day. −1 after two-decimal correlation coefficient indicates lag of one day.

In the first period (January 1, 1981 to March 31, 1982), about 40 percent (or 31 of the 78) cross-correlations were found significant at the 99 percent level. This increased to about 55 percent (or 43 of 78) in the second period (April 1, 1982 to June 30, 1983). Furthermore, the average magnitude of the correlation coefficient grew from .25 to .27 between the two periods. One reason for this increased correlation may well be that the present economy recovery in the United States started in the early part of the second subperiod, giving rise to optimism among investors in the industrialized countries.

In most cases, correlations found significant in the first period are also significant and have the same lag structure in the second period. This is true for 27 of the 31 cases, indicating that our findings are consistent.

An examination of our findings from the perspective of individual countries shows that the stock price movements of only one country, Italy, are entirely unaffected by stock market developments in any of the other countries either on the same trading day or lagged up to three months. All our findings presented in tables 8–4 through 8–7 also show that Italian stock market developments have no statistically significant impact on aggregate price developments in any of the other twelve countries we examined. This unique behavior of the Italian stock market has also been observed by Hilliard (1979) and by Panton, Lessig, and Joy (1976) who have characterized it as the most dissimilar among those studied.

An explanation of the absence of any statistically significant comovement between Italian stock prices and those in other countries is speculative. However, plausible explanations may focus on the fact that foreign investors do not play a significant role as buyers and sellers of Italian publicly traded stock. In addition, significant blocks of shares of large companies such as Montedison and Finsider are owned by the government; other large Italian companies such as Fiat, Olivetti, and Pirelli have dominant shareholder groups. Stocks of these companies have a significant weight in the Italian stock price index. However, prices of these stocks are more amenable to being "managed," while investing in these stocks is less attractive to foreign investors. Another point to consider is that few Italian stocks are listed on foreign exchanges and practically no foreign stocks are listed on Italian exchanges, thus eliminating arbitrage opportunities. All these factors combined provide a likely explanation for the independence of the Italian stock market developments from those in other countries.

Tables 8–4 through 8–7 show that French stock market developments are unaffected by and have no impact on market developments in other countries except the United States. Aggregate stock price changes in France are affected by the preceding day's developments on Wall Street with correlation coefficients of .20 and .26 for the two subperiods. The absence of any interdependence between the French stock market and exchanges in other European countries is surprising, particularly in view of France's economic inte-

Table 8–6
Lead–Lag Structure between Stock Indices, No Prewhitening, January 1, 1981 to March 31, 1982

	AUS	CAN	FRA	GER	ITA	JAP	NET	NOR	SIN	SWE	SWI	UK	US
Australia (AUS)													
Canada (CAN)	.37+1 .22+2												
France (FRA)	*	*											
Germany (GER)	.20 .28+1	.33−1	*	*									
Italy (ITA)	*	*	*	*									
Japan (JAP)	*	.22−1	*	.26	*								
Netherlands (NET)	*	.33−1	*	.23	*	.20							
Norway (NOR)	*	.17−1	*	*	*	*	*						
Singapore (SIN)	*	*	*	*	*	.17	*	*					
Sweden (SWE)	*	.21−1	*	*	*	*	*	*	*				
Switzerland (SWI)	*	.18−1	*	.25	*	.28	*	*	*	.18			
U.K. (UK)	.31+1	.26 .25−1	*	.28	*	.20	.28	.17+1	*	*	.17		
U.S. (US)	.25+1	.66	.20+1	.33+1	*	*	.32+1	.20+1	.19+1	.17+1	.20 .17+1	.17 .23+1	

Notes: * indicates no significant cross-correlation at any lag (99% level). +1 after two-decimal correlation coefficient indicates lead of one day. −1 after two-decimal correlation coefficient indicates lag of one day.

Table 8–7
Lead–Lag Structure between Stock Indices, No Prewhitening, April 1, 1982 to June 30, 1983

	AUS	CAN	FRA	GER	ITA	JAP	NET	NOR	SIN	SWE	SWI	UK	US
Australia (AUS)													
Canada (CAN)	.33+1 .17+2												
France (FRA)	.18	*											
Germany (GER)		.22−1	*										
Italy (ITA)	*	*	*	*									
Japan (JAP)	.30	.22 .26−1	.22	.26	*								
Netherlands (NET)	.23	.18 .37−1	.25	.35	*	.26							
Norway (NOR)	.21 .17+1	.33−1	*	.18	*	*	.27						
Singapore (SIN)	.20 .17−1	.26−1	.17+1	.21	*	.20	*	.24					
Sweden (SWE)	*	*	*	*	*	*	.18	*	*				
Switzerland (SWI)	.17	.17 .21−1	*	.34	*	.20	.21	.19	*	*			
U.K. (UK)	.17 .22+1	.27	*	.22	*	.31+1	.24 .28−1	*	.23+1	*	.20		
U.S. (US)	.37+1 .17+2	.56 .21+1	.26+1	.36+1	*	.40+1 .25+2	.48+1	.31+1	.31+1 .19+2	.22+1	.27+1	.22 .28+1 −.21+2	

Notes: * indicates no significant cross-correlation at any lag (99% level). +1 after two-decimal correlation coefficient indicates lead of one day. −1 after two-decimal correlation coefficient indicates lag of one day.

gration with other Common Market countries. France's degree of economic integration with other EEC countries is, however, due to a large extent to its agricultural sector, which does not play a significant role as determinant of stock price developments of major French companies. Similar to the situation in Italy, foreign investments in French securities are relatively small as are French holdings of foreign securities. In addition, French companies whose stocks play a significant role as determinants of the stock price index show a relatively low degree of international business involvement.

A third European country whose stock prices are not much affected by stock market developments in other countries is Sweden. Tables 8–4 and 8–5 show that Swedish stock price developments are weakly linked with market conditions in the United States, Canada, and Switzerland.

In contrast to the stock markets of Italy, France, and Sweden, stock price developments of all other investigated countries are significantly linked. Tables 8–4 and 8–5 show that changes in the U.S. stock price index cause statistically significant stock price changes in the same direction in all other countries (except Italy) on the following day as well as the same day in Canada and the United Kingdom. The interdependence between the U.S. and U.K. stock markets is particularly interesting. Since the London exchange closes before New York opens, the zero lag implies that New York actually lags London by one day (with correlation coefficients of .17 and .20 for the two subperiods). In addition, the United States leads the U.K. by one day. As expected, a high degree of interdependence exists between the U.S. and Canadian stock price developments on the same day (with coefficients of .66 and .55). Because of this linkage, Canadian stock price changes show up as interdependent with those of other countries that are affected and led by U.S. stock price developments.

Our findings provide evidence of the comovement among stock price indices in the same direction and on the same day among the major European exchanges in the U.K., Germany, Switzerland, and the Netherlands. The statistically strongest comovement on the same day exists between the U.K. and Dutch stock indices. The degree of synchronization between these two countries' stock indices is explainable by the role stocks of companies such as Shell and Unilever play on the U.K. and Dutch exchanges. In addition, our findings show that a change in the U.K. stock index affects a change of the Dutch index in the same direction the following day. A likely cause of this situation is the extensive speculative trading in stocks of large multinational companies listed on the U.K. and Dutch exchanges by two groups of investors: those that have access to information on stock price developments during trading hours and those that make decisions about buying and selling of stocks of companies such as Shell or Unilever based on information about closing prices in these stocks. The findings concerning the stock price developments in the U.K. and the Netherlands may also be reflective of the growing role stocks of large multinational companies play in "homogenizing" aggregate stock price developments among countries.

An interesting aberration occurs in the Japanese market between the two periods. In the first period, it is uncorrelated with the U.S. market. However, in the second period, it strongly lags the U.S. market at both one and two days. Also, the same-day correlation with the U.K. index in the first period shifts to a significant lag of one day in the second period. In both periods, Japan is significantly correlated with Canada when lagged one day. Also, Japan is significantly correlated with Germany, the Netherlands, Singapore, and Switzerland at no lag.

In general, the findings are consistent with the efficient market hypothesis. The results reveal four incidences with significant correlations of lags of two days or more, none of which appeared in both subperiods. In the second period, the London index and Tokyo SE New Index lag the Dow Jones significantly (with correlation coefficients of $-.20$ and $.24$, respectively) on the second trading day. Although with a slightly weaker correlation, the Australian index also appears to be lagging the Canadian index after one day. Note that some of the one-day lagged correlations may provide opportunities for arbitrage gain depending on the opening and closing times of the exchanges. The Dutch stock index, for example, lags the U.K. index by one day in both subperiods in spite of having similar opening and closing times. The longest statistically significant lag was discovered for the Norwegian stock market, which has the smallest capitalization of the thirteen markets studied. As table 8–4 shows, the Norwegian industrial index lags the Dow Jones significantly by seven trading days during the first subperiod. However, no similarly long lag was found to exist during the second subperiod.

The findings presented in tables 8–4 through 8–7 reveal the existence of significant interdependencies of stock price movements among the major stock markets around the world and a series of consistent lead–lag relationships. Besides providing evidence of the increasing integration of global equity markets, the findings have two major ramifications. (1) The considerable comovement among national stock market indices implies an erosion of the benefits to be derived from an internationally diversified equity portfolio. (2) The documentation of consistent lead–lag relationships implies certain market inefficiencies, particularly with regard to the smaller equity markets and the existence of unexploited arbitrage opportunities. Concerning the latter, one must, however, note some reservations. (1) It may well be that the transaction costs incurred by engaging in appropriate trading schemes will outweigh potential trading profits. (2) As already mentioned, Scholes and Williams (1977) and Roll (1981) have shown that infrequent trading of stocks included in a stock market index may give rise to substantial lags in the index itself. (3) This chapter centers on an examination of the interdependencies among stock market indices. An individual investor is normally unable to trade an indies without trading the range of securities it is composed of. In order to identify unexploited arbitrage opportunities with certainty, one would have to compare prices of individual stocks. This topic awaits further research.

Limitations of This Chapter and Suggestions for Further Research

This chapter provides evidence of a high degree of interdependence among stock price developments of the major stock markets around the world and of the leading role exerted by stock market developments in the United States. Major causes for these situations are the increasing economic integration between the industrialized countries, largely unrestricted capital flows among them, instantaneous information availability worldwide, and sensitivity to the benefits to be derived from an internationally diversified investment portfolio. Yet, our findings show that some of the stock markets (notably those of Italy, France, and Sweden) are essentially unaffected by stock market developments in other countries. Although we believe that the latter findings can be explained by various stock market characteristics (such as market size, trading frequency of various stocks, and government stockholdings in major companies), one must not overlook a wide range of other country-specific characteristics that may have an impact on the findings presented in this chapter. For example, differences in the industry structure among various countries or specific exogenous random shocks (such as the failing of a major corporation of banking institution) with different impacts in various countries may also be causal factors for low correlation among the countries' co-movements in stock price indices.

The findings presented in this chapter may also be contaminated by differences in transaction costs involved in buying and selling stock in various countries. Transition cost artifacts may well play a noticeable role in the existence or absence of stock market interdependencies among various countries.

A major constraint of this chapter is the exclusion of differences in real interest rates, variations in dividend strategies among countries, and the exclusion of exchange rate fluctuations from the data base. No adjustments have been made in the data base on account of these factors. One can argue that interest rate and dividend differentials among countries are rather low and not subject to daily fluctuations and thus can be safely ignored. In contrast, exchange rate fluctuations can have a major effect on stock market developments, particularly from the perspective of the international investors. Changes in a national stock price index may be the result, at least in part, of changing stock market conditions in other countries and stock-market–related information sets. However, the seeming interdependence among stock markets of different countries (or the lack of it) may also be the result of exchange rate developments. In order to be truly certain about the real effect of stock price changes in one country on stock market developments in other countries, one would have to eliminate changes in the demand for stock and their effect on aggregate stock prices on account of exchange rate fluctuations. Adler and Horesh (1974, p. 1361) have pointed out that under very restrictive assumptions that cannot be found in the real world (such as homogeneous expectations of investors, completely unrestricted international capital flows, the absence of default risk and transaction costs, and a perfect forward exchange market), exchange rate fluctuations could be ignored since they would not impair the analysis of the interdependence among national capital markets. Since these assumptions are not realistic, an empirical investigation of the synchronization and comovement among the stock markets of various countries must thus account for the impact of exchange rate fluctuations. In this chapter, the analysis of exchange rate fluctuations and their effect on daily stock price developments in thirteen countries has been ignored because of computational complexities. An investigation of this issue involving only two countries is under way and will shed some light on the impact of exchange rate fluctuations on the interdependence of stock markets.

Conclusions

This chapter differs from the existing literature in two main ways. First, a more comprehensive and current data base is used. Second, ARIMA model building was applied to identify potential lead–lag relationships. Our results show that significant and positive correlations exist in daily stock price movements between major industrialized countries. Contrary to previous studies, this holds both for inter- and intracontinental comparisons. The leading role of the U.S. market is also verified by our sample, with more than 75 percent of the indices included lagging the Dow Jones by one day.

Most of the lead–lag relationships found are consistent with what we should expect due to the differences in opening and closing times of the exchanges; that is, markets adjust immediately to new information about movements in other stock markets around the world. However, a few of the lags observed appear to be sufficiently long to provide opportunities for arbitrage gains and it is tempting to conclude that our results are evidence of market inefficiencies. As discussed above, such hasty conclusions may prove to be wrong due to infrequent trading of stocks included in the indices, transaction costs, and the effects of exchange rate fluctuations. Furthermore, the long lags discovered were not consistent over time. Future researchers seeking to identify potential inefficiencies are advised to use individual stock prices instead of indices. It would also be a great advantage to use data having a higher frequency of observations than days.

References

Adler, Michael, & Reuven Horesh, "The Relationship among Equity Markets: Comment," *Journal of Finance,* September 1974.

Agmon, Tamir, "The Relationship among Equity Markets in the United States, United Kingdom, Germany, and Japan," *Journal of Finance,* September 1974.

Box, George E. P., & Gwilym M. Jenkins, *Time Series Analysis, Forecasting, and Control.* San Francisco: Holden Day, 1970.

Branch, Ben, "Common Stock Performance and Inflation: An International Comparison," *Journal of Business,* January 1974.

Granger, Clive W. J., & Oskar Morgenstern, *Predictability of Stock Market Prices.* Lexington, Mass.: Lexington, 1970.

Granger, Clive W. J., & Paul Newbold, "Spurious Regressions in Econometrics," *Journal of Econometrics,* no. 2, 1974.

Hilliard, Jimmy E., "The Relationship between Equity Indices on World Exchanges," *Journal of Finance,* March 1979.

Lessard, Donald, "World, Country, and Industry Relationships in Equity Returns," *Financial Analysts Journal,* January-February 1976.

Levy, Haim, & Marshall Sarnat, "International Diversification of Investment Portfolios," *American Economic Review,* September 1970.

Panton, Don B., V. Parker Lessig, & O. Maurice Joy, "Comovement of International Equity Markets: A Taxonomic Approach," *Journal of Financial and Quantitative Analysis,* September 1976.

Ripley, Duncan M., "Systematic Elements in the Linkage of National Stock Market Indices," *Review of Economics and Statistics,* August 1973.

Roll, Richard, "A Possible Explanation of the Small Firm Effect," *Journal of Finance,* September 1981.

Scholes, Myron, & Joseph Williams, "Estimating Beta from Nonsynchronous Data," *Journal of Financial Economics,* no. 5, 1977, pp. 309–28.

9

Multiple Time-Series Analysis of National Stock Markets and Their Structure: Some Implications

Sarkis J. Khoury
Bajis Dodin
Hirokazu Takada

ABSTRACT

This chapter examines the dependence between the financial markets of the major developed countries. It identifies the leading market(s) and measures the strength and length of their lead. In addressing the above issues, the chapter conducts an empirical investigation applying multiple time-series analysis to daily national indices from five financial markets. The empirical analysis showed that the United States equity market leads those of Canada, Europe, and Japan. The financial markets of Europe and Japan lag behind the United States generally by one day. Contemporaneous correlation exists between the United States and Canada and also among France, Germany, and Japan. The United States's lead has been expressed in functional forms which can be used to forecast index prices in France, Germany, and Japan. The implications of the results are that a U.S. capital market index can be used as an index for the world financial markets, assuming markets are integrated.

The literature on the relationship across equity markets and on international asset pricing is still open for further investigation despite recent significant contributions. Some of the major issues requiring more rigorous investigation are: (1) the dependence between the financial markets, (2) the direction of causality if, in fact, dependence exists, (3) whether the dependence between the financial markets (if any) can be expressed in a functional form (that is, can it be modeled in a way that allows an international specu-

The authors acknowledge the excellent computational help of Tsou Tai-Houn, Statistics Department, University of California, Riverside. This chapter benefitted considerably from the comments of anonymous referrees.

lator to earn above-average rates of return on a consistent basis?), and (4) implications of the existence or the absence of a lead–lag relationship.

Several theoretical and empirical papers have dealt with the above issues. A thorough review of all the studies up to 1983 regarding international financial markets is provided by Adler and Dumas (1983).

Solnik (1974) was one of the early writers on international diversification. He showed that internationally diversified portfolios containing more than thirty stocks had half the risk of a well-diversified portfolio made up of strictly U.S. securities.

Agmon (1974) applied regression analysis to monthly data from four developed countries (Germany, Japan, Britain and the United States) and showed that the integrated market hypothesis cannot be rejected. This built on earlier work by Ripley (1973), who used factor analysis to show that over one-half of the movement in a country's index can be explained by factors endogenous to the country. Agmon's results were later supported by Panton, Lessig, and Joy (1976), who used cluster analysis to demonstrate structural stability and a high degree of similarity between the international financial markets.

The issue of market segmentation or integration was also the subject of a study by Stehle (1977). He tested whether stocks traded on the New York Stock Exchange were priced nationally or internationally. The results of the study were not conclusive. Stehle was unable to reject either the segmented or the integrated model.

Hilliard (1979) used spectral analysis to examine the international equity market indices during an international financial crisis. He examined daily averaged data from ten world markets (Amsterdam, Frankfurt, London, Milan, New York, Paris, Sydney, Tokyo, Toronto, and Zurich) for the period of July 7, 1973, to April 30, 1974, which includes the October 1973 Arab–Israeli war and the resulting oil embargo. His tests led him to conclude that the world markets reacted independently to the financial crisis despite the existence of some contemporaneous correlations between the intracontinental markets. Furthermore, Hilliard's tests ruled out a lead–lag relationship between the financial markets with the exception of having New York lead Amsterdam by one day. Also, Hilliard did not use his results to draw any inferences about the pricing of assets in an international context.

Solnik (1977) in another study argued that market segmentation was caused by investment barriers and that the most efficient way to test for imperfection is to isolate a market imperfection and examine its effects on pricing risky assets. This is what Errunza and Losq (1985) investigated. Barriers to international investments are introduced in an international capital market producing what Errunza and Losq refer to as mild segmentation. This is the case if the securities of *country 1* are eligible for *country 2* investors while the opposite is not true. Their primary conclusions are that the eligible securities are priced as if the financial markets are integrated and the ineligible securities of *country 2* command a super-risk premium proportional to the conditional market risk. Using monthly total return data for the years 1976–80 from nine less-developed countries and the United States, the test results, using cross-sectional regression analysis, provided tentative support to the mild segmentation hypothesis, even though more empirical investigation was recommended since their tests were not conclusive.

A recent paper by Cho, Eun, and Senbet (1984) used interbattery factor analysis to test the validity of arbitrage pricing theory in an international context. The cross-sectioned tests led the authors to reject the joint test that the international capital market is integrated and that the asset pricing theory (APT) is internationally valid. A more recent study relevant to the issue of the correlations between the financial markets was the work of Eun and Resnick (1984). The authors estimated the international correlation matrix using the full historical model (global mean model), the mean models (national mean model and industry mean model), and the index models (single index models and multi-index model). Two sets of monthly data, each consisting of eighty nonoverlapping firms chosen from eight different countries, representing twelve different industries, and covering the period January 1973 to December 1982, were used to select the preferred model. The performance measures were the mean squared forecast error (MSE) and the stochastic dominance frequency (SDF). The national mean model was shown to be consistently superior to the other models. However, the superiority of the national mean model did not lead to identifying the direction of causality between the international markets.

With the exception of the Hilliard study, none of the preceding studies dealt with the time lag structure and the direction of causality of price movements, both of which are critical issues in answering the questions raised above. For instance, if the U.S. stock market consistently leads the other major stock markets of the world (up or down), if the time lag is, say, one day, and if such a lag structure does not allow for abnormal profits, then it can be argued that the domestic capital asset pricing model or the domestic arbitrage pricing theory, whichever is superior, is possibly all that is necessary for pricing risky assets. To our knowledge, the issues of causality and time lag structures in the international financial markets have not been treated in the literature. Again, with the exception of Hilliard's study which uses spectral analysis, the papers discussed thus far rely on econometric analysis, mostly regression analysis, for their empirical tests, which may not be sufficient in determining the direction of causality and the lag structure between international financial markets.

This chapter deals with the issues of causality, correlation, and time lags between international financial markets. It employs the multiple time-series (MTS) methods in analyzing international stock market data. MTS, given stationarized time series, is capable of detecting the direction of causality between the time series and capable of measuring the correlation and the time lags between the international markets represented by the time series. In so doing, we can arrive at conclusions as to whether past data is of value for forecasting the future and if past patterns are likely to continue in the future. In this respect, time-series analysis becomes a more flexible and interesting tool.

The major difference between multiple times-series analysis and conventional econometric methods lies in the fact that, in the case of MTS, researchers do not require a priori assumptions in order to specify the structural form. Modern time-series model building of vector processes consists of three stages: identification, estimation, and diagnostic checking. In contrast to the econometric approach, time-series analysts explicitly rely on data to determine the model specification (or identification). The aim of many time-series analysts using a time domain approach is to find a parsimonious representation of the data-generating process. However, this does not necessarily mean that time-series analysis is free from assumptions. Stationarity is required for each time series prior to identification and estimation, and the residuals need to be white noise. Also, the functional form is assumed to be linear. Nonetheless, most of these assumptions belong to a statistical domain and are subject to various statistical tests. Therefore, the time series methodology reduces the need for subjective judgment or a priori assumptions from the researchers.

The other important factor, besides the analysis method, in determining the lead, lag, and correlation structures between international markets is the data. Since we are dealing with lags, it was believed that the data should not be aggregated with respect to the time element. Therefore, we preferred the use of daily data; this is the nationally averaged stock market prices. Nationally averaged stock prices are known, as demonstrated by Eun and Resnick (1984), to reflect the international correlation structure of the financial markets more than any other averaged data. The data used are dollar-denominated prices across countries, which helps avoid the exchange rate effects.

A discussion of the data is presented in the following section. In the subsequent section, we present the methodology and plan of analysis. Empirical results and interpretations are the subject of the next section. Conclusions and suggestions for further investigations are the subject of the final section.

Data

The data used in this chapter were provided by Capital Research Company (CRC), a multinational corporation based in Geneva, Switzerland. The company compiles data on major market indices and publishes it under *Capital International Indices (CII)*.

The stock market indices compiled by CRC are similarly designed. They are adjusted using the same formula, which is a combination of Laspeyres weighted arithmetic average and the chain-link concepts. The *CII* have the same base (January 1, 1970 = 100). For the purpose of full comparability of the index values, the U.S. dollar was used as the common denominator.

The data consisted of five time series representing the five major stock markets in the developed world, those of the countries shown in table 9–1. Companies included in the indices were selected with reference to national and industrial representation. The comprehensive nature of the indices is seen through the data of table 9–1.

The data are daily national averages starting on December 31, 1974, and ending on December 27, 1983. This period covers various economic cycles and major international events including the end of the Vietnam war and rise and decline of OPEC. The time series have been adjusted by deleting some entries so as to guarantee that each country has an entry on a given date. This takes care of data gaps caused by holidays and other nonworking days. The accuracy of the data was verified through digital plots and direct examination of the data printout.

Data from the five countries were used in the univariate and multivariate time-series analyses. The section "Empirical Results" shows both these analyses.

Methodology and Plan of the Analysis

As mentioned earlier, time-series analysis methods are used in the empirical investigation. The purpose of the time-series analysis is to determine the structure or form of the models on the basis of the empirical evidence. Interest in time-series analysis was stimulated by Box and Jenkins (1976) and Nelson (1973) with their contributions to univariate time-series analysis. As discussed in the above references, the modeling procedure of a univariate time series requires three steps: (1) the identification of the order of the model, (2) estimating the parameters of the model, and (3) a diagnostic checking to guard against misspecification and search for the direction of improvements. The final model is known as the autoregressive integrated moving average (ARIMA) model.

The methodology of the univariate time-series analysis has been extended to the multivariate time series, which deals with a vector of time series instead of one time series. Akaike (1974) calls it state space process. Akaike has shown that any autoregressive moving average (ARMA) process has a state space presentation and, conversely, that any state space process may be expressed in any ARMA form. Akaike uses the minimum information criterion in order to choose the order of the model.

Table 9–1
Coverage of Five Indices

Stock Market Index (Country)	Number of Companies Included	Market Value of Companies Included as of June 29, 1984 ($ billion)	Market Coverage of the Indices (Percent of Total Market Value)
Canada	72	64.6	56.6
France	76	24.2	59.7
Germany	56	50.5	62.8
Japan	20	332.8	60.0
United States	462	879.6	59.5

The state space representation of a stationary multivariate time series X_t of dimension r is of the form

$$Z_t = F Z_{t-1} + G e_t \tag{9.1}$$

where Z_t is a vector of process of dimension s, whose first components comprise X_t and whose remaining components contain all additional needed information to forecast values of Z_t; F is an s-by-s transition matrix; G is an s-by-r input matrix; and e_t is a sequence of independent r-dimensional random vectors with common variance matrix Σ and mean zero.

Based on the data, the procedure can select a state space form for the time series; that is, a form for F and G. Specifically, a sequence of vector autoregressive models is fit using the Yule-Walker equations, and the order is selected for which an information criterion (AIC) is minimized. This order is then taken as the number of lags into the past to use in a canonical correlation analysis.

In this analysis, the sample canonical correlations of the past with an increasing number of steps into the future are computed. Variables that yield large correlations are added to the state vector; those that yield small correlations are excluded from further consideration. The importance of the correlation is judged on the basis of another information criterion.

Once the form is decided, the free parameters are estimated by maximizing an approximate likelihood function that is based on the same autocovariance matrix.

In applying the above methodology to the data described in the previous section, we followed the following steps.

1. Identify the univariate ARIMA models for the five stock markets through the modeling process of identification, estimation, and diagnostic checking.

2. Apply the multiple time-series analysis to the stationarized time series. Models for each country are identified and direction of causality between the variables is detected through the processes of parameter estimation and diagnostic checking. Forecasting performance of each model is determined through comparison between the actual versus predicted values using the hold-out observations.

3. Interpret the structure of the identified models and parameters of the variables. The issues stated at the outset of this chapter are discussed in this context.

This plan of analysis is applied to the latest 500 observations of the data set. This reduction of the data was necessary since analyzing the original record, which consists of 9 years of daily observations, may contain too many unknown factors implicated in the model. However, preliminary analysis involving the 9-year data set was conducted to make sure that we are not losing accuracy by limiting our final analysis to the latest 500 observations (those of the past 2 years). The results of the 9-year data set agreed with those using the 500 observations. Out of the 500 observations, 450 are used in determining the models; the remaining 50 observations are held out for testing the forecasting performance of the models.

Empirical Results and Interpretation

The univariate time-series method was applied to the data set. The identified univariate models for the variables are contained in table 9–1. All of the parameters are significant at the .05 level. For diagnostic checking, the Portmanteau test was conducted, and the chi-square values for each residual series are included in table 9–2, all of which are less than the critical values. Also, the autocorrelation functions (ACF) of each residual were visually inspected, and no significant spikes were detected. Thus, both of the diagnostic checkings reject the hypothesis that the residual series are not white noise. The degree of difference was determined with much care to eliminate nonstationary components in the series, since multiple time-series analysis requires all input series to be stationary.

STATESPACE, an SAS program based on the state space representation of Akaike, was applied to five countries: Canada, Germany, France, Japan and the United States. It estimates the identified model and then forecasts future values based on the final model.

The estimation phase started with the full or unrestricted model. The insignificant parameters were eliminated from the full model and the rest of the parameters were estimated again to obtain the final, restricted model. This procedure is analogous to the method of backward elimination of variables in the stepwise regression. Table 9–3 shows the final forms of the re-

Table 9–2
Univariate Models of Market Value Indices for Five Countries

Country	Model[a]	Residual Test[b]
United States	$US_t = US_{t-1} + {}^eUS_t$	$^2(24) = 25.04$
Canada	$CA_t = 1.224CA_{t-1} - 0.224CA_{t-2} + {}^eCA_t$	$^2(23) = 25.56$
France	$FR_t = FR_{t-1} + {}^eFR_t$	$^2(24) = 24.67$
Germany	$GR_t = GR_{t-1} + {}^eGR_t$	$^2(24) = 18.62$
Japan	$JP_t = JP_{t-1} + {}^eJP_t$	$^2(24) = 24.30$

[a]Parameters are significant at the .05 level.
[b]The chi-square values for each residual series are less than critical values, indicating that the residuals are white noise.

stricted models for the five countries under consideration. Rearranging the entries in table 9–3 provides the following models:

United States: $US_t = US_{t-1} + e_{US_t}$

Canada: $CA_t = 0.238US_{t-1} + 1.093CA_{t-1} - 0.238US_{t-1} - 0.093CA_{t-2} + e_{CA_t}$

France: $FR_t = 0.295US_{t-1} + 1.111FR_{t-1} - 0.89GR_{t-1} - 0.295US_{t-2} - 0.111FR_{t-2} + 0.089GR_{t-2} + e_{GR_t}$

Germany: $GR_t = 0.433US_{t-1} - 0.184FR_{t-1} + GR_{t-1} - 0.433US_{t-2} + 0.184FR_{t-2} + e_{GR_t}$

Japan: $JP_t = 1.322US_{t-1} + JP_{t-1} - 1.322US_{t-2} + e_{JP_t}.$

It is clear from the above models that the United States market leads all the other four markets, while none of these other countries leads the U.S. market. If the time differences between the U.S. market and the markets of France, Germany, and Japan are incorporated, then the real time lead is more than one day. This conclusion is consistent with Hilliard's finding for the New York-Amsterdam markets; however, it contradicts Hilliard's conclusion for the other intercontinental lead–lag relationships. The U.S. lead is very strong in the case of Japan, but it is weaker for Germany, France, and Canada. The U.S market leads these markets by one day.

The weak U.S. lead over the Canadian market warranted the investigation of the residual correlation matrix of the model at lag zero to test for the existence of contemporaneous correlations; the residual correlation matrix is given in table 9–4. Indeed, the off-diagonal elements indicate a contemporaneous correlation between the United States and Canada and a weaker one between the United States, France, Germany, and Japan. The residual corre-

Table 9–3
Multivariate Models of Market Value Indices for Five Countries

Z_t	$=$	F					Z_{t-1}	$+$	G					e_t
$1 - B)US_t$		0	0	0	0	0	$(1 - B)US_{t-1}$		1	0	0	0	0	e_{US_t}
$1 - B)CA_t$		0.238	0.093	0	0	0	$(1 - B)CA_{t-1}$		0	1	0	0	0	e_{CA_t}
		(0.063)	(0.042)											
$1 - B)FR_t$	$=$	0.295	0	0.111	−0.089	0	$(1 - B)FR_{t-1}$	$+$	0	0	1	0	0	e_{FR_t}
		(0.035)		(0.045)	(0.029)									
$1 - B)GR_t$		0.433	0	−0.184	0	0	$(1 - B)GR_{t-1}$		0	0	0	1	0	e_{GR_t}
		(0.051)		(0.053)										
$1 - B)JP_t$		1.322	0	0	0	0	$(1 - B)JP_{t-1}$		0	0	0	0	1	e_{JP_t}
		(0.171)												

Notes: B denotes the backward shift operator defined by $BZ_t = Z_{t-1}$. Figures in parentheses are standard errors of the parameter estimates.

lation matrix indicates a contemporaneous correlation between France, Germany, and Japan. The contemporaneous correlations between the United States and Canada and between France and Germany are consistent with Hilliard's findings for the intracontinental correlation.

The lead of the U.S. market over the markets of Japan, Germany, and France is not disputable; the entries of table 9–4 reaffirm the magnitude of the lead detected in table 9–3. It is interesting to observe that the European markets interact with the Japanese market on a daily basis, while the U.S. market does not respond to the information obtained from the Japanese and European markets hours before its opening. However, the Japanese market appears to respond positively to what has happened in the U.S. market just hours before its opening. The U.S. lead over the Canadian market is also apparent from table 9–3, but from table 9–4, it appears that the lead is instantaneous due to the geographical proximity of the two countries, cross-direct investments, and other factors. The contemporaneous correlation between Europe and Japan may be caused by all markets responding positively to the behavior of the U.S. market in the previous day which again affirms the U.S. market lead.

The contemporaneous correlation between European markets and Japan dilutes the argument that the U.S. lead is just a temporal structure of closing times across markets. Despite the fact that the time difference between Europe and Japan is larger than that between the United States and Europe, neither did the European markets lead Japan, nor vice versa. Indeed, both markets are contemporaneously correlated.

The clear lead of the U.S. stock market over the other financial markets implies that the U.S. market can be used as a leading indicator for the other world financial markets. An international speculator may benefit from this

Table 9–4
Residual Correlation Matrix from the Model at Lag = 0

	U.S.	Canada	France	Germany	Japan
U.S.	1.000	0.650	0.120	0.125	0.168
Canada		1.000	0.265	0.283	0.287
France			1.000	0.571	0.485
Germany				1.000	0.532
Japan					1.000

lead by concentrating on the U.S. market to learn about the risks and returns of the other markets for the following day. Naturally, more information about the financial markets in Europe or Japan reduces the investor's risk and may improve his return. In short, the U.S. lead may not change the riskiness of a U.S. asset, but it may reduce the trading risk of an international speculator.

The usefulness of the above results in an international asset pricing framework is significant. The consistent lead of the U.S. market over major European and Japanese financial markets implies that the U.S. stock market index may serve as an adequate proxy for the world market. This should not be surprising considering that the western economies are becoming increasingly interdependent and that the national indices we have examined contain largely multinational companies with operations covering the five countries used in the multivariate analysis. This is consistent with the findings of Errunza and Senbet (1981) that the multinational corporation is an excellent conduit for international portfolio diversification. A financial analyst can, therefore, use the U.S. stock market index as a proxy for world equity markets in an international capital asset pricing model (CAPM) or APT.

The remaining issue to deal with is whether the knowledge of a U.S. lead will allow a speculator to earn above-average rates of return from speculation in the international markets by going short in Europe and Japan the day after the U.S. market has declined and long the day after the U.S. market has risen. The time difference, transactions costs, low average value of daily changes in the value of market indices, rigidity of many speculative and investment strategies, and lingering aversion by professionals to shifting funds from one financial center to another (foreign) center almost instantaneously discouraged us from using various filter rules to measure speculative rates of returns.

The use of the identified models for each country as a forecasting tool is investigated utilizing the hold-out sample. Plots of the comparison between actual and predicted values for each country are shown in figures 9–1 through 9–5. Each plot shows the univariate model prediction, denoted in the figures by the letter "S;" the multivariate model prediction, denoted by

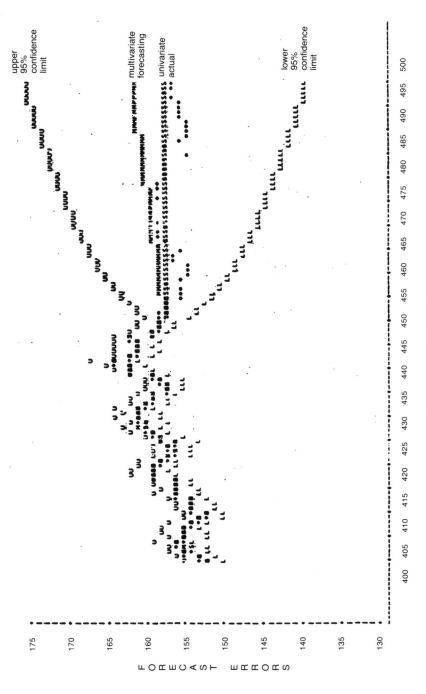

Figure 9–1. United States

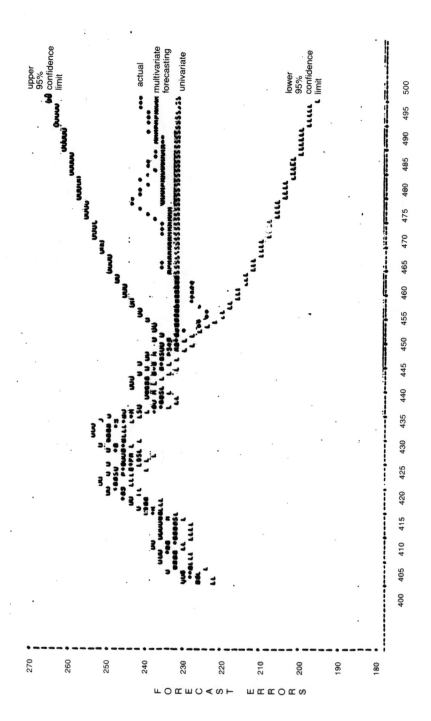

Figure 9–2. Canada

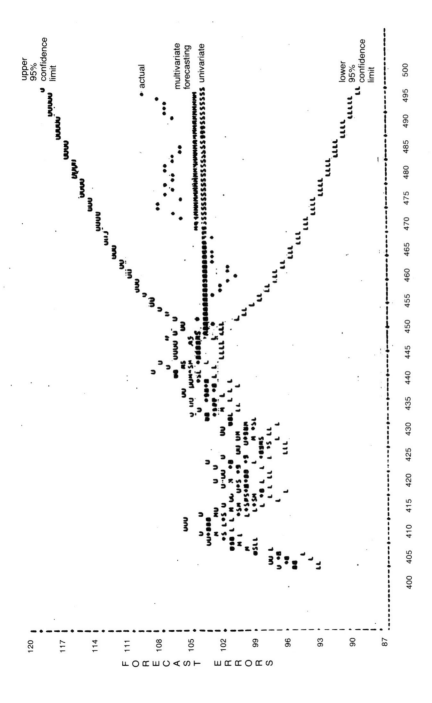

Figure 9–3. France

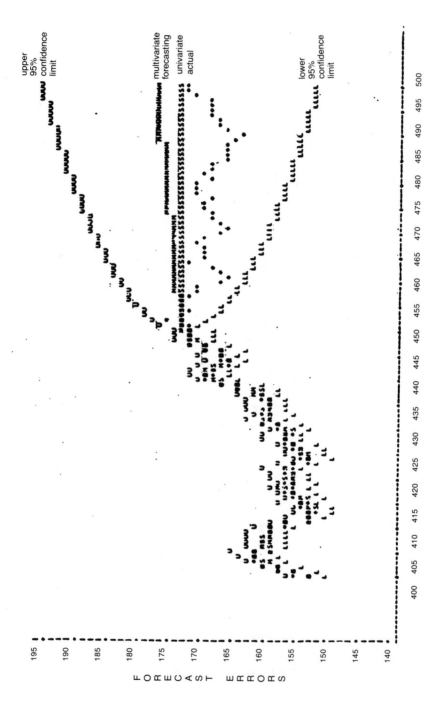

Figure 9–4. Germany

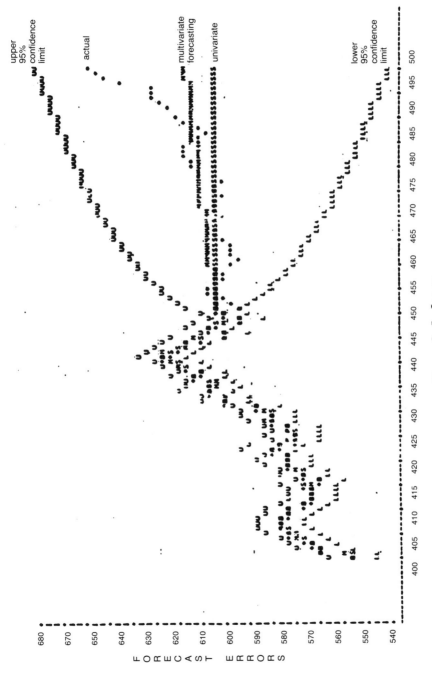

Figure 9–5. Japan

the letter "M;" the actual index, denoted by "*;" the 95 percent upper confidence limit, denoted by "U;" and the 95 percent lower confidence limit denoted by "L."

Figure 9–1, representing the U.S. market, shows that the univariate model resulted in a random walk model; therefore, a univariate prediction exhibits a straight line. Figure 9–2, representing the Canadian market, shows that the multivariate model predicts a general trend of the actual values closer than the univariate model. Figure 9–3, representing the French market, shows that although the discrepancy between the univariate and multivariate predictions is small, the multivariate model captures an upward trend of a price index better than the univariate model. Figure 9–4, representing the German market, contrary to the plots of the other countries, shows that the multivariate model does not perform well; this might be due to the change of a general trend of the actual values from an upward trend to a downtrend or stable trend. Finally, figure 9–5, representing the Japanese market, shows that the multivariate model forecasts an upward trend better than the univariate model.

Summary and Conclusions

The correlation structure between international financial markets has been modeled through a series of time-series analyses that begins with the univariate identification of the variables in the data set, followed by the multivariate time-series analysis by the STATESPACE method.

Analyzing the five capital markets led to the conclusion that the U.S. market leads the other four markets. The Japanese, French, and German markets lag behind the United States by one day, while in the case of Canada, the lead is contemporaneous. It was also noticed that the markets of Japan, Germany, and France have a high contemporaneous correlation, perhaps caused by all three markets responding to the U.S. lead in a similar fashion. However, international speculators may be able to use such a lead to their advantage, possibly in better timing their sales or purchases in a given market. The more significant implication of the findings is that the U.S. stock market index may well serve as an adequate proxy for the world index in a CAPM or APT framework.

The presence of correlation, no matter what the size and the direction of the lag, is neither a necessary nor a sufficient condition for market integration, however. No hard conclusions can be made, based on our results regarding the integration or segmentation hypothesis in the international equity markets. Low correlations could exist even in perfectly integrated markets. High correlations can exist in a segmented market. However, very high correlations among returns on *similar* assets do indicate a degree of market integration. The market indices we have utilized are value-weighted, but that is the extent of the similarity. Should the construction in terms of industry grouping have been the same across national equity markets, some conclusions could have been drawn with regard to a market segmentation or integration. This must await another study by the authors.

Measuring the advantage that an international speculator may generate from the above lead or developing a speculative trading rule requires further time-series analysis involving less aggregated data. The data employed in this investigation is not aggregated in the sense of time, but is aggregated in other aspects since they are nationally averaged. Analyzing a particular industry or asset across countries may result in more specific conclusions and reaffirm the direction of causality. It is not clear if the above conclusion holds for all industries or whether it is stronger for some and weaker, if not reversed, for others. Investigation of these issues is pending the acquisition of the appropriate data.

References

Adler, M., & B. Dumas, "International Portfolio Choice and Corporation Finance: A Synthesis," *Journal of Finance* (June 1983), 925–84.

Agmon, T., "The Relations among Equity Markets in the United States, United Kingdom, Germany, and Japan," *Journal of Finance* (September 1974), 839–55.

Akaike, H., "Markovian Representation of Stochastic Processes and Its Application to Analysis of Autoregressive Moving Average Processes," *Annals of the Institute of Statistical Mathematics* (1974), 363–87.

———, "Canonical Correlations Analysis of Time Series and the Use of an Information Criterion," in R. Mehra & D. G. Lainiotis (eds.), *Advances and Case Studies in System Identification.* New York: Academic Press (1976).

Box, G. E. P., & G. M. Jenkins, *Time Series Analysis: Forecasting and Control,* second edition. San Francisco: Holden-Day (1976).

Cho, D. Chinhyung, Cheol S. Eun & Lemma W. Senbet, "International Arbitrage Pricing Theory: An Empirical Investigation." Working paper, Graduate School of Business, University of Wisconsin-Madison (October 1984).

Errunza, Vihang, & Etienne Losq, "International Asset Pricing under Mild Segmentation: Theory and Test," *Journal of Finance* (March 1985), 105–24.

Errunza, Vihang, & Lemma W. Senbet, "The Effects of International Operations on the Market Value of the Firm: Theory and Evidence," *Journal of Finance,* (May 1981), 401–17.

Eun, Cheol, S., & Bruce G. Resnick, "Estimating the Correlation Structure of International Share Prices," *Journal of Finance* (December 1984), 1311–24.

Hilliard, Jimmy, "The Relationship between Equity Indices on World Exchanges," *Journal of Finance* (March 1979), 103–13.

Nelson, Charles R., *Applied Time Series Analysis for Managerial Forecasting.* San Francisco: Holden Day (1973).

Panton, D., V. Lessig & O. Joy, "Co-movement of International Equity Markets: A Taxonomic Approach," *Journal of Financial and Quantitative Analysis* (September 1976), 415–32.

Ripley, D. M., "Systematic Elements in the Linkage of National Stock Market Indices," *Review of Economics and Statistics* (August 1973), 356–61.

Solnik, B. H., "The International Pricing Risk: An Empirical Investigation of the World Capital Market Structure," *Journal of Finance* (1974), 365–78.

———, "Testing International Asset Pricing: Some Pessimistic Views," *Journal of Finance* (May 1977), 503–12.

Stehle, R., "An Empirical Test of the Alternative Hypothesis of National and International Pricing of Risky Assets," *Journal of Finance* (May 1977), 493–502.

10
The Pricing of Derivative Assets in Foreign Exchange Markets

Krishna Ramaswamy
Suresh M. Sundaresan

ABSTRACT

Using the dynamic version of the purchasing power parity, interest rate parity theorem, and the Fisherian relationships, we specify stochastic processes for spot exchange rates and interest rate differentials. These processes permit the expected rate of appreciation of the spot exchange rate to be affected by nominal interest rate differentials which themselves follow a mean-reverting process. Using such a specification, we develop two models of pricing forward contracts and futures contracts on foreign currencies. Some testable implications are derived and discussed.

There has been sizable and rapid growth in the number of available assets and in the volume of trading in foreign exchange markets since the introduction of floating exchange rates. The market for forward contracts on foreign exchange, primarily supported by institutions, coexists with the growing market for futures and option contracts on the organized exchanges. In addition, there has been a surge of interest in currency swaps and in the market for bonds whose payoffs depend on the values of stated currencies.

The theory dealing with the valuation of these derivative assets follows from the application of valuation models for forward and futures contracts. Black (1976) provides a complete description of these contracts, and discusses the valuation of European options on these contracts. A forward contract commits the buyer and the seller to exchange a prespecified number of units of the underlying commodity at an agreed upon forward price at the maturity of the contract. The futures contract is similar in design but requires the buyer and seller to settle their profits and losses daily, so that the com-

We thank the participants at the Symposium on Recent Developments in International Banking and Finance, Lake Arrowhead, Calif. (April 1986), for their comments.

modity is exchanged at the price of the futures contract on the maturity date, which will equal the spot price on that date. The relationship between forward prices and futures prices has been studied by Cox, Ingersoll, and Ross (1981), Margrabe (1976), and Richard and Sundaresan (1981), employing arbitrage-based and utility-based approaches. The difference between forward and futures prices (of contracts maturing at date T) is related to the difference between the current values (at date t) of two contracts: (1) one that pays $B(t, T)^{-1}$ units of spot commodity at date T and (2) one that pays $\prod_{s=t}^{T-1}$ $B(s, s + 1)^{-1}$ units of the spot commodity at date T, where $B(u, v)$ is the price at date u of \$1 payable at v. The current value of the first contract is equal to the forward price, while that of the second is equal to the futures price. The difference between forward and futures prices can also be expressed as a function of the conditional covariances between futures price changes and the rates of return on default-free bonds. When the term structure is nonstochastic, these prices are identical. (See, for example, Black, 1976).

Cornell and Reinganum (1981) provide evidence on the central propositions concerning the difference between forward and future prices, using three- and six-month data on these prices for five currencies. They conclude that the average difference over their sample period is not different from zero in either statistical or economic senses. French (1983) provides evidence on these propositions using forward and futures prices from the markets for silver and copper. He finds that

> There are significant differences between these prices. The average difference is generally consistent with the predictions of both arbitrage and utility-based models. However, these models are not helpful in explaining intrasample variations in the futures-forward price differences.

Both these studies employed estimates of the conditional covariance between futures price changes and bond returns from data over their sample periods. Furthermore, both studies used the (unconditional) average of the differences between forward and futures prices in their tests. Because neither study had a formal model of futures pricing available, attention was restricted to the sign and the average magnitude of the difference over the entire sample. It is useful, then, to develop valuation models of futures and forward contracts that will enable us to relate these price differences over time to prevailing levels of relevant state variables that determine the individual prices.

In this chapter, two models for the valuation of futures and forward contracts on foreign currencies are developed. Both models employ the spot exchange rate and the nominal interest rates in the two countries as relevant (state variables) descriptors; both models are consistent with lack of arbitrage opportunities and are consistent within an equilibrium framework. In keeping with the spirit of contingent claims pricing and in employing continuous time, continuous state space models, we make assumptions on the stochastic processes driving these state variables that are economically meaningful and that lead to tractable solutions. The process assumed for the dynamics of the spot exchange rate incorporates the feature that the expected appreciation (or depreciation) of this rate will depend on the prevailing levels of the interest rates in the two countries.

The rest of the chapter is organized as follows. The next section briefly examines the dynamics of the spot exchange rate, starting from its determinants, the indices for the price levels in the two countries. The price of a forward contract is linked to the interest rate parity theorem, and the characterization of forward and futures contracts along the arguments of Cox, Ingersoll, and Ross (1981) is provided. The two valuation models are developed in the subsequent section, and their properties are discussed in detail. The final section discusses conclusions.

The following notation is employed throughout the chapter. Variables with an asterisk as superscript refer to the values of those variables in the foreign country.

$V(t)$:   the spot exchange rate at date t ($/DM).

$B(t, T)$:   the dollar price at date t of $1 payable at time T.

$B^*(t, T)$:   the DM price at date t of 1 DM payable at time T.

$p(t), p^*(t)$:   the index of the price levels in the two countries at date t in units of local currency per unit of the composite consumption good.

$H(t)$:   the futures price ($/DM) quoted at date t for a futures contract maturing at date T.

$G(t)$:   the forward price ($/DM) quoted at date t for a forward contract maturing at date T.

$r(t), r^*(t)$:   the annualized interest rates on default-free and instantaneously maturing loans in the two countries.

y, y^*:   the expected instantaneous inflation rates in the two countries.

The Behavior of Spot Exchange Rates and the Relationship between Forward and Futures Prices

It is useful to consider the determinants of the dynamic behavior of the spot asset, here foreign currency, and the implications of models well known in international finance for forward and futures prices. In this section, these issues are discussed briefly, with a view of their future use in developing the models in the next section.

Assume a two-country world with no barriers to goods or financial flows. Individuals consume a single good or basket of goods across both countries. The prices of this good are defined as $p(t)$ and $p^*(t)$ at date t in the domestic and foreign currencies, respectively. Absent any nontraded goods or frictions, the current spot exchange rate $V(t)$ is given by purchasing power parity (PPP) as

$$V(t) = p(t)/p^*(t) \tag{10.1}$$

The dynamic behavior of the spot exchange rate depends on the corresponding behavior postulated for the two price levels. Suppose that the price levels in the two countries evolved continuously according to the following stochastic differential equations:

$$dp = ypdt + p\sigma(p)dz \tag{10.2}$$
$$dp^* = y^*p^*dt + p^*\sigma(p^*)dz^*$$

where $z(t)$ and $z^*(t)$ are standard Wiener processes. In equation 10.2, y and y^* represent the expected inflation rates in the two countries, and may themselves evolve in a stochastic manner. The variance rate of unanticipated inflation is given by $\sigma^2(p)$ and $\sigma^{*2}(p^*)$. We shall assume neutrality of money in a strong sense: that $z(t)$ and $z^*(t)$ are uncorrelated with the evolution of all real variables in the economies and with each other, and that the processes which drive $y(t)$ and $y^*(t)$ inherit these properties as well. By using Itô's lemma, it follows that

$$dV = V[y - y^* + \sigma^{*2}(p^*)]dt + V[\sigma(p)dz - \sigma^*(p)dz^*] \tag{10.3}$$

The expected rate of change in the spot exchange rate is related to the difference between the inflation rates in the two countries and to the variance rate of the unanticipated change in the foreign price level. If we add the further assumptions that the expected real interest rates in the two countries are equal, then the difference $y - y^*$ can be replaced by the difference in the nominal interest rates for instantaneously maturing loans. Equation 10.3 then implies that the spot exchange rate can appreciate or depreciate, depending on the levels of y and y^* (or, equivalently, depending on the nominal rates). This is economically a slightly more meaningful implication than that resulting from the assumption of a *lognormal* diffusion for the spot exchange rate—which implies a *secular* appreciation or depreciation of the currency.

We derived the process 10.3 for the spot exchange rate by assuming the validity of the static version of the purchasing power parity (PPP) result. The bulk of the empirical evidence, however, seems to suggest that there are significant deviations from the PPP, especially in the short run. It turns out that the process specified in 10.3 can accommodate certain types of deviations from the PPP.

Consider now the real price of a unit discount bond that pays one unit of consumption good at date T. Assuming a representative consumer with a time-additive von Neumann Morgenstern utility function $u_t(_t)$ where c_t is consumption at date t, the real price of this bond at date t is given simply by the expected marginal-rate-of-substitution–weighted real payoff:

$$E_t[u'_T(\tilde{c}_T)/u'_t(c_t)]$$

The real price of a nominal bond with a payoff of \$1 at date T is given by

$$\frac{B(t,\,T)}{p(t)} = E_t\left[\frac{u'_T(\tilde{c}_T)}{u'_t(c_t)} \cdot \frac{1}{\tilde{p}(T)}\right] \tag{10.4}$$

and given the exogenous nature of the stochastic process for the price level and the inflation rate, the nominal price of a nominal bond paying \$1 at date T is

$$B(t,\,T) = E_t\left[\frac{u'_T(\tilde{c}_T)}{u'_t(c_t)}\right]E_t[p(t)/\tilde{p}(T)\}, \tag{10.5}$$

which says that the nominal bond price is equal to the real bond price multiplied by the expectation of the inverse of the growth in the price level.

Cox, Ingersoll, and Ross (1981, proposition 1) demonstrate that the price $G(t)$ of a forward contract maturing at date T is given by the current value of a contract that pays $B(t,\,T)^{-1}$ units of the underlying commodity at T. In this context, then, the real price of a forward contract on the foreign currency is given by

$$\frac{G(t)}{p(t)} = E_t\left[\frac{u'_T(\tilde{c}_T)}{u'_t(c_t)} \cdot \frac{B(t,\,T)^{-1}\tilde{V}(T)}{\tilde{p}\,(T)}\right] \tag{10.6}$$

where the second term in the expectation is the real payoff (under their proposition) to the hypothetical contract, and the first represents the familiar state price. Employing the purchasing power parity theorem, the nominal forward price is given by

$$G(t) = \frac{V(t)}{B(t,\,T)}\,E_t\left[\frac{u'_T(\tilde{c}_T)}{u'_t(c_t)} \cdot \frac{p^*(t)}{\tilde{p}^*(T)}\right]. \tag{10.7}$$

If we assume that the movements in the foreign price level and the foreign inflation rate are uncorrelated with the real shocks that affect domestic consumption, then

$$G(t) = \frac{V(t)}{B(t, T)} E_t\left[\frac{u_T'(\tilde{c}_T)}{u_t'(c_t)}\right] E_t[p^*(t)/\tilde{p}^*(T)]. \tag{10.8}$$

However, the familiar interest rate parity theorem (IRPT) shows that with no frictions in financial and forward markets,

$$G(t) = V(t)\frac{B^*(t, T)}{B(t, T)}. \tag{10.9}$$

Employing equation 10.5 and comparing the two relations above, it follows that the real bond prices (and hence real rates) will be equal in both countries if the foreign price level is uncorrelated with real variables and if arbitrage conditions permit the IRPT to hold. This implication of equality of real rates is useful in specifying the process for the exchange rate in terms of *observable* nominal rates.

The extension of the arguments (in linking theorems on futures prices from an arbitrage-based framework) to futures prices is more complicated. Cox, Ingersoll, and Ross (1981, proposition 2) demonstrate that the price $H(t)$ of a futures contract maturing at date T is the current value of a contract that pays $\prod_{s=t}^{T-1} \tilde{B}(s, s + 1)^{-1}$ units of the commodity at date T. In this context, the real price of a futures contract on the foreign currency is given by

$$\frac{H(t)}{p(t)} = E_t\left\{\frac{u_T'(\tilde{c}_T)}{u_t'(c_t)} \cdot \left[\prod_{s=t}^{T-1} \tilde{B}(s, s + 1)^{-1}\right] \cdot \frac{\tilde{V}(T)}{\tilde{p}(T)}\right\} \tag{10.10}$$

where the second term is the real payoff to the hypothetical contract. Employing PPP, the nominal price of the futures contract is

$$H(t) = p(t)E_t\left\{\frac{u_T'(\tilde{c}_T)}{u_t'(c_t)} \cdot \left[\prod_{s=t}^{T-1} \tilde{B}(s, s + 1)^{-1}\right] \cdot \frac{1}{\tilde{p}^*(T)}\right\} \tag{10.11}$$

Incorporating the exogenous nature of the foreign price level and simplifying, the futures price can be written as

$$H(t) = \frac{V(t)B^*(t, T)}{B(t, T)} \cdot E_t\left[\frac{u_T'(\tilde{c}_T)}{u'(c_t)} \cdot \prod_{s=t}^{T-1} \tilde{B}(s, s + 1)^{-1}\right] \cdot E_t[p(t)/\tilde{p}(T)]. \tag{10.12}$$

The first term on the right-hand side is the forward price, $G(t)$, so that relation 10.2 says that the futures-to-forward price ratio is given by the product of the real value of a bond that pays $\prod_{s=t}^{T-1} B(s, s+1)^{-1}$ units of consumption good at date T times the expectation of the inverse of the growth rate in the domestic price level. It is easy to show that this ratio is unity if $B(s, s+1)$ is nonstochastic for each s.

These arguments show that the imposition of PPP and IRPT, together with the characterization of futures and forward contracts, require, first, that the dynamics of the spot exchange rate depend on nominal interest rate differentials across the two countries, and second, that the futures-forward price difference depends on the future one-period interest rates and the future spot exchange rate. We proceed to build these economic characteristics in the context of specific foreign exchange valuation models in the next section.

Valuation of Forward and Futures Contracts on Currencies

The development of models of forward and futures prices on foreign currencies requires the specification of relevant state variables that describe the stochastic properties of the spot exchange rate, the price levels, and the properties of nominal bond prices in the underlying currencies. Two such models are developed in this section. We begin by specifying the valuation framework briefly in fairly general terms. We then proceed to specialize by modeling forward and futures for the two cases. It should be clear that the forward price is given directly (from IRPT) by the spot exchange rate level and the levels of the nominal bond prices in the two currencies. It follows that modeling the forward price is equivalent to specifying models for nominal bond prices in the two currencies. On the other hand, specifying a model for the futures price requires the specification of models of the price level in addition to a description of the evolution of nominal bond prices. Our objective is to construct models that are at once tractable and economically plausible, although the usefulness of these models must eventually rest on their predictive ability.

Let $\underline{x} = (x_{1t}, x_{2t}, \ldots x_{nt})'$ be a vector of n state variables evolving continuously that completely characterize the current state of the world. Let μ_i be the expected (local) change in state variable x_i; let $\text{cov}(x_i, x_j)$ represent the local covariance of changes in $\underline{x}_i$ with changes in $\underline{x}_j$. In this framework the equilibrium forward price $G(\underline{x}_t, t)$ is given (from IRPT) as

$$G(\underline{x}_t, t) = V(\underline{x}_t, T) \frac{B^*(\underline{x}_t, t, T)}{B(\underline{x}_t, t, T)} \tag{10.13}$$

where the dependence of the forward price G, the spot price V, and the nominal bond prices B and B^* on the state vector $\underline{x}$ is explicitly recognized. In equation 10.13, the forward contract matures at date T, and the nominal unit discount bonds mature at T also. In the context of currency forwards, the vector $\underline{x}$ must contain, among other things, the price levels p and p^* or the variables that determine these levels.

Cox, Ingersoll, and Ross (1981) have shown under general conditions that the equilibrium futures price $H(\underline{x}_t, t)$ satisfies

$$\frac{1}{2} \sum_{j=1}^{n} \sum_{i=1}^{n} H_{x_i x_j} \left[\text{cov}(x_i, x_j) \right] + \sum_{j=1}^{n} H_{x_j} (\mu_j - \phi_j) + H_t = 0 \quad (10.14)$$

$$H(\underline{x}_T, T) = V(\underline{x}_T, T) \quad (10.15)$$

In the valuation equation 10.14, the ϕ_j's, $j = 1, 2, \ldots n$ represent the factor risk premiums for each of the state variables and they will depend on the preference of investors in the economy. Note that the terminal condition on the valuation equation requires that the futures price equal the spot price on the maturity date. It should be stressed that the forward price in equation 10.13 also depends on the factor risk premiums, because they will appear in the nominal bond prices B and B^*.

This formulation is exceedingly general. In order to obtain explicit formulae for the forward and futures prices, additional restrictions need to be placed on the state vector $\underline{x}$, and assumptions need to be made regarding the associated factor risk premiums.

To keep the problem tractable, the factor risk premiums are assumed to be identically equal to zero. This assumption, in the context of the bond prices B and B^*, is equivalent to assuming that the local expectations hypothesis holds. (For a discussion of this, see Cox, Ingersoll & Ross, 1981). That is, the expected instantaneous holding period returns on default-free bonds of all maturities are equal to the return on an instantaneously maturing bond.

To develop the prices of derivative assets on foreign currencies in a useful manner, we need to specify this vector in terms of observable variables. Following on the arguments in the previous section, we specify the vector $\underline{x}_t$ in terms of the spot exchange rate $V(t)$ and the instantaneous nominal interest rates $r(t)$ and $r^*(t)$ in the domestic and foreign currencies. While in principle, one would like to accommodate the effects of other variables, such as the price levels in the two countries, such a step involves considerable complexity in valuation. In this context, the spot exchange rate and the two interest rates are variables that one can observe. Thus, our specification enhances the testability of the results.

Essentially, the term structure of interest rates in the domestic (foreign) country is assumed to be a function of $r(r^*)$ only. In general, the evolution of the state of the system is governed by the following system of stochastic differential equations which are jointly Markov:

$$\frac{dV}{V} = (\alpha_1 dt + \sigma_1 dz_1) \tag{10.16}$$

$$dr = \alpha_2(r)dt + \sigma_2(r)dz_2 \tag{10.17}$$

and

$$dr^* = \alpha_3(r^*)dt + \sigma_3(r^*)dz_3 \tag{10.18}$$

In equations 10.16, 10.17, and 10.18, $[z_i(t), t > 0, i = 1, 2, 3]$ represents independent standard Wiener processes. The functions $\alpha_1(\cdot)$ and $\sigma_1(\cdot)$ are assumed to depend on r and r^* but not on V. The restrictions to be placed on the functions $\alpha_i(\cdot)$ and $\sigma_i(\cdot)$ will largely depend on prior economic reasoning and one's view of the nature of interrelationship between $V(t)$, $r(t)$, and $r^*(t)$. We present two equilibrium models below, which differ in terms of the restrictions they place on these functions. As we shall see, fewer restrictions are necessary to solve for the equilibrium forward price, whereas the solution of the futures price requires us to place additional restrictions.

Model 1

In this model, we assume that

$$\alpha_1(\cdot) \equiv \alpha_1(r - r^*)$$
$$\sigma_1(\cdot) \equiv \sigma_1 > 0$$
$$\alpha_2(\cdot) \equiv \kappa_2(\mu_2 - r)$$
$$\sigma_2(\cdot) \equiv \sigma_2 > 0$$
$$\alpha_3(\cdot) \equiv \kappa_3(\mu_3 - r^*)$$
$$\text{and } \sigma_3(\cdot) \equiv \sigma_3 > 0.$$

The terms α_1, σ_1, σ_2, κ_2, μ_2, κ_3, μ_3, and σ_3 on the right-hand side are all positive scalars.

The domestic (foreign) spot rates of interest follow a mean-reverting behavior, with μ_2 (μ_3) serving as the long-run mean rate and $\kappa_2(\kappa_3)$ as the speed of adjustment toward that long-run mean rate. The variance of the changes in the domestic (foreign) spot rate is assumed to be independent of the level of the rate and is denoted by σ_2^2 (σ_3^2). The structure that we have imposed on the spot exchange rate dynamics is consistent with our discussion in the previous section: the expected proportionate change in the spot exchange rate is linear function of the interest rate differential. Thus if $r > r^*$, the spot exchange rate is expected to appreciate; if $r < r^*$, it is expected to decline.

It is noteworthy that our formulation admits deviations from the PPP. If $\alpha_1 > 1$, then the expected proportionate change in the spot exchange rate may be greater than the interest rate differentials. On the other hand, if $\alpha_1 < 1$, then the expected proportionate change in the spot exchange rate may be less than the interest rate differential. The variability of the proportionate changes in the spot exchange rates is assumed to be a constant. Under these assumptions, we can explicitly solve for the equilibrium bond prices as shown below:

$$B(r, t, T) \equiv \exp\left[\frac{1}{\kappa_2}(1 - e^{-\kappa_2\tau})(R_\infty\right.$$

$$\left. - r) - \tau R_\infty - \frac{\sigma_2^2}{4k_2^2}(1 - e^{-\kappa_2\tau})^2\right] \quad (10.19)$$

where

$$\tau = T - t, \quad (10.20)$$

and $R_\infty \equiv \left(\mu_2 - \dfrac{\sigma_2^2}{\kappa_2^2}\right)$ is the limiting yield-to-maturity on a perpetual discount bond.

In a completely analogous manner, we can solve for the foreign discount bond price. By substituting these prices in equation 10.13, we can solve for the equilibrium forward exchange rate, as shown below:

$$G(\underline{x}, \tau) = V(t) \exp\left[\frac{1}{\kappa_3}(1 - e^{-\kappa_3\tau})(R_\infty^* - r^*) - \frac{1}{\kappa_2}(1 - e^{-\kappa_2\tau})(R_\infty\right.$$

$$\left. - r) - \tau(R_\infty^* - R_\infty) - \frac{\sigma_3^2}{4\kappa_3^2}(1 - e^{-\kappa_3\tau})^2 + \frac{\sigma_2^2}{4\kappa_2^2}(1 - e^{-\kappa_2\tau})^2\right]$$

$$(10.21)$$

The forward exchange rate is a decreasing function of the foreign spot rate of interest and an increasing function of the domestic spot rate of interest. As the volatility changes in the domestic (foreign) interest rate increases, the forward exchange rate decreases (increases). The term structure of forward rates can be upward-sloping, humped, or downward-sloping depending upon the location of the interest rate differential relative to other parameters. Formally,

$$G_\tau = G[(r - r^*) + (\mu_2 - R_\infty)(1 - e^{-\kappa_2\tau})\kappa_2$$
$$- (\mu_3 - R_\infty^*)(1 - e^{-\kappa_3\tau})\kappa_3]. \quad (10.22)$$

If $\kappa_2 = \kappa_3$, then we can make sharper predictions about the term structure of forward rates, for in this case the above expression simplifies to:

$$G_\tau = G\{(r - r^*) + \kappa_2(1 - e^{-\kappa_2\tau})[(\mu_2 - R_\infty) - (\mu_3 - R_\infty^*)]\}. \quad (10.23)$$

Let $x(t) \equiv r - r^*$ denote the interest rate differential. For the assumed process $x(t)$ can take on positive or negative values. The second term in the square bracket is positive or negative depending on whether $(\mu_2 - R_\infty)$ is greater or less than $(\mu_3 - R_\infty^*)$. For positive values of $x(t)$, the term structure is always upward-sloping if $(\mu_2 - R_\infty)$ is greater than $(\mu_3 - R_\infty^*)$. It is downward-sloping or humped if $(\mu_2 - R_\infty)$ is less than $(\mu_3 - R_\infty^*)$. Similar comments apply when $x(t)$ is negative. By estimating the parameters of the stochastic process specified for $x(t)$, one can test the implications of our theory for the term structure of forward rates.

We now turn our attention to the pricing of futures exchange rates. In the context of the present model, the valuation equation 10.14 is a three–state-variable partial differential equation, which is difficult to solve either numerically or analytically. But the futures exchange rate can be obtained analytically by assuming that $\kappa_2 \equiv \kappa_3 \equiv \kappa$. In this special case, the interest rate differential $x(t)$ serves as a sufficient state variable for both $r(t)$ and $r^*(t)$. To see this, note that

$$x(t) = r(t) - r^*(t) \quad (10.24)$$

By applying Itô's lemma, we get

$$dx(t) = \kappa(\hat{\mu} - x)dt + \hat{\sigma}d\hat{z}(t) \quad (10.25)$$

when

$$\hat{\mu} \equiv \mu_2 - \mu_3 > 0 \text{ (by assumption)}$$

and

$$\hat{\sigma}^2 \equiv \sigma_2^2 + \sigma_2^2 - 2\rho\sigma_2\sigma_3 > 0 \,.$$

Under the hypothesized assumptions, equations 10. 16 and 10.25 completely summarize the state of the system. The evolution of $x(t)$ and 10.25 depends only on the current level of $x(t)$. In a similar way, the evolution of $V(t)$ depends on the current levels of $V(t)$ and $x(t)$. Thus, the equilibrium futures exchange rate may be written as a function of the triple $[V(t), x(t), \tau]$. Note that unlike the valuation of forward exchange rates, the pricing of futures exchange rates requires us to specify the evolution of the spot exchange rate. At this juncture, we will be using the restrictions placed on $\alpha_1(\cdot)$ and $\sigma_1(\cdot)$.

The futures exchange rate is given by

$$H(t) = V(t) \, a(\tau) \, \exp [b(\tau)x(t)]. \tag{10.26}$$

$$b(\tau) = \frac{\alpha_1}{\kappa}(1 - e^{-\kappa\tau}) > 0 \tag{10.27}$$

and

$$a(\tau) = \exp\left\{\left(\frac{1}{2}\frac{\alpha_1^2\hat{\sigma}^2}{\kappa^2}\right)\left[\left(\frac{1}{2\kappa} - \frac{1}{2\kappa}e^{-2\kappa\tau}\right) + \tau + \frac{2}{\kappa}(e^{-\kappa\tau} - 1)\right]\frac{-(\kappa\mu + \hat{\sigma}_{12})\alpha_1}{\kappa}\left[\tau - \frac{1}{\kappa}(1 - e^{-\kappa\tau})\right]\right\} \tag{10.28}$$

There are two distinct ways in which the futures exchange rate differs from the forward exchange rate. First, the futures exchange rate is affected by the expected rate of change of the spot exchange rate, whereas the forward rate is not. Second, the futures exchange rate is influenced by the covariance between the proportionate change in the spot exchange rate and the interest rate differentials. These are potentially refutable implications. These conclusions rely critically on the assumption that the speed of adjustment factor is the same in both countries.

Model 2

We now turn to an alternative model of futures and forward exchange rate determination. This model differs from the previous one in two ways: first, the variance of the proportionate change in the spot exchange rate is allowed to depend on the interest rate differentials. Second, the term structure of interest rates in the two countries is assumed to be driven by the respective spot rates which follow a mean-reverting diffusion with the variance of the changes proportional to the level of the rates. Formally, we represent the restrictions as shown below:

$$\alpha_1(\cdot) \equiv \alpha_1(r - r^*)$$
$$\sigma_1^2(\cdot) \equiv \sigma_1^2 x$$
$$\alpha_2(\cdot) \equiv \kappa_2(\mu_2 - r)$$
$$\sigma_2^2(\cdot) \equiv \sigma_2^2 r$$
$$\alpha_3(\cdot) \equiv \kappa_3(\mu_3 - r^*)$$
$$\text{and } \sigma_3^2(\cdot) \equiv \sigma_3^2 r^*$$

Our specification under model 2 once again permits deviation from the PPP. The deviation is identical to the one considered under model 1. The specification used for the unanticipated proportionate changes in the spot exchange rates is different in this model; we assume that the variability of the changes in the spot exchange rates is proportional to the level of the rate. In a similar way, we have assumed that the interest rate differential follows a mean-reverting process with the variability of the changes proportional to the level of the interest rate differential.

The forward exchange rate can be represented in terms of the state variables, (V, r, r^*), by substituting the domestic and foreign discount bond prices in terms of r and r^*, respectively. For the assumed stochastic process, the discount bond prices have been derived by Cox, Ingersoll, and Ross (1985). Using these prices, it can be shown that the forward exchange rate is a decreasing function of the domestic spot rate of interest. As the volatility of the foreign spot rates increases, the foreign discount bond prices go up, thereby driving the forward exchange rates up. The term structure of the forward exchange rates cannot be easily characterized, although when $\kappa_2 = \kappa_3$ and $\sigma_2 = \sigma_3$, it depends only on the interest rate differential.

The determination of the futures exchange rates in our equilibrium setting requires us to place further restrictions. In effect, we need to assume that r and r^* are driven by a common state variable y which follows a mean-reverting square root diffusion. Thus,

$$r = \beta y$$

and

$$r^* = \beta^* y$$

where β and β^* are positive scales. Then

$$dx(t) = d(r - r^*) = (\beta - \beta^*)dy$$

Under this assumption, the interest rate differential and the spot exchange rate are sufficient to describe the state of the system. Let

$$dx = \hat{\kappa}(\hat{\mu} - x)dt + \hat{\sigma}\sqrt{x}\,d\hat{z}(v) \tag{10.29}$$

The parameters of the stochastic process for $x(t)$ are linked to those of r and r^*. In this economy, the equilibrium futures exchange rate is given by the expression below:

$$H(t) = V(t)\hat{A}(\tau)\exp[\hat{G}(\tau)x] \tag{10.30}$$

where

$$\hat{G}(\tau) \equiv \frac{4\alpha_1(1 - e^{\gamma\tau})}{\{[\sigma_{12} - \hat{\kappa}) + \gamma] - [\sigma_{12} - \hat{\kappa} - \gamma]e^{\gamma\tau}} \tag{10.31}$$

$$\gamma \equiv \sqrt{(\sigma_{12} - \hat{\kappa})^2 - 4\alpha_1\hat{\sigma}^2} > 0 \tag{10.32}$$

and

$$\hat{A}(\tau) = \left[\frac{1}{\gamma} e^{1/2\,[(\sigma_{12} - \hat{\kappa}) - \gamma]\tau} \{[(\sigma_{12} - \kappa) \right.$$
$$\left. + \gamma]\,(1 - e^{\gamma\tau}) + re^{\gamma\tau}\} \right]^{-2\hat{\kappa}\hat{\mu}/\hat{\sigma}^2} \tag{10.33}$$

Futures exchange rates are increasing in $V(t)$ and are explicitly influenced by the covariance between the proportionate changes in spot exchange rates and interest rate differentials. The logarithm of the futures premium is independent of the current spot exchange rate and depends on the time to maturity of the futures contracts and the interest rate differentials in a nonlinear way.

Conclusion

Using PPP, IRPT, and Fisherian relationships, this chapter stressed the importance of modeling the link between the evolution of the spot exchange rates and the nominal interest rate differentials. Two equilibrium models were presented that incorporated the link between the spot exchange rate and the interest rate differential. In the first model, the variance of the rate of change in the spot exchange rate and the variance of the nominal interest rate differentials were assumed to be constant. In the second model, these variances were assumed to be proportional to the nominal interest rate differentials. For both models, closed-form solutions for the prices of foreign exchange forward contracts and futures contracts were obtained.

References

Black, F. (1976), "Pricing of Commodity Contracts," *Journal of Financial Economics* 3, 167–79.

Cornell, B., & M. R. Reinganum (1981), "Forward and Futures Prices: Evidence from the Foreign Exchange Markets," *Journal of Finance* 36(12), 1035–45.

Courtadon, G. (1981), "Numerical Methods in the Valuation of Options and Corporate Liabilities with Interest Rate Uncertainty." Unpublished manuscript. Evanston, Ill.: J. L. Kellog Graduate School of Management, Northwestern University.

Cox, J. C., J. E. Ingersoll & S. A. Ross (1981), "A Re-examination of the Traditional Hypothesis about the Term Structure of Interest Rates," *Journal of Finance* 35, 769–99.

——— (1981), "The Relationship between Forward and Futures Prices," *Journal of Financial Economics* 9, 321–46.

——— (1985), "A Theory of the Term Structure of Interest Rates," *Econometrica* 53, 385–407.

French, K. R. (1983), "A Comparison of Futures and Forward Prices," *Journal of Financial Economics* 12, 311–42.

Garman, M. B., & S. W. Kohlhagen (1983), "Foreign Currency Option Values," *Journal of International Money and Finance* 2, 231–38.

Margrabe, W. (1976), A Theory of Forward and Futures Prices. Working paper. Philadelphia, Pa.: Wharton School, University of Pennsylvania.

Richard, S. F., & M. Sundaresan (1981), "A Continuous Time Equilibrium Model of Forward Prices and Futures Prices in a Multi-Good Economy," *Journal of Financial Economics* 9, 347–72.

11
Foreign Currency Options: A Survey

J. Orlin Grabbe

ABSTRACT

This chapter is a survey of foreign currency option pricing. Since the literature is incomplete, I will attempt to fill in a number of gaps in the theory in addition to summarizing existing results. The first part defines the conceptual types of foreign currency options, including options on spot, options on futures or forwards, futures-style options on spot, and futures-style options on futures. The second part surveys pricing equations for European FX options, including variants such as Boston options and range forward contracts. The third part shows pricing procedures and relationships for American FX options. It also introduces the concept of a "first passage" option, a type of option that has appeared in some currency swap contracts. The final part looks at the practical application of pricing models. It summarizes some important risk-management concepts and looks at the empirical evidence.

This chapter is a survey of foreign currency option pricing. Since the literature is incomplete, I will attempt to fill in a number of gaps in the theory in addition to summarizing existing results. The first part defines the conceptual types of foreign currency options, including options on spot, options on futures or forwards, futures-style options on spot, and futures-style options on futures. The next part surveys pricing equations for European FX options, including variants such as Boston options and range forward contracts. The following part shows pricing procedures and relationships for American foreign exchange (FX) options. It also introduces the concept of a "first-passage" option, a type of option that has appeared in some currency swap contracts. The final part looks at the practical application of pricing models. It summarizes some important risk-management concepts and looks at the empirical evidence.

Types of Foreign Currency Options

There are sixteen basic option types, representing the intersection of the sets {call, put}, {American, European}, and {option on spot, option on futures, futures-style option on spot, futures-style option on futures}. The location of the types currently traded is noted in table 11–1.

A *call on spot* is a contract between a buyer and a writer whereby the call buyer pays a price (the call "premium") to the writer in order to acquire the right, but not the obligation, to purchase a given amount (the call "size") of one currency from the writer at a purchase price (the call "strike price") stated in terms of a second currency. A *put on spot* is a contract between a buyer and a writer whereby the put buyer pays a price (the put "premium") to the writer in order to acquire the right, but not the obligation, to sell a given amount of one currency (the put "size") to the writer at a sale price stated in terms of a second currency (the put "strike price"). For exchange-traded options, a clearing house or clearing corporation guarantees performance of all option contracts by becoming the writer to every customer who is a buyer and the buyer to every customer who is a writer.

The *expiration date* of an option is the calendar day beyond which an option contract is no longer valid or binding. The buyer of an option is said to "exercise" the option if the buyer takes advantage of his or her right to purchase (if the option is a call) or to sell (if the option is a put) at the option strike price.

An *American* option is a call or put option that gives the buyer the right to exercise the option on the expiration date or on any business day prior to the expiration date. A *European* option is a call or put option that gives the buyer the right to exercise the option only on the expiration date.

A *call on futures* is a contract between a buyer and a writer whereby the call buyer pays a price (the call "premium") to the writer in order to acquire the right, but not the obligation, to go long an exchange-traded FX futures contract at an opening price (the call "strike price") stated in terms of a second currency. If the buyer of a call on futures exercises his or her right to go long a futures contract, the writer of the option must go short the futures contract.

A *put on futures* is a contract between a buyer and a writer whereby the put buyer pays a price (the put "premium") to the writer in order to acquire the right, but not the obligation, to go short an exchange-traded FX futures contract at an opening price (the put "strike price") stated in terms of a second currency. If the buyer of a put on futures exercises his or her right to go short a futures contract, the writer of the option must go long the futures contract.

By extension, a *call on forward* is a contract that gives the buyer the right to go long an interbank forward contract, while a *put on forward* is a contract that gives the buyer the right to go short an interbank forward contract.

Table 11–1
Types of Traded FX Calls and Puts

	European	*American*
Option on spot	CBOE, OTC	PHLX, LSE, OTC, IOCC
Option on futures	Not traded	CME
Futures-style option on spot	Not traded	LIFFE
Futures-style option on futures	Not traded	Not traded

CBOE: Chicago Board Options Exchange
CME: Chicago Mercantile Exchange
IOCC: Member exchanges of the International Options Clearing Corporation
LIFFE: London International Financial Futures Exchange
LSE: London Stock Exchange
OTC: Over-the-counter
PHLX: Philadelphia Stock Exchange

A *futures-style call on spot* is a contract between a buyer and a writer whereby the call buyer agrees to pay a daily cash flow to the writer in an amount equal to any decrease in the market value of the call (the call "premium"), the call writer agrees to pay a daily cash flow to the buyer in an amount equal to any increase in the market value of the call, and, in addition, the writer gives the call buyer the right, but not the obligation, to purchase a given amount (the call "size") of one currency from the writer at a purchase price (the call "strike price") stated in terms of a second currency. A *futures-style put on spot* is a contract between a buyer and a writer whereby the put buyer agrees to pay a daily cash flow to the writer in an amount equal to any decrease in the market value of the put (the put "premium"), the put writer agrees to pay a daily cash flow to the buyer in an amount equal to any increase in the market value of the put, and, in addition, the writer gives the put buyer the right, but not the obligation, to sell a given amount (the put "size") of one currency to the writer at a selling price (the put "strike price") stated in terms of a second currency.

A *futures-style call on futures* is a contract between a buyer and a writer whereby the call buyer agrees to pay a daily cash flow to the writer in an amount equal to any decrease in the market value of the call (the call "premium"), the call writer agrees to pay a daily cash flow to the buyer in an amount equal to any increase in the market value of the call, and, in addition, the writer gives the call buyer the right, but not the obligation, to go long an exchange-traded FX futures contract at an opening price (the call "strike price") stated in terms of a second currency. A *futures-style put on futures* is a contract between a buyer and a writer whereby the put buyer agrees to pay a daily cash flow to the writer in an amount equal to any decrease in the market value of the put (the put "premium"), the put writer agrees to pay a daily cash flow to the buyer in an amount equal to any increase in the market value of the put, and, in addition, the writer gives the put buyer the right, but not the obligation, to go short an exchange-traded FX futures contract at an opening price (the put "strike price") stated in terms of a second currency.

Several points should be clear from the option definitions.

1. There are two sides to each option contract: the buyer who obtains the option right to exercise and the writer who issues this right.

2. From the buyer's perspective, a call is an option to buy or go long, while a put is an option to sell or go short.

3. From the writer's perspective, a call is an obligation to sell or go short (if the buyer exercises), while a put is an obligation to buy or go long (if the buyer exercises).

4. An option on spot involves an up-front cash payment of the premium from the buyer to the writer, and, in addition, a subsequent exchange of currencies if the buyer exercises the option.

5. An option on futures involves an up-front cash payment of the premium from the buyer to the writer, and, in addition, a subsequent futures position in which the buyer and writer are on opposite sides if the buyer exercises the option.

6. A futures-style option does not involve an up-front payment between the buyer and the writer. Instead, the buyer goes long the option premium and the writer goes short the option premium, and there is a daily cash flow between buyer and writer in a manner similar to a futures contract. The futures-style option is not purely a futures contract on the option premium, however. The option buyer has the right to exercise the option into the underlying asset (spot currency or an FX futures contract).

7. Any of the above options can be American or European. The option is European if it can only be exercised on the final day, the expiration day. An American option can also be exercised on any business day prior to expiration.

Pricing Equations for European Foreign Currency Options

Options are priced by arbitrage relationships. The value of a foreign currency option is independent of anyone's expectation regarding the future movement of the spot rate. In this respect, option valuation can be compared to the valuation of forward contracts. Forward contracts are priced by reference to spot contracts using the interest parity theorem, where the relevant interest rates are Eurocurrency rates. Given a spot contract and two Eurocurrency deposits, one can (subject to bid/asked spreads) create the exact equivalent of a forward rate. If this "synthetic forward" rate is different from the market forward rate, a riskless profit can be made by buying at the low price and simultaneously selling at the high. This arbitrage relation is independent of future movements of the spot rate. In the same way, options are priced by creating a portfolio that duplicates the properties of the option. The value of the option is identical to the value of this portfolio or "synthetic option." For FX options, the duplicating portfolio is composed of a combination of domestic and foreign currency discount bonds. An FX call may be created by issuing domestic currency liabilities and purchasing foreign currency assets, while an FX put may be created by issuing foreign currency liabilities and purchasing domestic currency assets.

That options in general could be priced by an arbitrage relationship was the key insight of Fisher Black and Myron Scholes (1973). To obtain the arbitrage relationship, they made three special assumption: the logarithm of the price of the underlying asset follows a Levy-Wiener process, the standard deviation (volatility) rate of the process is known over the life of the option, and there are no transactions costs. The latter assumption allows for continuous adjustment of the portfolio that duplicates the option payoff states. Many of the practical problems faced by FX option market-makers stem from the failure of these special assumptions to hold in the real world. Nevertheless, employment of option formulae has proved not only useful but also mandatory as option markets have increased in efficiency. A small bid/asked spread around the model price suffices to cover transactions costs and to compensate for the risk of noncontinuous hedging as well as for uncertain or random volatility.

Prior to Black and Scholes, options were valued by calculating the discounted expected value of their future cash flows. The two approaches are not incompatible if a restriction is placed on the probability distribution under which expectations are taken.

Options on Spot

The basics of pricing European options on spot are given in Grabbe (1983) and Garman and Kohlhagen (1983). The notation of table 11–2 will be used to summarize these and other results. Assume that ln S follows a Wiener-Levy process. Roughly speaking, this implies that spot rates have a lognormal distribution and that the sample path is continuous (no jumps). Assume also that both domestic (r) and foreign (r^*) interest rates are constant. If r and r^*

Table 11–2
Notation

c	value of European call on one unit of spot exchange
p	value of European put on one unit of spot exchange
C	value of American call on one unit of spot exchange
P	value of American put on one unit of spot exchange
c^*	value of European call on one unit of futures/forwards
p^*	value of European put on one unit of futures/forwards
C^*	value of American call on one unit of futures/forwards
P^*	value of American put on one unit of futures/forwards
$c+$	value of futures-style European call on one unit of spot
$p+$	value of futures-style European put on one unit of spot
$C+$	value of futures-style American call on one unit of spot
$P+$	value of futures-style American put on one unit of spot
c^*+	value of futures-style European call on one unit of futures
p^*+	value of futures-style European put on one unit of futures
C^*+	value of futures-style American call on one unit of futures
P^*+	value of futures-style American put on one unit of futures
B	current price of a pure discount (or zero-coupon) bond paying one unit of domestic currency at maturity
B^*	current price of a pure discount (or zero-coupon) bond paying one unit of foreign currency at maturity
$S(t)$	domestic currency price of spot foreign currency
$F(t,T)$	domestic currency price of forward exchange, with the contract maturing at $t+T$
T	the option term to maturity
X	the option strike price
v	the annualized standard deviation (volatility) rate of the logarithm of the underlying asset price

are continuously compounded rates, then the prices of domestic (B) and foreign (B^*) currency discount bonds can be written as

$$B = \exp(-rT)$$
$$B^* = \exp(-r^*T).$$

The instantaneous standard deviation rate of ln S is v. If the price c of a call option on spot is assumed to be a twice-continuously differentiable function of the spot rate, then a proposition in stochastic calculus called Ito's lemma may be used to construct a portfolio of bonds that duplicates the option payoff. According to Garman and Kohlhagen, the construction process under the assumption of constant interest rates show that the option value follows the partial differential equation

$$\frac{1}{2} v^2 S^2 \frac{\delta^2 c}{\delta S^2} + (r - r^*)S\frac{\delta c}{\delta S} - rc = \frac{\delta c}{\delta T}, \qquad (11.1)$$

with the boundary constraint

$$c = \max[0, S - X] \text{ at } T = 0. \tag{11.2}$$

The Feynman-Kac solution of this partial differential equation is significant.[1]

$$c = \exp(-rT) \int_{\ln X}^{\infty} [\exp(y) - X] \, f(y; mt, v\sqrt{T}) \, dy \tag{11.3}$$

where

$$y = \ln S$$
$$m = r - r^* - \frac{1}{2}v^2$$
$$f(y; mT, v\sqrt{T}) = [1/(v\sqrt{2\pi T})] \exp[-(y - mT)^2/2v^2T].$$

Notice carefully the proper interpretation of this integral solution. It looks just like the discounted expected value of the option payoff states at expiration, where the mean and variance of the normal density f are mT and v^2T, respectively. But, that interpretation would be misleading. The normal integral arises in determining the proportion of domestic and foreign currency bonds in the duplicating portfolio. There is no assumption that the mean drift of $\ln S$ will actually be mT. However, the form of the integral solution does show that taking the discounted expected value will lead to the proper option valuation formula, but only if the actual rate of drift in the objective probability distribution is first placed with a "risk neutral" equivalent.[2]

Taking the integral in equation 11.3, we obtain

$$c = \exp(-r^*T)SN(d1) - \exp(-rT)XN(d2)$$

or

$$c = SB^*N(d1) - XBN(d2). \tag{11.4}$$

where

$$d1 = \{\ln(S/X) + [(r - r^*) + .5 \, v^2] \, T\}/v\sqrt{T} = [\ln(SB^*/XB)$$
$$+ .5 \, v^2T]/v\sqrt{T}$$
$$d2 = \{\ln(S/X) + [(r - r^*) - .5 \, v^2]T\}/v \, \sqrt{T} = [\ln(SB^*/XB)$$
$$- .5 \, v^2T]/v \, \sqrt{T}$$
$$N(d) = (1/\sqrt{2\pi}) \int_{-\infty}^{d} \exp(-x^2/2) \, dx$$

Equation 11.4 expresses the option formula in the form of the duplicating portfolio of domestic and foreign currency bonds. The foreign currency bond price is B^*, the number of foreign currency bonds is $N(d1)$, while the domestic currency value of the foreign currency bonds is $SB^*N(d1)$. The price of a domestic currency bond is B, while the number of bonds is $-XN(d2)$, for a total position in domestic currency bonds of $-XBN(d2)$. The negative sign denotes a short position or borrowing.

An inspection of $N(d1)$ and $N(d2)$ shows that the amounts of foreign and domestic currency bonds are themselves function of the time to maturity T as well as the current value of the spot rate S. Hence, the bond portfolio must be adjusted continuously in order to duplicate the option payoff.

Given a solution for the call, the European put on spot may be priced by the put-call conversion equation (Grabbe, 1983)

$$p = c - SB^* + XB . \tag{11.5}$$

This leads to the solution

$$p = XB[1 - N(d2)] - SB^*[1 - N(d1)] . \tag{11.6}$$

If bond prices (or interest rates) are treated as stochastic instead of constant, then the relevant partial differential equation (Grabbe, 1983) for a call on spot becomes

$$\frac{1}{2}\left[v_1^2 (SB^*)^2 \frac{\delta^2 c}{\delta(SB^*)^2} + 2\rho\, v_1\, v_2 \frac{\delta^2 c}{\delta(SB^*)\delta B} (SB^*B) + v_2^2\, B^2 \frac{\delta^2 c}{\delta B^2} \right] = \frac{\delta c}{\delta T} \tag{11.7}$$

where v_1 is the standard deviation rate of $\ln(SB^*)$, v_2 is the standard deviation of $\ln(B)$, and ρ represents their correlation coefficient. The boundary constraints are equation 11.2 and

$$c - \frac{\delta c}{\delta(SB^*)} (SB^*) - \frac{\delta c}{\delta B} B = 0. \tag{11.8}$$

The solution in this case is also given by equation 11.4, except that v must be reinterpreted as the average volatility of $\ln F(t,T)$ over the life of the option (as $T \to 0$). When bond prices are stochastic, there is a cross-correlation between bond prices (interest rates) and spot rate movements. For European options, the relevance of this cross-correlation for pricing is entirely embodied (through interest parity) in the movement of the market price of forward exchange.

Next, we address *range forwards*. Let S^* be the spot rate at some date in the future. Consider a contract between a buyer and a seller under whose terms the buyer will be required to purchase foreign currency and pay a domestic currency price of $X1$ if $S^* \geq X1$, S^* if $X1 > S^* > X2$, or $X2$ if $X2 \geq S^*$. Such a contract is termed a *range forward* contract. The investment banking firm of Salomon Brothers began offering range forward contracts in 1985. It is easy to show that the purchase of a range forward with a maximum price of $X1$ and a minimum price of $X2$ is equivalent to buying a European call on spot and selling a European put on spot, where the strike price on the call is above that on the spot.

Consider an option portfolio which consists of a long position in a European call on spot $c(F, X1)$ and a short position in a European put on spot $p(F, X2)$, where the option strike prices $X1$ and $X2$ are chosen in such a way that

$$X1 > F > X2$$

and

$$C(F, X1) = p(F, X2).$$

The current value of the position is $c - p = 0$, while at expiration, for a spot rate of S^*, the value will be

	value of long call	value of short put	total cost of FX
$S^* \geq X1$	$S^* - X1$	0	$X1$
$X1 > S^* > X2$	0	0	S^*
$X2 \geq S^*$	0	$(X2 - S^*)$	$X2$

For spot values between $X1$ and $X2$, the holder of this option position will be required to pay the expiration spot rate in order to receive foreign exchange, since the value of the two options will be zero. Otherwise, the holder will exercise the call and pay a maximum of $X1$, or else have the put exercised against the position and be required to pay a price of $X2$ for the exchange received.

The seller of the range forward contract must chose $X1$ and $X2$ so that the values of the call and put are equal, and, hence, there will be no premium payment for the range forward contract. (When dealing at a spread, the market-maker will sell a range forward at a zero price with $X1$ and $X2$ chosen so that the net value to the buyer is slightly negative.)

Options on Futures/Forwards

For futures contracts expiring at the same time as the option, European options on futures have the same values as the equivalent European options on spot. At maturity, which is the only time a European option can be exercised, the futures price will have converged to the spot price, and, hence, either option could only be exercised into the same underlying asset. Hence, equations 11.4 and 11.6 give the respective values of the European call and put on FX futures. These equations may be given a more convenient representation.

In doing so, we will treat futures and forward prices as equivalent, and related to the spot price by interest parity. Even though the daily marking-to-market of futures contracts can theoretically cause forward and futures prices to diverge, empirically FX futures and forwards do not differ in any material way.[3] For discount bonds expiring at the same time as the forward or futures contract, we may write the interest parity equation as

$$F(t, T) = SB^*/B. \tag{11.9}$$

Equation 11.4 then may be rewritten as

$$c^* = B[FN(d1) - XN(d2)]. \tag{11.10}$$

where

$$d1 = (\ln(F/X) + .5 \ v^2T)/v \ \sqrt{T},$$
$$d2 = [\ln(F/X) - .5 \ v^2T]/v \ \sqrt{T}.$$

Equation 11.9 may also be used to express the put-call conversion equation 11.5 in the form

$$p^* = c^* + B(X - F), \tag{11.11}$$

yielding as the value of a European put on futures/forwards

$$p^* = B\{X[1 - N(d2)] - F[1 - N(d1)]\}. \tag{11.12}$$

Note that these formulae require that the futures/forward contract mature on the option expiration date.

Futures-Style Options

Futures-style options involve no initial premium transfer from the buyer (long side) to the writer (short side). The buyer does not lose and the writer does not receive the value of the interest paid on the premium over the life of the option. Hence, the future payoff states of the option are not discounted. The buyer will be willing to go long the option premium at a higher price, and the writer will insist on going short at a higher price.

This observation suffices to write the value of the futures-style European call on either spot or futures/forwards as

$$c+ \; = \; c^* + \; = \; FN(d1) - XN(d2), \qquad (11.13)$$

while the put-call conversion equation and the put value become

$$p+ \; = \; p^* + \; = \; c + [X - F] = c^* + \; + \; [X - F], \qquad (11.14)$$

$$p+ \; = \; p^* + \; = \; X[1 - N(d2)] - F[1 - N(d1)]. \qquad (11.15)$$

The call equation 11.13 represents the solution of the partial differential equation (interpreting c as either $c+$ or $c^* +$)

$$\frac{1}{2} v^2 S^2 \frac{\delta^2 c}{\delta S^2} + (r - r^*) S \frac{\delta c}{\delta S} = \frac{\delta c}{\delta T}, \qquad (11.16)$$

with the usual boundary constraint 11.2.

Now consider *Boston options*. A slight variation of an option on forward or futures contracts is the Boston option introduced by the Bank of Boston.[4] A Boston option involves either a long forward contract plus a put option on the forward or a short forward contract plus a call option on the forward. The option in either case allows one to walk away from the forward contract. The option premium part of a Boston option is paid at option *maturity.* Hence the option payoff states are not discounted when calculating the option premium.

The premium payment for the option on the forward thus corresponds precisely to the value of a European futures-style option on futures ($p^* +$ for a put or $C^* +$ for a call). Equation 11.14 should also make clear that a Boston option (the combination of the forward and option on forward) corresponds in value to a futures-style option on futures/forwards. A long forward plus a put is equivalent to a call option, while a short forward plus a call is equivalent to a put option.

Alternative Probability Assumptions

The pricing formulae above were derived on the assumption that logarithms of the relevant asset prices followed Levy-Wiener processes, which implies that differences in price logarithms have normal distributions. Empirical exchange rate data are leptokurtic, however. There are proportionally more very small changes and more very large changes than would be expected if the data were normal, but fewer changes in the intermediate ranges of the distribution. This has led some to conclude that log changes in spot or forward rates have Levy stable (sometimes called "stable Paretian"), but nonnormal distributions.[5]

The construction of option-pricing models under the assumption of a Levy stable distribution poses a number of problems, the principal one being that the sample path of a nonnormal stable process is not continuous. Thus, one cannot derive the theoretical option value by an arbitrage argument as done in the derivation of equation 11.1. One might, however, choose to assume a relevant rate of drift (a value for m) and take discounted expected values of the option payoff states. But if $y = \ln S$ has a nonnormal stable distribution, then the expected value of $S = \exp(y)$ is undefined except in one special case.[6]

McCullough (1984) takes advantage of this special case in proposing a pricing equation for European FX options on spot under the Levy stable assumption. Purchasing power parity is assumed, and the spot rate is determined as the ratio of domestic and foreign purchasing powers, which in turn have maximally skewed nonnormal stable distributions. The FX option on spot is then priced by its discounted expected value as

$$c = B[F \, I(d1) - X \, I(d2)], \tag{11.17}$$

where $I(d1)$ and $I(d2)$ are functions of F, X, and B, as well as the stable distribution parameters. The formula has an aesthetically pleasing similarity to 11.10. The objection to the formula is that it depends on purchasing power parity and, moreover, requires a particular formulation of purchasing power parity.[7]

Vankudre (1984) has obtained stock option pricing results assuming either a Pareto or a beta distribution. The pricing equations are utility-based and require the assumption of constant relative risk aversion. If Vankudre's results are adjusted to apply to foreign currency options (Ghosh, 1985), the formulae for European calls on spot become

$$c = (SB^* - XB)G(d), \tag{11.18}$$

for the Pareto distribution—$G(d)$ being a function of S, X, B, B^*, and the Pareto distribution parameters—and

$$c = SB^*H(d1) - XBH(d2), \tag{11.19}$$

for the beta distribution—$H(d1)$ and $H(d2)$ being functions of S, B, B^*, and the beta distribution parameters. The corresponding put prices may be obtained from equation 11.5.

Pricing American FX Options

American Boundary Constraints

American options differ from European ones in that they may be exercised at any time prior to expiration. This implies that an American option must be at least as valuable as the corresponding European option, since one may choose arbitrarily to hold an American option to maturity. This is indicated in table 11–3 by the inequality which sets the American call value greater than or equal to the European value, the latter being expressed in terms of the formulae summarized in the previous section. Since an American call option may be exercised at any time, its value must be also at least as great as the difference between the underlying asset price and the strike price, as indicated by the second inequality in table 11–3. A similar table is easily constructed for put options, so I will confine the discussion here to calls.

The American boundary conditions in table 11–3 can be used to tell us if a particular type of American call has a value strictly greater than the corresponding European call. If exercised, the value of an American call option is exactly equal to the difference between the underlying asset price and the exercise price. Thus an American call would never be exercised early if this immediate exercise value were less than the value of the corresponding European call.

For the futures-style option on futures, we note that

$$FN(d1) - XN(d2) \geq F - X. \qquad (11.20)$$

An exercised futures-style option on futures has a value of $F - X$, which is never greater than the European value. The value of early exercise is thus zero, and the American futures-style option on futures has the same value as the European equivalent, $C^* + = c^* +$, as noted in figure 11–1.

In the remaining cases, the early-exercise boundary constraint can be strictly greater than the European value. If B, $B^* < 1$ (interest rates are positive), then for *some value* of S sufficiently large,

$$S - X > B[FN(d1) - XN(d2)], \qquad \text{some } S, \qquad (11.21)$$

while for *some value* of F sufficiently large,

$$F - X > B[FN(d1) - XN(d2)], \qquad \text{some } F. \qquad (11.22)$$

Table 11–3
Boundary Constraints on American Calls

	European Value	American Boundary Constraint
Option on spot	$B[FN(d1) - XN(d2)]$	$\geq B[FN(d1) - XN(d2)]$ $\geq S - X$
Option on futures	$B[FN(d1) - XN(d2)]$	$\geq B[FN(d1) - XN(d2)]$ $\geq F - X$
Futures-style option on spot	$FN(d1) - XN(d2)$	$\geq FN(d1) - XN(d2)$ $\geq S - X$
Futures-style option on futures	$FN(d1) - XN(d2)$	$\geq FN(d1) - XN(d2)$ $\geq F - X$

Hence there is a *positive probability of early exercise*. This positive probability gives the American call a value strictly greater than the corresponding European call for calls on spot $(C > c)$ and calls on futures $(C^* > c^*)$.

The remaining relationships shown in figure 11–1 for American FX options may be obtained as follows. For $B < 1$, the inequality

$$FN(d1) - XN(d2) > B[FN(d1) - XN(d2)], \qquad (11.23)$$

gives the American futures-style option on spot a value greater than the value of the American option on spot $(C+ > C)$ and gives the American futures-style option on futures a value greater than that of the American option on futures $(C^*+ > C^*)$.
The fact that either

$$F - X \geq S - X \quad \text{or} \quad F - X \leq S - X \qquad (11.24)$$

makes the value relationship between American calls on spot and American calls on futures ambiguous. Whether the boundary constraint on one of the options is subsumed depends on whether the forward rate is at a premium or a discount. If interest rates are constant, then in the event $S - X > F - X$, the call on spot will be more valuable $(C > C^*)$, while if $F - X > S - X$, the call on futures will be more valuable $(C^* > C)$. The same conclusions are not possible if interest rates are stochastic, because there is then a positive probability that the forward rate will move from a premium to a discount or move from a discount to a premium.

Equations 11.20 and 11.23 show that a futures-style option on spot has a value, for $B < 1$, greater than that of an option on futures $(C+ > C^*)$. The future-style option on spot has the additional constraint that $C+ \geq S - X$, yielding (for stochastic interest rates) the further relations $C+ > c+$ and $C+$

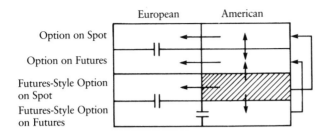

European   American

Option on Spot

Option on Futures

Futures-Style Option
on Spot

Futures-Style Option
on Futures

——▶ : Arrow points to option with lower value.

=   : Options have equal values.

◀—▶ : Relative value between options can go either way, depending on relation between
       Eurocurrency rates on deposits denominated in the two currencies.

▨▨▨ : Most valuable (hence, most expensive) contract.

Source: Reproduced from J. Orlin Grabbe, *International Financial Markets*. New York:
Elsevier Science, 1986.

Note: Values are for similar options only. (That is, both options are calls or both are puts;
strike prices and dates of expiration are identical.) When applying these relationships to
traded options, keep in mind that International Monetary Market options expire a week
earlier than PHLX, LSE, CBOE, and LIFFE options.

Figure 11–1. Value Relationships among Types of FX Options

$> C^* +$. (The special case of constant interest rates and $S - X < F - X$
would give the results $C+ = c+$ and $C+ = C^* +$.)

*Perpetual American FX Options and First-Passage
Options*

Under the assumption that the logarithm of the spot rate follows a Wiener-
Levy process, the value of an American FX call on spot may be obtained as
the solution of equations 11.1 and 11.2 with the additional boundary
condition

$$C \geqslant S - X. \qquad (11.25)$$

An integral solution of this boundary value problem is not known, but numerical prices may be generated by a variety of techniques. An approach that
approximates the Wiener-Levy process by a multiplicative binomial process
is considered in the following section. An explicit integral solution can be
given in the special case of a perpetual American FX option, which is an
option that never matures. Its solution (which will provide additional insight

into American FX options generally) will be obtained from the pricing equation for another option type, a *first-passage option*.

First-passage options are neither American nor European. Consider an FX contract of the following form. Company A and company B trade currencies at a current spot rate of $1.50/British pound. The reverse trade at the same rate will take place at some future date. Meanwhile, in the event that the spot rate rises to $1.65/British pound, company A will immediately pay company B $.15/British pound. What is the value of company A's contingent obligation to pay $.15/British pound to company B? Consider an option contract with a strike price X which pays off an amount $Z_\mu - X$ at the time of the first occurrence of $S = Z_\mu$, provided this event takes place prior to option maturity. Otherwise, the option pays nothing and expires worthless. We will designate such an option contract a *first-passage call*. In our example, company A's obligation to company B can be priced as a first-passage call with X = $1.50 and Z_μ = $1.65. A *first-passage put* is similar, except that it pays $X - Z_d$ at the time of the first occurrence of $S = Z_d$, provided this event occurs prior to maturity.

Under the assumption that $\ln S$ follows a Wiener-Levy process, the usual hedging argument shows that the value of a first-passage call, c^Λ, is goverened by the partial differential equation 11.1 (substituting c^Λ *for c* in the equation) and has the boundary constraints

$$c^\Lambda = Z_\mu - X, \, S = Z_\mu, \tag{11.26}$$

$$c^\Lambda = 0, \, \text{for } T = 0, \, S \neq Z_\mu. \tag{11.27}$$

An integral solution of this problem may be given as

$$c^\Lambda = (Z_\mu - X) \int_o^T \exp(-rt) \, f(t; \, z, \, m) \, dt \tag{11.28}$$

where

$$z = \ln(Z_\mu/s)$$
$$f(t; \, z, \, m) = [z/(v \, \sqrt{2\pi t^3})] \, \exp[-(z - m)^2/2v^2 t].$$

Here f is a one-sided Levy stable density with characteristic exponent equal to ½. Both the mean and variance of t are undefined (infinite). Calculation of this integral (Grabbe, 1985) shows that

$$c^{\Lambda} = [Z_{\mu} - X] \left[\frac{Z_{\mu}}{S}\right]^{m/v^2} \left[\left(\frac{Z_{\mu}}{S}\right)^{\theta} N(d_1) + \left(\frac{Z_{\mu}}{S}\right)^{-\theta} N(d_2)\right],$$

$$d_1 = \frac{\ln(S/Z_{\mu}) - v^2\theta^T}{v\sqrt{T}}$$

$$\theta = \frac{\sqrt{m^2 + 2rv^2}}{v^2} \tag{11.29}$$

$$d_2 = \frac{\ln(S/Z_{\mu}) + v^2\theta^T}{v\sqrt{T}}.$$

Letting $T \to \infty$, the value of a perpetual first-passage call becomes

$$c^{\Lambda}_{\infty} = (Z_{\mu} - X)\left(\frac{Z_{\mu}}{S}\right)^{m/v^2 - \theta} \tag{11.30}$$

The value in equation 11.30 corresponds to the value of an FX option that never matures and that will be exercised when and only when $S = Z_{\mu}$. This perpetual first-passage call differs from a perpetual American FX call on spot only in that in the latter case, the optimal exercise level Z_{μ} may be freely chosen. Thus, the value of a perpetual American FX call may be obtained by maximizing c^{Λ} over Z_{μ}. Applying this procedure to equation 11.30, we discover that the maximum is obtained at $Z_{\mu} = \infty$, for $(m/v^2) - \theta \geqslant -1$ (Grabbe, 1985). In that case, the value of the perpetual American FX call on spot is $C_{\infty} = S$. For $(m/v^2) - \theta < -1$,

$$C_{\infty} = (Z^*_{\mu} - X)\left(\frac{Z^*_{\mu}}{S}\right)^{\dfrac{r - r^* - \frac{1}{2}v^2 - \sqrt{(r - r^*)^2 + v^2(r + r^*) + \frac{1}{4}v^4}}{v^2}} \tag{11.31}$$

where

$$Z^*_{\mu} = X\left[\frac{r^* + \sqrt{(r - r^*)^2 + v^2(r + r^*) + \frac{1}{4}v^4} - \left(r - \frac{1}{2}v^2\right)}{r^* + \sqrt{(r - r^*)^2 + v^2(r + r^*) + \frac{1}{4}v^4} - \left(r + \frac{1}{2}v^2\right)}\right].$$

Equation 11.31 represents the solution to the partial differential equation

$$\frac{1}{2} v^2 S^2 \frac{\delta^2 c}{\delta S^2} + (r - r^*) S \frac{\delta c}{\delta S} - r c = 0, \tag{11.32}$$

with the boundary condition 11.26. Similar results can be obtained for puts.

Sample values of perpetual American FX options are given in table 11–4, for $S = X = 35$ and $v = .12$. We see that for $r = r^* = .10$, the values of the perpetual American call and put are equal: $c_\infty = P_\infty = 3.434$. The call will be exercised at the critical level $Z_\mu^* = 45.736$, while the put will be exercised at $Z_d^* = 26.784$. If the foreign interest rate falls to .01, the value of the call rises to $C_\infty = 24.909$ and the critical level for call exercise rises to 377.772, while the value of the put falls to $P_\infty = 0.983$ and the critical level for put exercise rises to 32.427. These results highlight the impact of the interest differential on the critical exercise level.

Binomial Pricing Procedure

The previous section showed that explicit pricing equations may be given for perpetual American options. The lack of an integral solution in the other cases requires a numerical approach for generating prices. An approach due to Cox, Ross, and Rubinstein (1979) values American options under the assumption of a multiplicative binomial process. Their approach can be treated either as an alternate probability assumption or as a discrete time approximation to the continuous time Wiener-Levy process. Here I will derive the relevant evaluation equations for the different types of American FX options.

Let S represent the level of the spot rate in the current time interval, while F is the price of forward exchange for delivery in the following time interval. Assume that the spot rate follows a binomial process with proportional jumps between time intervals of u or $d = 1/u$. Given the current spot value of S, at the next time interval, the value will be Su with probability q, or Sd with probability $1 - q$. The current value of an American option on spot is C. If the option is exercised immediately, it will have a value $C = S - X$. If the option is held until the next time interval, the value will be C_μ corresponding to Su, or C_d, corresponding to Sd.

We may determine the value of the U.S. option C by creating a portfolio whose net payoff duplicates the net payoff to the option. For an option purchased this period and sold next period, the net payoff is $C_\mu - C$ with probability q, or $C_d - C$ with probability $1 - q$.

Consider a purchase of a units of forward exchange at the price F, along with an investment of b units of domestic currency at the one-period rate of interest r. The payoff to this portfolio in the next time period will be $a(Su -$

Table 11–4
Perpetual American FX Option Values

s = 35				x = 35	v = .12	
r	r*	C_∞	z_u^*	P_∞	z_t^*
.10	.10	3.434	45.736	3.434	26.784
.10	.05	10.208	79.045	1.564	30.995
.10	.01	24.909	377.772	0.983	32.427
.05	.10	1.564	39.522	10.208	15.498
.01	.10	0.983	37.777	24.909	3.243

$F) + rb$, with probability q, or $a(Sd - F) + rb$, with probability $1 - q$. In order that these payoffs duplicate those available from the purchase of an option, it is necessary that

$$C_\mu - C = a(Su - F) + rb$$
$$C_d - C = a(Sd - F) + rb.$$

Solution of these equations shows that a and b must be chosen such that

$$a = (C_\mu - C_d)/S(u - d)$$
$$b = (C_\mu - C)r - (C_\mu - C_d)(u - F/S)/r(u - d).$$

Since investment in the strategy has the same net payoff as holding the option for another period, the value of retaining the option for another period is equal to the domestic currency amount invested in the portfolio. But the total domestic currency amount investment in the portfolio is b. Hence

$$c = \max[b, S - X] . \tag{11.33}$$

Substituting this relation into the previous equation and solving for C, we obtain

$$C = \max(\{C_\mu[(F/S - d)/(u - d)] + C_d[(u - F/S)/(u - d)]\}/(1 + r), S - X).$$

This last equation may be written in the simplified form

$$c = \max \{kC_\mu + (1 - k)c_d]/(1 + r), S - X\} \tag{11.34}$$

where

$$k = (F/S - d)/(u - d). \tag{11.35}$$

The variable k may be interpreted as a probability, since $0 < k < 1$. However, it is important to keep in mind that this interpretation is solely for convenience. The real probabilities were given by q and $1 - q$, while k and $1 - k$ are only "as if" probabilities that arise from the duplicating portfolio. They are sometimes called "risk-neutral" probabilities because they have the property that

$$F = kSu + (1 - k)Sd.$$

With probabilities k and $1 - k$, the forward rate is the expected value of next period's spot rate. There is, however, no assumption that the same is true with respect to the actual probabilities q and $1 - q$.

Notice that this procedure gives us a way of valuing the American option prior to expiration. At expiration $C_\mu = \max[Su - X, 0]$ and $C_d = \max[Sd - X, 0]$. Hence, we may explicitly solve for C at the time period prior to expiration. Given values of C for the time period prior to expiration, we may solve for C two time periods prior to expiration, and so on, working backward in a dynamic programming fashion.

For options on futures, C^*, a similar argument to that above leads to equations 11.34 and 11.35 being replaced with

$$C^* = \max \{kC_\mu + (1 - k)C_d]/(1 + r), F - X\} \tag{11.36}$$

$$k = (1 - d)/(u - d). \tag{11.37}$$

For futures-style options on spot, $C+$, the equation becomes

$$C+ = \max \{kC_\mu + (1 - k)C_d], S - X\}, \tag{11.38}$$

where k is given by equation 11.35. Finally, for futures-style options on futures, C^*+, the pricing equations are 11.37 and

$$C^*+ = \max \{kC_\mu + (1 - k)C_d], F - X\}. \tag{11.39}$$

U.S. *FX* puts are priced in an analogous manner, the value of the put at each stage being the maximum of the immediate exercise value of the put or the amount b invested in the duplicating portfolio. Equation 11.33 is replaced with

$$P = \max[b, X - S], \tag{11.40}$$

and so on for the other equations.

In practice, this procedure requires that the actual time interval to option expiration be broken into discrete pieces. If we divide the time interval T into n smaller pieces, each with length T/n, then u and d may be written in terms of a volatility parameter v as

$$u = \exp(v \sqrt{T/n}), \qquad d = 1/u. \tag{11.41}$$

Cox, Ross, and Rubenstein (1979) show that as n goes to infinity, the value of an option following a multiplicative binomial process will converge to the value of a similar option following a Wiener-Levy process.

Other Pricing Procedures

The procedure above approximated the normal distribution (of log prices) by a binomial distribution. Other procedures follow either an alternative approximation to the normal, substitute a finite difference equation for the partial differential equation, or directly approximate an exact analytical solution.

A technique due to Parkinson (1977) utilizes a trinomial approximation to the normal distribution. In the "as-if" or "risk-neutral" probability interpretation of the solution to equation 11.1, if the current value of the logarithm of the underlying asset price is $\ln W$, then after the passage of T/n units of time, the asset price logarithm is distributed normally with mean $\ln W + mT/n$ and with variance $v^2 T/n$. The Parkinson technique involves replacement of the normal distribution with three transition probabilities corresponding to three discrete movements in the price logarithm—an up jump, a down jump, or no change. This technique is equivalent to the binomial pricing technique if we view the trinomial probabilities as stemming from a binomial distribution. Corresponding to an up jump Wuu would be a probability k^2; to a down jump Wdd, a probability $(1 - k)^2$; and to no change, a probability $2k(1 - k)$. The Parkinson approach was adapted for American foreign currency options on spot by Bodurtha and Courtadon (1984).

The technique of Schwartz (1977) involves substituting a finite difference equation for the option partial differential equation. The resulting equation can be written in a form that values the option as the maximum of either its immediate exercise value or as a weighted average of three future option values corresponding to three future prices of the underlying asset. The weights in this case cannot be interpreted as probabilities, however, since they may take negative values.

A final approach relies on an analytical solution to equations 11.1, 11.2, and 11.25. Geske and Johnson (1984) value an American option as a series of European compound options. The value of an American option is the maximum of either its immediate exercise value or the value of a European option whose possible payoff values in the next instant of time are the values of other European options. Geske and Johnson are able in this way to derive an analytical solution for the value of an American call option:

$$C = S\ C(1) - X\ C(2)\ , \qquad (11.42)$$

where $C(1)$ and $C(2)$ are each composed of an infinite number of terms. The first of this infinite number of terms involves the univariate normal distribution; the second, the bivariate normal; the third, the trivariate normal; and so on for the *n*-variate normal as $n \to \infty$. The solution is made practical through a polynomial approximation technique which involves calculating only the normal, bivariate normal, and trivariate normal distributions. This approach to American foreign currency option pricing has been used by Shastri and Tandon (1984).

Market Practice and Empirical Evidence

Empirical Tests of the Market Pricing of FX Options

Empirical tests of rational FX option pricing have either focused on boundary constraints (for example, was an option sold at less than its exercise value?) and rational relationships between options (such as put-call conversion) or else have compared market prices to model prices. The first type of test is the least ambiguous (because the boundary relationships do not involve any probability assumption), but it is also the least interesting, because option boundary relationships are automatically satisfied by any correctly derived FX option pricing model, whether or not the model probability assumption is valid. The use of FX option pricing models in the market is widespread. Thus, to a large extent, empirical "tests" of an option pricing model represent a comparison of the researcher's model with those used in the market. Or, assuming the models in use in the market are the same as those of the researcher, the empirical study simply measures the effects of transactions costs and market adjustments to the risks of noncontinuous hedging and stochastic volatility.

Shastri and Tandon (1985) do tests of pricing relationships for FX options on spot, using data from the Philadelphia Stock Exchange (PHLX) over the period December 1982 to November 1983. A number of violations of option boundary conditions were found, and even though the authors do not consider transactions costs explicitly, the size of the reported violations would rule out transactions costs as the source of the apparent market inefficiency. The authors' data set is, however, composed of spot rates at the close of trading along with option settlement prices. The PHLX typically chooses the last trade price as the settlement price; for infrequently traded option, the last trade price may be well outside the market bid–asked range at the close of trading. The use of settlement prices instead of actual transactions prices would appear to be the major source of the observed violations.

Bodurtha and Courtadon (1986) use actual option transactions prices along with contemporaneous spot rates and take transactions costs explicitly into account. Their data, also for the PHLX, spans the period February 1983 to September 1984. Virtually no violations of rational boundary conditions were reported. Their results were similar to those of Shastri and Tandon (1984), however, if settlement prices were used or transactions costs ignored. Their results indicate that the exchange-based market is efficient with respect to option boundary conditions.

The question of market efficiency with respect to theoretical option pricing is a more difficult question. Both Shastri and Tandon (1984) and Bodurtha and Courtadon (1984) look at divergences between option transactions prices and model prices. Shastri and Tandon price PHLX American options on spot using the Geske-Johnson technique, and using as model inputs contemporaneous spot rates and Eurocurrency interest rates. Volatility was estimated in two forms—as a historical moving average volatility calculated from the previous forty trading days and as the implied volatility of the nearest at-the-money option from the previous trading day. The use of implied volatility resulted in model prices more closely corresponding to market prices and also proved superior in generating profits through simulated trading.

Some systematic divergences relating either to time-to-maturity or exercise price were observed between the Shastri-Tandon model prices and market prices. Relative to the model, the market undervalued in-the-money options and overvalued out-of-the money options. In addition, long-maturity calls (puts) tended to be more overvalued (undervalued) than short-maturity calls (puts). To see if these divergences represented exploitable profit opportunities, the authors used the model in a trading simulation exercise that involved selling (buying) overpriced (underpriced) options along with delta-hedging in the spot market. They were able to generate excess profits by this procedure, if trades were assumed to take place at actual transaction prices, but not if trades were executed at posted bid and asked prices. The authors conclude that the market is efficient from the point of view of nonmembers of the exchange, but there may be profit opportunities from the point of view of floor traders who are able to deal at prices undercutting the posted bid–asked spread.

Similar tests are performed by Bodurtha and Courtadon (1984) on PHLX date from February 1983 to September 1983. Employing the Parkinson technique, Bodurtha and Courtadon (1986) price PHLX options using as inputs contemporaneous spot rates, the U.S. treasury bill rate, and the implied foreign interest rate calculated from the FX futures contract corresponding to option maturity. Their treatment of interest rates biases their results, because the interest parity theorem giving the relation between FX spot and forward rates normally does not hold for treasury bill rates.[8] Since the Eurodollar rate is typically at a spread of a percentage point above the treasury bill rate, their calculation implies an option value that is too large.[9] The authors choose as their volatility input an implied volatility chosen so as to minimize the sum of squared deviations between market prices and model prices for all put and call options traded on the particular currency the previous day. They find that, relative to the model, the market undervalues in-the-money and at-the-money options, but prices out-of-the-money options fairly.

Model pricing using alternative probability distributions has been performed by McCullough (1984) and Ghosh (1985). Ghosh compares the Pareto and beta models to the lognormal. Based on PHLX data, he finds that both the Pareto and beta perform on average significantly worse than the lognormal. Hence, neither of the former distributional assumptions appears to offer an attractive alternative for practical option pricing. Based on McCullough's results, however, the assumption of a nonnormal Levy stable distribution may fare considerably better. McCullough does not test his formulation against empirical data, but pricing tables show that out-of-the-money options are given greater value under the stable assumption than they are under the normal. This would seem to accord with the empirically observed market "overpricing" of out-of-the-money options as found by models derived with a normality assumption. Whether the *magnitude* of the stable model increase in value accords with the magnitude of market "overpricing" remains a subject for future empirical research.

Option Concepts and Partial Derivatives

Many of the problems associated with the practical task of managing an options book involve the concepts of delta, gamma, theta, and lambda. These variables are easily calculated from the explicit formulae given above for European options or approximated by one of the numerical techniques used for American options.

The option *delta* is the partial derivative of the option value with respect to the price of underlying asset. It expresses, in terms of value movement, the underlying asset equivalent to the option. Market-makers who wish to avoid FX risk and live off the bid–asked spread calculate the net delta of their total option portfolio and take an offsetting position in the spot, forward, or futures market, leaving their book "delta-neutral" (a net delta of zero). The value of their portfolio will not change with respect to a small change in the price of the underlying asset.

For such a procedure to be completely effective (risk-free), the option delta would have to be constant. If the option delta were constant over the entire range of the underlying asset, then both option pricing and risk management would be a simple affair. The price of a European call option on spot would be homogeneous of degree one in the spot price:

$$c = \frac{\delta c}{\delta S} S = (\text{delta}) \ S \ . \tag{11.43}$$

If such were the case, however, options would not be options. The limited liability feature of a long option position requires that the delta of an in-the-money option fall as the price of the underlying asset moves in the direction of the strike price, and rise as the price of the underlying asset moves away from the strike price. Hence, the option delta is not constant over varying levels of the price of the underlying asset. A delta-neutral position faces the risk that the delta will change. Such risk may be measured from the gamma.

The option *gamma* is the partial derivative of the option delta with respect to the price of the underlying asset. An equivalent definition is that the option gamma is the second partial derivative of the option *value* with respect to the price of the underlying asset. The gamma expresses the rate at which the delta moves. The risk of delta movement is, however, a function not only of the rate of delta movement (gamma) but also of the probability of changes in the underlying asset price. The probability of asset price changes is given by the currency volatility. The total risk is thus a function of both the volatility and the option gamma. One measure of this risk is

$$\frac{1}{2} v^2 S^2 \frac{\delta^2 c}{\delta S^2} = \frac{1}{2} (\text{volatility})^2 \ S^2 \ (\text{gamma}) \ . \tag{11.44}$$

The option *theta* is the partial derivative of the option value with respect to the passage of time. It represents the decay in the option value over time if the underlying asset price remains unchanged. Note that time flow is inverse to the term to maturity. For a European call on spot,

$$\text{theta} = \frac{-\delta c}{\delta T} \ . \tag{11.45}$$

The theta represents the income stream to an option writer.[10] Some have been puzzled by the concept of a futures-style option, wondering what is the advantage to the writer of such an option given that there is no up-front premium. The answer is simple: futures-style options have higher thetas than the equivalent ordinary options.

From equation 11.1, we see that the value of an FX call on spot (American or European) may be written in the form

$$c = [(r - r^*)/r] \text{ (delta) } (S)$$
$$+ (1/r) \frac{1}{2} \text{ (volatility)}^2 S^2 \text{ (gamma) } + (1/r)\text{(theta)}. \quad (11.46)$$

The value of an option may be expressed as the sum of its constant delta value [(delta)(S)] multiplied by the capitalized interest differential [(r − r*)/r], plus the capitalized value of its delta risk [(1/r) times equation 11.44, plus the capitalized value of its theta [(1/r) theta]. The last term is always negative for American options.

All of the pricing models dealt with in this chapter have relied on a known option volatility for their derivation. But, most option market practitioners believe volatilities are stochastic. In the absence of a correctly derived option pricing equation for stochastic volatility, practitioners bootstrap the existing models by using frequently updated volatility estimates. The risk they face from changing volatility is thus captured in the concept of the lambda. The option *lambda* is the partial derivative of the option value with respect to volatility. This partial derivative is usually large, representing the extreme sensitivity of option values to the underlying volatility. Some simulation results by Hull and White (1985) suggest that the risk associated with stochastic volatility is in some cases more important than the risk of changing deltas: a lambda hedge may be more important than a gamma hedge.

Altering option pricing models and procedures to account for stochastic volatility promises to be a fruitful area for future research.

Notes

1. See Gihman and Skorohod (1972).
2. See Cox and Ross (1976) for a general discussion of this point.
3. The source of theoretical divergence arises from stochastic interest rates, as explained in Cox, Ingersoll, and Ross (1981). Cornell and Reinganum (1981) and Park and Chen (1985) find little empirical divergence between FX forwards and futures prices.
4. See Cicchetti (1985).
5. See Cornell and Dietrich (1978), Ghosh (1985), McFarland, Pettit, and Sung (1982), So (1982), and Westerfield (1977) for empirical evidence on exchange rate data. Stable distributions, defined in Levy (1937), are called "stable Paretian" by Mandelbrot (1963). The normal distribution is itself one member of the class of stable distributions, so the alternative hypothesis focuses on the nonnormal members.

6. The exceptional case consists of the "maximally skewed" nonnormal stable distributions having the property that one of the tail probabilities falls to zero even more rapidly than in the case of a normal distribution. Details are supplied in Mc-Cullough (1984).

7. Purchasing power parity assumptions are criticized in Grabbe (1986, chapter 8). McCullough's derivation requires the further property that the forward rate be written as the ratio of expected purchasing powers, $F = E(1/P_2)/E(1/P_1)$. The alternative formulation that the forward rate is the expected value of the ratio of purchasing powers, $F = E[(P_1/P_2)]$, is not allowed.

8. See Grabbe (1986, chapter 4), for a discussion of the relevant interest rates for interest parity in the FX market.

9. This is most easily seen in the European case. Equations 11.10 and 11.12, which give the values of both European options on spot and European options on futures, show that if the forward rate F is held constant, but the domestic bond price B is increased (by using the lower t-bill rate), the values of the call and put rise. Bodurtha and Courtadon hold the futures price constant, since they use interest parity to calculate a foreign interest rate from the spot, forward, and t-bill rates.

10. The theta is *not* the same as the "time-value" of an option, as the latter term is used in the market. The time-value is simply the option premium minus the immediate exercise value of the option. As such, time-value is not a very useful concept.

References

Black, F., & M. Scholes, "The Pricing of Options and Corporate Liabilities," *Journal of Political Economy*, 81 (May 1973), 637–54.

Bodurtha, James, & Georges R. Courtadon, "Empirical Tests of the PHLX's Foreign Currency Options Market." Columbus: The Ohio State University, August 1984.

———, "Efficiency Tests of the Foreign Currency Options Market," *Journal of Finance*, 41 (March 1986), 151–62.

Brennen, Michael J., & Eduardo S. Schwartz, "The Valuation of American Put Options," *Journal of Finance*, 32 (May 1977), 449–62.

Cicchetti, Claude, "The Beauty of the Boston Option," *Euromoney*, February 1985.

Cornell, Bradford, & J. K. Dietrich, "The Efficiency of the Market for Foreign Exchange under Floating Exchange Rates," *Review of Economics and Statistics*, 60 (February 1978), 111–20.

Cornell, Bradford, & Marc C. Reinganum, "Forward and Futures Prices: Evidence from the Foreign Exchange Markets," *Journal of Finance*, 36 (December 1981), 1035–45.

Cox, J. C., J. E. Ingersoll & S. A. Ross, "The Relationship between Forward and Futures Prices," *Journal of Financial Economics*, 9 (December 1981), 321–46.

Cox, J. C., & Stephen A. Ross, "The Valuation of Options for Alternative Stochastic Processes," *Journal of Financial Economics*, 3 (January 1976), 145–66.

Cox, J. C., Stephen A. Ross & Mark Rubinstein, "Option Pricing: A Simplified Approach," *Journal of Financial Economics*, 7 (September 1979), 229–63.

Garman, Mark B., & Steven W. Kohlhagen, "Foreign Currency Option Values," *Journal of International Money and Finance*, 2 (December 1983), 231–37.

Geske, R., & H. Johnson, "The American Put Valued Analytically," *Journal of Finance*, 39 (December 1984), 1511–24.

Ghosh, Alo, *Three Essays on the Microeconomics of International Finance*. Ph.D. dissertation. Philadelphia: University of Pennsylvania, 1985.

Gihman, I. I., & A. V. Skorohod, *Stochastic Differential Equations*. Berlin: Springer-Verlag, 1972.

Grabbe, J. Orlin, *International Financial Markets*. New York: Elsevier Science, 1986.

———, "The Pricing of Call and Put Options on Foreign Exchange," *Journal of International Money and Finance*, 2 (December 1983), 239–53.

———, "The Pricing of First-Passage and Perpetual American Options." Philadelphia: Dept. of Finance, Wharton School, University of Pennsylvania, January 1985.

Hull, John, & Alan White, "Hedging the Risks from Writing Foreign Currency Options." Faculty of Administrative Science, York University, 1985.

Levy, Paul, *La Théorie de l'Addition des Variables Aléatoires*. Paris: Gauthier-Villars, 1937.

Mandelbrot, Benoit, "The Variation of Certain Speculative Prices," *Journal of Business*, 36 (October 1963), 394–419.

McCullough, J. Houston, "The Value of Options with Log-Stable Uncertainty." Columbus: The Ohio State University, November 1984.

McFarland, James W., Richardson Pettit & Sam K. Sung, "The Distribution of Foreign Exchange Price Changes: Trading Day Effects and Risk Measurement," *Journal of Finance*, 37 (June 1982), 693–715.

Park, Hun Y., & Andrew H. Chen, "Differences between Futures and Forward Prices: A Further Investigation of the Marking-to-Market Effects," *Journal of Futures Markets*, 5, no. 1 (1985), 77–88.

Parkinson, Michael, "Option Pricing: The American Put,"*Journal of Business*, 50 (January 1977), 21–36.

Priestly, Sarah, "Forward Forex Now Offers More Flexibility," *Euromoney Corporate Finance*, 15 (February 1986).

Schwartz, Eduardo S., "The Valuation of Warrants: Implementing a New Approach," *Journal of Financial Economics*, 4 (January 1977), 79–93.

Shastri, Kuldeep, & Kishore Tandon, "Arbitrage Tests of the Efficiency of the Foreign Currency Options Market," *Journal of International Money and Finance*, 4(1985), 455–68.

———, "Valuation of American Options on Foreign Currency." Graduate School of Business, University of Pittsburgh, March 1984.

So, Yuk-Chow (Jacky), "The Stable Paretian Distribution of Foreign Exchange Rate Movement, Nonstationarity and Martingale: An Empirical Analysis." Ph.D. dissertation. Columbus: The Ohio State University, 1982.

Vankudre, P., "Option Pricing in Discrete Time." Philadelphia: Dept. of Finance, Wharton School, University of Pennsylvania, 1984.

Westerfield, Janice Moulton, "An Examination of Foreign Exchange Risk under Fixed and Floating Rate Regimes," *Journal of International Economics*, 7(May 1977), 181–200.

12
Foreign Exchange Option Pricing with Log-Stable Uncertainty

J. Huston McCulloch

ABSTRACT

This chapter applies the stable Paretian option pricing formula developed by the author to the case of options on foreign exchange. The chapter assumes that the underlying uncertainty in terms of fundamental value is entirely negatively skewed and that any covariance between the value of the asset being priced and the numeraire asset takes the form of a log-additive term that contributed equally to the value of both assets. The results are a more robust model for pricing options on foreign exchange, assuming purchasing power parity to hold.

The value of an option on a foreign currency (or on any other speculative asset, for that matter) depends crucially on the shape of distribution of the underlying asset's future price. Two different distributions with the same mean and variance could give very different probabilities that the option will be in the money on its maturity date. Conditional on the information that the option does happen to be in the money on the maturity date, they could also differ substantially in terms of how far in the money the option is expected to lie.

In order to make the evaluation of such an option manageable, it is therefore necessary to make strong assumptions concerning the types of probability distribution that are likely to be encountered. Bachelier (1900, reprinted 1964) used the central limit theorem to restrict the option pricing problem to the normal (Gaussian) distribution. He observed that the unanticipated change in an asset's price that accumulates over the life of an option is the sum of the (more or less) independent and identically distributed (IID) random shocks that occur day by day and minute by minute. These shocks are themselves the cumulative outcome of the transactions of millions of agents.

The author is grateful to the Philadelphia Stock Exchange for financial support and to James Bodurtha for invaluable assistance.

In Bachelier's day, it was believed that only the normal distribution could plausibly result from an infinite sum of IID random variables, and his normality assumption (modified later to log-normality so as to keep the asset value positive) has dominated the option pricing literature ever since. Grabbe (1983) and Garman and Kohlhagen (1983) thus employ a lognormal assumption to evaluate options on foreign currencies, both employing a variation on the famous Black-Scholes (1973) log-stable option pricing formula.

However, Lévy (1937) derived a generalized central limit theorem stating that an infinite sum of IID random variables can, in fact, result in a distribution drawn from a broader class known as the *stable distributions*. The normal is just one special, limiting case of these distributions.

According to a recent survey of the modern international finance literature by Adler and Dumas (1983, p. 935), "The currently prevailing hypothesis . . . is that the distributions of the exchange rates belong to the stable, infinite variance class." Research by Moulton (1977), McFarland, Pettit, and Sung (1982), So (1982), and others indicates that the "characteristic exponent" α of these distributions lies in the range 1.3 to 1.8, well below its Gaussian value of 2.0. These findings indicate that the distribution of foreign exchange rates has much heavier tails and higher peaks, relative to the shoulders, than does the normal distribution. Using a normal model to evaluate foreign exchange options would therefore tend to give higher implied volatilities for out-of-the-money foreign exchange options than for at-the-money options. Indeed, Bodurtha and Courtadon (1985) find this to be the case empirically.

In this chapter, we show how the general log stable European option pricing model of McCulloch (1985) can be applied to the case of foreign exchange rates. As it happens, the foreign exchange rate case is one in which certain special assumptions necessary for the general stable option pricing formula are particularly natural.

Stable Distributions

The stable distributions $S(x, \alpha, \beta, c, \delta)$ are completely characterized by four parameters: the *characteristic exponent* α, $0 < \alpha \leq 2$; the *skewness parameter* β, $-1 \leq \beta \leq 1$; the *standard scale* c, $0 < c < \infty$; and the *location parameter* δ, $-\infty < \delta < \infty$.

The characteristic exponent is an indicator of how leptokurtic, or heavy-tailed, the distribution is. Lower α means heavier tails and higher mode relative to the shoulders of the distribution. When $\alpha = 2$, its maximum permissible value, the normal distribution results. Thus, *all* the other stable distributions are heavier tailed than the normal.

The skewness parameter β is 0 when the distribution is symmetrical, positive when the distribution is skewed to the right, and negative when the distribution is skewed to the left.[1] As α approaches 2, β loses its effect and the distribution becomes symmetrical regardless of β.

The location parameter δ merely shifts the distribution left or right, and the scale parameter c expands or contracts the distribution about δ in proportion to c. Thus, if x has a stable distribution with parameters $(\alpha, \beta, c, \delta)$, the normalized variate $z = (x - \delta)/c$ will have a standardized stable distribution with parameters $(\alpha, \beta, 1, 0)$. In the Gaussian case, $\alpha = 2$, c^2 is half the variance. When $\alpha < 2$, the population variance is infinite, but c may still be used to measure scale in place of the familiar, but undefined standard deviation.

For $\alpha > 1$, δ is the mean of the distribution. For $\alpha \leqq 1$, the mean does not exist, but δ still serves as an index of location. In the symmetrical cases when $\beta = 0$, it equals the distribution's median for all permissible α values.

When $\alpha < 2$, one or both extreme tails of a stable distribution behave like a Pareto distribution. Thus, the non-Gaussian stable distributions are sometimes referred to as the *Paretian stable distributions*.

The time path of a continuous time process with IID Paretian stable increments is full of discontinuities (see McCulloch, 1978). This means that the famous arbitrage argument of Black and Scholes (1973) cannot be adapted to the option pricing problem under log-stable uncertainty. In order to evaluate these options, we must therefore go back to the drawing board and rebuild a model of foreign exchange rate determination and option pricing from scratch.

A Model of Spot and Forward Exchange Rates

Let P_1 and P_2 be the price levels in countries *1* and *2*, respectively, at future time *T*. Under purchasing power parity,[2] the exchange rate giving the value of one unit of currency *2* in terms of currency *1* at time *T* may be expressed as the ratio of the price levels:

$$X = \frac{P_1}{P_2}, \tag{12.1}$$

or, equivalently, as the ratio of the purchasing powers of the two currencies:

$$X = \frac{1/P_2}{1/P_1}. \tag{12.2}$$

If $\log P_1$ and $\log P_2$ are both stable with a common exponent α and skewness parameters β_1 and β_2 [so that $\log(1/P_2) = -\log P_2$ has parameter $-\beta_2$], then $\log X$ will also be stable, with the same exponent α and with skewness parameter β intermediate between β_1 and $-\beta_2$.[3]

Price level uncertainty itself is generally *positively* skewed. Astronomical inflations are very easily arranged, simply by throwing the printing presses into high gear, and this policy has a certain fiscal appeal to it. Comparable deflations would be fiscally intolerable, and are in practice unheard of. It is therefore reasonable to assume that $\log P_1$ and $\log P_2$ are both *maximally positively skewed;* that is, $\beta_1 = \beta_2 = +1$. This assumption still allows $\log X$ to have any intermediate value of β, since, as noted above, its skewness parameter must lie between that of $\log P_1$ ($+1$) and that of $-\log P_2$ (-1). Precisely where it lies in this range will depend on the relative uncertainties of the two price levels and on any interactions that may be present.

Under this maximal skewness assumption for the P_i's, the upper Paretian tail of $\log X$ will come entirely from P_1. In other words, the occurrence of an extraordinarily high exchange rate will more likely be due to a collapse in the value of the numeraire currency in country *1* than to a drastic deflation in country 2. Conversely, the lower Paretian tail of $\log X$ will come entirely from P_2. This means that the occurrence of an extraordinarily low exchange rate will more likely be due to an unexpected inflation in country *2* than to an unexpected deflation in country *1*.

It can be shown that if $\log X$ is stable, the lower Paretian tail of $\log X$ will give the distribution of X a mode (with density approaching infinity) at 0, as well as a second mode (unless its scale c is quite large) near $\exp(E \log X)$. Thus, log-stable distributions achieve the bimodality sought by Krasker (1980), all in terms of a *single* story about the underlying economic process. If currency 2 is depreciating rapidly in terms of purchasing power, the mode near 0 corresponding to continuing collapse will pull its expected future purchasing power down substantially below the upper mode corresponding to the off chance of stabilization.

We assume that in each country, inflation has two independent components: a country-specific component (representing the idiosyncrasies of national monetary policy) and an international component (representing the herd instincts of central bankers). Formally,

$$\log P_1 = u_1 + u_3 \tag{12.3}$$

and

$$\log P_2 = u_2 + u_3, \tag{12.4}$$

where u_i is independent and stably distributed with parameters (α, $+1$, c_i,

δ_i), for $i = 1, 2, 3$. We let α, β, c, and δ be the four parameters of the log exchange rate

$$\log X = u_1 - u_2. \tag{12.5}$$

The parameters β, c, and δ can be computed from α and the c_i and δ_i, using formulae in McCulloch (1985). These can be solved for c_1 and c_2 as follows:

$$c_1 = \left(\frac{1 + \beta}{2}\right)^{1/\alpha} c, \tag{12.6}$$

$$c_2 = \left(\frac{1 - \beta}{2}\right)^{1/\alpha} c. \tag{12.7}$$

Even though inflation is correlated across countries (in the sense of having a common international component), we assume that it is uncorrelated with real variables and, therefore, involves no systematic risk that is priced by the market. In this case, the forward exchange rate must set the expected profit (in terms of purchasing power) from forward speculation equal to zero. This implies:[4]

$$F = \frac{E(1/P_2)}{E(1/P_1)}. \tag{12.8}$$

Note that this expression is by no means equivalent to $E(P_1/P_2)$ or $E(P_1)/E(P_2)$. The forward exchange rate is the ratio of expected purchasing powers, not the expected ratio of purchasing powers or the ratio of expected price levels.

For most values of β, the expectation of a log-stable variate is infinite. The one exception is the case of $\beta = -1$, which is precisely the case we encounter in equation 12.8 above. In this case, there is a simple formula for the expectation of the exponential of a stable variate, recently discovered by the mathematician V. M. Zolotarev. Using this formula, in conjunction with the formulae linking β, c, and δ of log X to the underlying c_i and δ_i, gives

$$F = e^{\delta_1 - \delta_2 + (c_1{}^\alpha - c_2{}^\alpha)\,\sec(\pi\alpha/2)} \tag{12.9}$$
$$= e^{\delta + \beta \cdot c^\alpha\,\sec(\pi\alpha/2)}$$

We assume that α, β, c, and F are observable, but that δ, c_i, and δ_i are not directly observable. Nevertheless, it turns out that we are able to infer all we need to know about these unobservable parameters from the observed ones, using equations 12.6, 12.7, and 12.9.

Note that equation 12.9 implies that for arbitrary β and for $\alpha > 1$ (so that the expectations in question exist),

$$E \log X - c^\alpha |\sec(\pi\alpha/2)| \leq \log F \leq E \log X + c^\alpha |\sec(\pi\alpha/2)|. \quad (12.10)$$

when $\alpha = 2$, equation 12.10 becomes

$$E \log X - \sigma^2/2 \leq \log F \leq E \log X + \sigma^2/2, \quad (12.11)$$

since $\sigma^2 = 2c^2$. Under log-normality, expression 12.11 is equivalent to Boyer's (1977) inequality:

$$1/E(1/X) \leq F \leq EX. \quad (12.12)$$

Inequalities 12.11 and, therefore, 12.12 do not hold for completely general joint lognormal distributions, but are ensured here by the assumption that international inflation uncertainty (u_3) is additive with a unit coefficient to both $\log P_1$ and $\log P_2$. In the general lognormal case, it can be shown (see McCulloch, 1980) that F may lie arbitrarily far above EX or below $1/E(1/X)$, even holding σ constant. The general bivariate log-stable case is much richer in possibilities than is the bivariate log-stable case, so we do not attempt to generalize expression 12.1 here. Inequality 12.12 itself is vacuously true in the log-stable case with $\alpha < 2$ and $|\beta| < 1$, since then $EX = E(1/X) = \infty$.

Option Pricing

Let C be the value, in terms of units of currency *1* to be delivered unconditionally at time *O*, of a European call option on one unit of currency *2* to be exercised at time T (but not before) with striking price X_0. Let r_1 be the default-free interest rate on currency-*1*–denominated loans with maturity T. A payment of C units of currency *1* today (time *0*) is thus equivalent to an unconditional payment of $Ce^{r_1 T}$ units at time T.

If $X > X_0$, the profit on the call option will be $X - X_0 - Ce^{r_1 T}$ units of currency *1*. If $X < X_0$, the profit will be $-Ce^{r_1 T}$. Again assuming that inflation has no systematic risk, the expected profit, measured in purchasing power, of a position in the option must be zero. Letting $P(P_1, P_2)$ represent any joint probability distribution for the two price levels (for which the relevant expectations exist), this condition can be stated

$$\int_{X>X_O} \frac{X - X_O}{P_1} dP(P_1, P_2) - Ce^{r_1T} \int_{\text{all }X} \frac{1}{P_1} dP(P_1, P_2) = 0. \quad (12.13)$$

Solving for the call value C,

$$C = e^{-r_1T} \left[\frac{F}{E(1/P_2)} \int_{X>X_0} \frac{1}{P_2} dP(P_1, P_2) \right.$$
$$\left. - \frac{X_0}{E(1/P_1)} \int_{X>X_0} \frac{1}{P_1} dP(P_1, P_2) \right]. \quad (12.14)$$

In order to apply equation 10.14 to the special stable case defined by equations 12.3 and 12.4, we first define $S(z)$ and $s(z)$ to be the standard maximally positively skewed stable distribution and density functions; that is, $S(z) = S(z; \alpha, +1, 1, 0)$ and $s(z) = S'(z)$. It can then be shown[5] that equation 12.14 becomes

$$C = Fe^{-r_1T + c_2^\alpha \sec(\pi\alpha/2)} I_1 - X_0 e^{-r_1T + c_1^\alpha \sec(\pi\alpha/2)} I_2, \quad (12.15)$$

where

$$I_1 = \int_{-\infty}^{\infty} e^{-c_1z} s(z) \left\{ 1 - S\left[\frac{c_2z - \log \dfrac{F}{X_0} + \beta c^\alpha \sec(\pi\alpha/2)}{c_1} \right] \right\} dz \quad (12.16)$$

and

$$I_2 = \int_{-\infty}^{\infty} e^{-c_1z} s(z) S\left[\frac{c_1z - \log \dfrac{F}{X_0} + \beta c^\alpha \sec(\pi\alpha/2)}{c_2} \right] dz \quad (12.17)$$

Equation 12.15 gives the value of the call option as a function of the contractual exercise price X_0, the market observations F and r_1, and the three stable distribution parameters α, β, and c. (Recall that c_1 and c_2 may be calculated from α, β, and c by means of equations 12.6 and 12.7.) Note that we do not actually need to know δ, since all we need to know about it is contained in F through 12.9. Note also that the international component of inflation, u_3, completely drops out. It can be shown (McCulloch, 1980) that in the normal case $\alpha = 2$, equation 12.14 leads to Grabbe's and Garman and

Kohlhagen's variant of the Black-Scholes formula and that equation 12.15 is therefore generally equivalent to it with $\alpha = 2$, regardless of the value of β we feed into it.

If the forward exchange rate F happens to be unobserved, we may use the spot exchange rate S to construct a proxy for it by means of the covered interest arbitrage formula

$$F = S\, e^{(r_2 - r_1)T}, \tag{12.18}$$

where r_2 is the foreign (country 2) interest rate on default-free loans of maturity T. Furthermore, the value P of a European put option giving one the right to sell one unit of currency 2 at striking price X_0 may be evaluated using equation 12.15, along with the put–call arbitrage condition

$$P = C + (X_0 - F)\, e^{-r_1 T}. \tag{12.19}$$

Numerical Option Values

Table 12–1 through 12–4 give the interest-incremented value, in terms of currency *1*, of an option on an amount of currency *2* equal in value (at the forward price) to 100 units of currency *1*.[6] For example, if currency *1* is the dollar and currency *2* is the mark, the tables give the value, in dollars and cents to be paid at the maturity of the option, of an option on $100 worth of marks. This value is a function solely of X_0/F and the three distribution parameters; it does not further depend at all on r_1, r_2, X_0, or F.

Table 12–1 holds α and β fixed at 1.5 and 0.0, while c and X_0/F vary. C declines as X_0 increases relative to F, and increases with c. Note that a call (or put) on $1 worth of marks at fraction $\dfrac{X_0}{F}$ of the forward dollar price of marks is equivalent to a put (or call) on DM $\dfrac{X_0}{F}$ worth of dollars at $\dfrac{F}{X_0}$ times the forward DM price of dollars, and that this constrains the values in table 12–1. With $c = 0.10$, for example, a call on $100 worth of marks at $X_0/F = .5$ is worth $50.240 (to be paid at maturity). Formula 12.19 implies that a put on $100 worth of marks at half the forward price of marks is worth $0.240, paid on maturity. This is the same option as a call on $50 at double the forward price of dollars. A call on $100 at double the forward price is therefore worth $0.480, and a call on 100 DM worth of dollars at double the forward price is worth about 0.480 DM. Since $\log X$ and $\log 1/X$ have the same α and c, but opposite β (here zero), a call on $100 worth of marks at $X_0/F = 2.0$ should also be worth $0.480, and we see that it is, within rounding error. Values of $X_0/F < 1$ are therefore redundant. (With $\beta \neq 0$, we would of course have to reverse its sign in performing this calculation.)

Table 12–1
Value of 100 $Ce^{r_1 T}/F$ When $\alpha = 1.5$ and $\beta = 0.0$

	X_0/F			
c	*0.5*	*1.0*	*1.1*	*2.0*
0.01	50.007	0.787	0.079	0.014
0.03	50.038	2.240	0.458	0.074
0.10	50.240	6.784	3.466	0.481
0.30	51.704	17.694	14.064	3.408
1.00	64.131	45.642	43.065	28.262

Tables 12–2 through 12–4 hold c fixed at 0.1 and allow α and β to vary for three values of X_0/F representing "at the money" (in terms of the forward price, not the spot price) with $X_0/F = 1.0$, "out of the money" but still on the shoulder of the distribution with $X_0/F = 1.1$, and "far out of the money" with $X_0/F = 2.0$.

In all three tables, we see that the value of the option increases briskly from its Black-Scholes-Grabbe value as α declines from 2.0. When $\alpha = 2$, β has no effect on the option value, even though the story in terms of the inflation uncertainty of the two currencies is changing, and even though the position of the forward price is changing relative to $E \log X$. (The values for $\alpha = 2.0$ reported here were, as a check, computed independently by the same numerical procedure we used to obtain the sub-Gaussian values, even though they are theoretically equivalent to Garman and Kohlhagen's and Grabbe's variant of the Black-Scholes formula.)

When the option is at the (forward) money as in table 12–2, we see that for $\alpha < 2.0$, β has a symmetrical effect on the value of the option, and that its effect is slightly U-shaped.

When the option is sufficiently out of the money, we see in tables 12–3 and 12–4 that the value of the call option tends to increase with β with only a few exceptions when $X_0/F = 1.1$.

The importance of small deviations from normality is readily apparent from these tables. Note in table 12–1 that with $c = 0.01$ and $X_0/F = 2.0$, the call option on \$100 worth of foreign currency is still worth \$0.014 when $\alpha = 1.5$ and $\beta = 0$. In this case, the log forward price is about 69.3 scales below the log of the striking price. When $\alpha = 2.0$, a c of 69.3 is equivalent to about 49.0 standard deviations. In this case, the Black-Scholes option value is approximately $\$3.7 \times 10^{-528}$.[7] If the true α is even a little less than 2.0, we would therefore expect the Black-Scholes formula and its variants to greatly underestimate the value of options with a low probability of exercise. In equation 12.15, we derive a relatively simple limiting value for such options.

Table 12–2
Value of 100 $Ce^{r_1 T}/F$ When $c = 0.1$ and $X_0/F = 1.0$

			β		
α	-1.0	-0.5	0.0	0.5	1.0
2.0	5.637	5.637	5.637	5.637	5.637
1.8	6.029	5.993	5.981	5.993	6.029
1.6	6.670	6.523	6.469	6.523	6.670
1.4	7.648	7.300	7.157	7.300	7.648
1.2	9.115	8.455	8.137	8.455	9.115
1.0	11.319	10.200	9.558	10.200	11.319
0.8	14.685	12.893	11.666	12.893	14.685

Table 12–3
Value of 100 $Ce^{r_1 T}/F$ When $c = 0.1$ and $X_0/F = 1.1$

			β		
α	-1.0	-0.5	0.0	0.5	1.0
2.0	2.211	2.211	2.211	2.211	2.211
1.8	2.271	2.423	2.590	2.764	2.944
1.6	2.499	2.772	3.123	3.510	3.902
1.4	2.985	3.303	3.870	4.530	5.175
1.2	3.912	4.116	4.943	5.957	6.924
1.0	5.605	5.391	6.497	8.002	9.410
0.8	8.596	7.516	8.803	11.019	13.067

Table 12–4
Value of 100 $Ce^{r_1 T}/F$ When $c = 0.1$ and $X_0/F = 2.0$

			β		
α	-1.0	-0.5	0.0	0.5	1.0
2.0	0.000	0.000	0.000	0.000	0.000
1.8	0.000	0.055	0.110	0.165	0.220
1.6	0.000	0.160	0.319	0.477	0.634
1.4	0.000	0.351	0.695	1.032	1.361
1.2	0.000	0.691	1.354	1.991	2.604
1.0	0.000	1.287	2.488	3.619	4.689
0.8	0.000	2.333	4.438	6.372	8.164

Implicit Parameter Values

Formula 12.2 gives the value of a call option as a function of three distribution parameters (α, β, and c) that cannot be directly observed. If we are willing to assume that the distribution of the log of the underlying asset price is symmetric, so that $\beta = 0$, we are still left with two unobserved parameters.

In this case, if we observe the market value of an option at one striking price, we can solve 12.20 implicitly to obtain an implicit scale $\hat{c}$ for any given value of α. In principle, the market price of a second option at a different striking price will define a second schedule of implicit scale parameters. The intersection of the two schedules gives implicit parameter values ($\hat{\alpha}$, $\hat{c}$) that explain these two option prices. If the perceived asset distribution is truly log-symmetric stable, and if the market is really using our formula, the implicit parameter schedule for any third option should pass through the same point ($\hat{\alpha}$, $\hat{c}$).

It would be far beyond the scope of this chapter to provide definitive empirical implicit stable parameter values for actual options. However, for the sake of illustration only, we will show how this might be done.

On September 17, 1984, call options on 100 West German marks were selling at $0.85 with a striking price of $33.00, and at $.03 with a striking price of $39.00.[8] On the same day, the futures price (which for present purposes is an adequate proxy for a pure forward price) for one December DM was $0.3328, so that the X_0/F ratios were 0.9916 and 1.1719, respectively. The bid-asked mean discount rate on U.S. t-bills maturing in mid-December was 10.37 percent, which is equivalent to a continuously compounded, 365-day annual rate of 10.65 percent. The interest-incremented call prices per $100 (forward) worth of DM were therefore $2.623 and $0.093, respectively, assuming $T = 0.25$ year.

These are American options that can be exercised before final maturity rather than pure European options. Nevertheless, the fact that the DM was at a forward premium (the spot price was only $.3234) makes early exercise on an out-of-the-money or at-the-money call option unlikely. In any event, the American feature is probably adding only a small amount to the value of the option.

Figure 12–1 plots implicit parameter schedules for the two options as if they really were European options, under the maintained assumption $\beta = 0$. For each option, three lines are plotted: the center one is based on the quoted option price and the other two on the quoted price plus or minus $.005, the rounding error in the quotations.

At $\alpha = 2.0$, the near-the-money option has an implicit scale of 0.0583, with a range of 0.0566 to 0.0599. The out-of-the-money option has an implicit scale of 0.0388, with a range of 0.0385 to 0.0390. Clearly, the two option prices are inconsistent with a normal distribution.

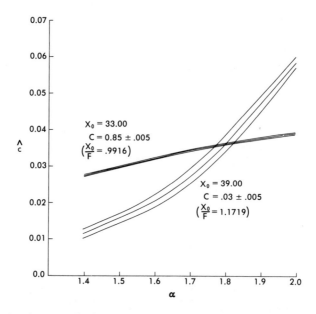

Implicit scale $\hat{c}$ is a function of α for two DM call options with the same maturity but different striking prices X_0. On this date, $F = 33.28\text{¢/DM}$, $S = 32.34\text{¢/DM}$, and $r_1 = 10.65$ percent. T is approximately 0.25 year. Parameter values of $\hat{\alpha} = 1.797$ (1.766–1.832) and $c = 0.0355$ (0.0345–0.0365) are consistent with the two options' market values, assuming $\beta = 0.0$.

Figure 12–1. Option Price

The two central lines intersect at $\hat{\alpha} = 1.797$ and $\hat{c} = 0.0355$. The rounding error on the two options accommodates a range of (1.766, 1.832) for $\hat{\alpha}$ and (0.0345, 0.0365) for $\hat{c}$.

If asymmetry is not assumed away, three option values would be necessary to identify α, β, and c. For any maintained value of β, $\hat{c}$ could be plotted as a function of β as above, for all three option values. Except at the true values of α, the three lines would not intersect at a single point. This determination would be most precise if the third option were well out on the tail opposite the second option.[9]

Conclusion

This chapter applies the stable option pricing formula developed in McCulloch (1985) to the special case of options on foreign exchange. In the general case, we were forced to make two special and somewhat awkward assumptions:

First, we had to assume that the underlying uncertainty, in terms of fundamental value (here purchasing power, but in general marginal utility), is entirely negatively skewed, that is, has skewness parameter $\beta = -1$. This assumption is necessary in order to make the expectations whose ratios define the forward price, as well as the integrals appearing in the option pricing formula, finite.

Second, we had to assume that any covariation between the value of the asset being priced and the numeraire asset (here currencies 2 and 1, respectively) took the form of a log-additive term u_3 that contributed *equally* to the value of both assets. Generally, we would want such a common term to be allowed to contribute different amounts of uncertainty to the two asset values. Unfortunately, the neat cancellation that occurs when the contributions are equal does not seem to take place in this more general case.

Although these special assumptions are admittedly a bit strained in the general case, they are actually quite natural in the foreign exchange rate case treated in the present chapter.

As noted in the text, the first assumption follows easily in the foreign exchange context from the observation that inflation uncertainty is highly positively skewed, in combination with a purchasing power parity theory about exchange rate determination. Indeed, the virtual impossibility of a hyperdeflation, coupled with the great facility of a hyperinflation, makes $+1$ the only natural value for inflation uncertainty, and, therefore, -1 the natural value for purchasing power uncertainty.

As for the second assumption, the tendency for central bankers to keep one eye on exchange rate stability and the other eye on domestic targets implies that individual countries will tend to import a common "global inflation" factor to which they add country-specific disturbances. Boyer (1977), in fact, bases his treatment of forward exchange rates on just such an assumption.

Thus, these two special assumptions, instead of entering through the back door as they do in the general case, are perfectly natural, and, in fact, almost compelling, in the foreign exchange context.

Notes

1. To be precise, we define the stable distributions in terms of their log-characteristic functions:

$$\psi(t) = \log E(e^{ixt})$$

$$= \begin{cases} i\delta t - |ct|^\alpha \left[1 - i\beta \, \text{sign}(t) \tan \dfrac{\pi\alpha}{2} \right], & \alpha \neq 1 \\[2em] i\delta t - |ct| \left[1 + i\beta \dfrac{2}{\pi} \, \text{sign}(t) \log|t| \right], & \alpha = 1. \end{cases}$$

See McCulloch [16] for discussion of alternative parameterizations and a partial survey of estimation techniques.

2. Purchasing power parity in terms of general price indices in fact performs very poorly, particularly on a short-run basis. (See, for example, Adler & Lehmann, 1983.) It is nevertheless useful for present purposes.

3. The precise mathematical relationships are presented in McCulloch (1985) and so are omitted here. Currency *1 (2)* corresponds to asset A_1 (A_2) in that model; marginal utilities have been replaced by purchasing powers in the present context.

4. Fama and Farber (1979, p. 647) add an adjustment for systematic risk to equation 12.3, but we make no attempt to incorporate this here. Essentially, we have a one-good economy in which the price levels are merely lottery drawings that have no correlation with any real uncertainty in the economy, even though they are correlated across countries. The currencies serve no real function, but there are nevertheless shadow prices at which excess demands for forward contracts and options on them are zero.

5. See McCulloch (1985) for details. Slightly modified formulae are necessary for the special cases $\alpha = 1$ and $|\beta| = 1$.

6. See McCulloch (1985) for details of computations. Option values are tabulated more extensively in McCulloch (1984).

7. Using an approximation for the limiting value of the Black-Scholes option formula developed in McCulloch (1985, footnote 19).

8. Philadelphia Exchange Foreign Currency Options, quoted in *Wall Street Journal*, September 18, 1984.

9. For this purpose, an out-of-the money put option may give better computational results than an in-the-money call.

References

Adler, Michael, & Bernard Dumas. "International Portfolio Choice and Corporation Finance: A Synthesis." *Journal of Finance* 38 (1983), 925–84.

Adler, Michael, & Bruce Lehmann. "Deviations from Purchasing Power Parity in the Long Run." *Journal of Finance* 38 (1983), 1471–87.

L. Bachelier. "The Theory of Speculation." In Paul H. Cootner (ed.), *The Random Character of Stock Market Prices*, pp. 497–500. Cambridge, Mass.: MIT Press, 1964. (Original article published in French, 1900.)

Black, Fischer, & Myron Scholes. "The Pricing of Options and Corporate Liabilities." *Journal of Political Economy* 8 (1973), 637–54.

Bodurtha, James N., Jr., & George R. Courtadon. "Tests of the American Option Pricing Model on the Foreign Currency Options Markets." Working paper. Columbus: The Ohio State University; and New York: New York University, 1985.

Russell S. Boyer. "The Relation between the Forward Exchange Rate and the Expected Future Spot Rate." *Intermountain Economic Review* 8 (1977), 14–21.

Fama, Eugene F., & André Farber. "Money, Bonds, and Foreign Exchange." *American Economic Review* 69 (1979), 639–49.

Garman, Mark B., & Steven W. Kohlhagen. "Foreign Currency Option Values." *Journal of International Business and Finance* 2 (1983), 231–37.

J. Orlin Grabbe. "The Pricing of Call and Put Options on Foreign Exchange." *Journal of International Money and Finance* 2 (1983), 239–53.

William S. Krasker. "The 'Peso Problem' in Testing the Efficiency of Forward Exchange Markets." *Journal of Monetary Economics* 6 (1980), 269–76.

Paul Lévy. *La Théorie de l' Addition des Variables Aléatoires.* Paris: Gauthier-Villars, 1937.

J. Huston McCulloch. "Continuous Time Processes with Stable Increments." *Journal of Business* 51 (1978), 601–19.

———. "Foreign Exchange Rate Determination in Efficient Markets under Purchasing Power Parity with Log-Normal Uncertainty, with Empirical Reference to the German Hyperinflation." Working paper. Columbus: The Ohio State University, 1980.

———. "Stable Option Tables." Working paper. Columbus: The Ohio State University, 1984.

———. "The Value of European Options with Log-Stable Uncertainty." Working paper. Columbus: The Ohio State University, July 1985.

———. "Simple Consistent Estimators of Stable Distribution Parameters." *Communications in Statistics,* in press.

McFarland, James W., R. Richardson Pettit, & Sam K. Sung. "The Distribution of Foreign Exchange Price Changes: Trading Day Effects and Risk Measurement. *Journal of Finance* 37 (1982), 693–715.

Moulton, Janice, (formerly Westerfield). "An Examination of Foreign Exchange Risk under Fixed and Floating Rate Regimes." *Journal of International Economics* 7 (1977), 181–200.

So, Yuk-Chow (Jacky). "The Stable Paretian Distribution of Foreign Exchange Rate Movement, Nonstationarity and Martingale: An Empirical Analysis." Unpublished Ph.D. dissertation. Columbus: The Ohio State University, 1982.

13

Future Contract Delivery and Volatility of Spot Exchange Rates

Mark R. Eaker
Dwight M. Grant

ABSTRACT

Empirical evidence is provided which indicates that currency futures market activity contributes to the volatility of the cash or spot foreign exchange market. The increased volatility is related to the delivery procedures of the futures market and consequently occurs on specific days.

The past ten years have seen increases in the volatility of exchange rate changes and in the development and use of new instruments with which to take foreign exchange positions. A traditional or standard interpretation of the latter phenomenon is that financial innovation has occurred to meet the changing needs created by a more volatile economic environment. Consequently, futures and options markets have developed to meet the increased need for hedging instruments on the part of firms.

A second and partially opposing view is that the development of alternative foreign exchange instruments has contributed to the volatility in the interbank market for foreign exchange. This view seems to be held by people in the trade and the press as indicated by the following quotes from articles in the *Wall Street Journal* which suggest that the futures market has a significant impact on the cash or interbank market:

> New currency instruments, such as options and futures, often trigger stampedes of buying and selling in the main foreign exchange markets, and the derivative markets are used not only by speculators but also by companies seeking to protect themselves from currency swings.[1]

The authors appreciate the comments of Henry Goldstein and the research assistance of Felicia Marston.

But there were other factors supporting the dollar as well, . . . and speculative buying on the International Monetary Market division of the Chicago
Mercantile Exchange.[2]

The *Wall Street Journal* articles describe no explicit transmission mechanism by which futures and options activities might have an impact on the
spot market. Two alternatives come to mind, one involving information processing and the other one generating trading activity. As the two are described
below, it will become apparent that the distinction between them is not clear-
cut. This chapter attempts to isolate and test the impact of the second alternative, futures trading activity which generates volume in the cash market.

The information processing view links the futures market to the spot
market through the market response to new information. It hypothesizes that
information is processed and embedded in prices more quickly in the futures
market than the spot market, which then reacts to futures market price
changes. This is a difficult position to support. The size of the spot market
dwarfs the futures market. Moreover, the spot market is a global market with
trading essentially twenty four hours a day. The larger, less restricted market
should be the more efficient and, to the extent that price changes in one
market lead those in the other, the lead market should be the interbank
market.

In a test of the information processing view, Clifton (1985) examined the
relationship between volume on the futures market and the range between
high and low prices on the interbank market. He found them to be highly
correlated although not causally related. Clifton's article offers some important insights into the difficulty of testing the information theory and to the
integration of the two markets.

The major weakness of Clifton's test is that the trading strategy he believes is responsible for the futures market activity is likely to have the same
impact in the interbank market. As Clifton points out, the same banks that
are active in the interbank market are active on the International Monetary
Market (IMM). Trading strategies used by participants in one market are the
same as those used by participants in the other. New information, whether it
is based on technical factors or fundamental economics, is going to be available simultaneously to traders in both markets. Factors leading to a decline
or increase in futures prices will at the same time lead to a decline or increase
in forward prices. Because the futures and forward markets are physically
distinct, there is the likelihood of small differentials arising, but, as Clifton
argues, those are eliminated by arbitrage across the two markets.

Proponents of the information view need to establish theoretically why
prices on the futures market would move before (or after) prices on the forward market and the length of time over which a price differential would
exist. Empirical tests would then determine if the differential did exist by
looking at transactional data on the two markets.

Clifton's analysis, for example, does not establish a convincing theoretical link. To be fair to Clifton, his empirical results emphasize correlation and not causality, indicating that he does not interpret his results to support the information view. Those results suggest that the two markets generally function as one market. Although Clifton compares volume on one market with price fluctuations on the other, it is likely that volume and price fluctuations on both markets are highly correlated. What Clifton's results demonstrate is that price volatility and volume are correlated. When volume is large on the futures market, the same factors make it large on the interbank market; when prices fluctuate greatly on the interbank market, the same factors make them fluctuate greatly on the futures market.

An alternative view of the impact on the spot market is that trading activities on the futures market lead to transactions on the spot market. If the resulting spot market transactions are sufficiently large and concentrated, the increased volume could contribute to increased price volatility. This research (Rogalski, 1978; Tauchen & Pitts, 1983) examines one potential case of this volume–price relationship: the impact of futures market delivery upon cash market price volatility. The next section describes the motives of users of futures contracts and argues that there is no apparent reason to expect their futures activities to affect the cash market on a daily basis. However, institutional factors suggest a transaction-related impact near delivery date. The following section describes test hypotheses, data, and results. The final section offers conclusions.

Futures Market Transactions

Participants in the futures market can be categorized as hedgers, speculators, and arbitrageurs. This is similar to the taxonomy used to describe participants in the interbank forward market. It serves the same purpose and suffers from the same shortcoming. The categories are a useful way to describe transactions, but, in fact, the same individuals will engage in more than one activity. Consequently, it is misleading to think of participants who perform only one function, although class *B* arbitrageurs on the futures markets are in fact restricted to a single activity. The question that needs to be addressed is whether any of these activities on the futures market lead to the volume effect on the spot market.

Hedging consists of taking foreign exchange positions for the purpose of reducing the volatility of wealth in future periods. In most cases, a hedger will take an offsetting position in a futures contract that matches the currency and maturity of an existing commercial exposure. At maturity, the proceeds of the commercial transaction can be used to meet the future obligation, or both positions can be reversed. In either case, the use of the futures contract hedge does not create a transaction on the spot market.

Speculation differs from hedging in that the speculator does not have an existing position. Both speculators and hedgers are motivated by differences in the expected future spot price and the current future price for the same maturity. Although risk reduction was the hedgers' goal, it is not the speculator's. Speculation involves taking either a long or short position in the futures contract and then closing it out at a subsequent date. Although it is possible for a speculator to hold the futures position until maturity and reverse the position on the spot market, it is not necessary. In addition, it would entail a different type of transaction which might be more costly to conduct. The expected pattern would be for the buyer (seller) of a futures position to sell (buy) an offsetting contract. The entire speculative transaction would occur on the futures market without spillover on the spot market. It is important to understand that the argument presented here focuses on the transaction aspect of speculation and not the information-processing aspect. Speculation on the futures market can be accomplished without a related transaction on the cash market.

The final type of transaction is arbitrage. The usual form of arbitrage described in foreign exchange discussions is interest arbitrage, but that is essentially an interbank market activity (Eaker, 1980). Arbitrage activities on the futures markets involve arbitraging price differentials between the futures market and the interbank forward market. Such activities, known as *class B arbitrage,* are tightly regulated. A class B arbitrageur can trade for no other purpose and must deal exclusively with one bank (Goldstein, 1983). Much of this activity is now being undertaken directly by major banks that have acquired seats on the IMM (Clifton, 1985).

Arbitrage of this nature involves monitoring the price relationship between futures and forwards. When contracts for the same maturity move out of equilibrium, arbitrageurs buy low and sell high, earning the differential as a riskless reward for monitoring. There is nothing in the set of arbitrage transactions itself that would lead to increased price volatility in the interbank market. In fact, arbitrage insures that information is impounded in prices in the two markets simultaneously or nearly so. However, there is a distinction between the futures and forward markets that might lead to increased activity in the spot market on the delivery date for each futures contract.

Futures contracts are "mark-to-market" arrangements which require position holders to post margin deposits as losses occur and allow them to remove profits as they arise. That is not true for the interbank market in which losses and profits are realized at maturity. When arbitrageurs take simultaneous positions in forwards and futures, they have locked in their arbitrage profit at maturity. However, interim price movements will lead to losses on one contract and offsetting profits on the other. Profits and losses on the futures contract will be realized immediately through the mark-to-market mechanism, but profits and losses on the forward contract will only be realized at maturity.

The arbitrageur can expedite the realization of the arbitrage profit by closing out the two positions once the contracts are back in price equilibrium. However, if equilibrium price movements subsequent to the arbitrage transactions generate profits in the futures market position, the arbitrageur might choose to hold his positions. He will realize the futures market profits as they occur, but will be able to defer the losses on the forward market until maturity, thus generating interest-free capital. Since futures contracts trade for a two-year period, while price movements over the life of a contract can be substantial, the benefit of deferring the arbitrage profit in favor of the mark-to-market advantage is realistic, although Goldstein suggests that such opportunities are infrequent.

On the futures market, buyers of contracts determine whether the contract results in delivery. If an arbitrageur has a long position in futures and prices are rising, he will hold until maturity and take delivery, using the currency to meet his short obligation on the forward market. Sellers of futures contracts will have to deliver; unless they already have cash positions, they will have to acquire currency in the spot market. That transaction represents the link, albeit tenuous, between the futures market and the spot interbank market. The next section presents empirical tests related to the volatility effect.

Empirical Tests and Results

It is not possible to test directly the effect of arbitrage-related transactions because there is no way to measure the volume of arbitrage activity. The tests in this section will focus on the price behavior in the interbank spot market near the delivery dates for the futures contracts. There are two arguments for focusing on the delivery date. First, if the activity hypothesis is correct and arbitrage-related transactions as described above are responsible, then the impact will occur near the delivery date. Second, futures trading volume on other dates has no direct relationship with the spot market. The open interest at the close of trading on the Monday before delivery is an indication of the amount of futures-generated activity that will show up in the interbank market. Some of the delivered currency might come from previously acquired positions, however, so the final open interest figure is only a proxy for generated spot transactions.

Delivery procedures require that delivery be made on the third Wednesday of the month in which the contract matures. Delivery is made at a bank in the country of issuance. Notification of an obligation to deliver is made at 11:00 A.M. on the Monday before delivery, which is the last day of trading.

In order to make delivery, a holder of a short futures position would have to acquire spot currency on either Monday or Tuesday.

If delivery were made in the United States, the spot transaction would have to take place on Monday because funds clear after two days. Overseas, the funds are cleared in one day so that spot transactions made on Tuesday would meet the Wednesday delivery requirement (McRae & Walker, 1980). As a consequence of the delivery and clearing procedures, any effect of delivery-related transactions on the cash market should occur on Tuesday, the day before delivery.

The first set of tests examines whether the mean and variance of percentage price changes near delivery days differ from changes in other days. Near delivery day is operationalized to be delivery day, the day before delivery day, and two days before delivery day. For each of those days, the variance and means of percentage price change were calculated and compared with the variance and means for all other days. The hypotheses are that the mean and variance on the day before delivery should be greater than on other days because that is the day on which futures-generated spot transactions occur. Conversely, the mean and variance on delivery day and two days prior to delivery should not differ from the mean and variance on other days.

To test the hypotheses, data were collected on closing interbank rates for five currencies: the Canadian dollar, German mark, Japanese yen, Swiss franc, and British pound for the period from January 1, 1977 through December 21, 1983. These currencies represent the only ones continuously traded on the International Money Market during that period. The total sample has 2,002 observations, but the sizes of the two comparison groups differ substantially because there are only four delivery days in each year. Delivery day (D), the day before delivery $(D - 1)$, and two days before delivery $(D - 2)$ each have twenty eight observations. An F test was used to determine if the variances for the three days near delivery differed from variances on other days and a T test was used to compare the means. Table 13–1 provides the results.

For four of the five currencies, the means on $D - 1$ are larger and statistically different than the means on all other days. None of the means on either D or $D - 2$ is statistically different. That is a strong result that indicates that future market delivery requirements do have an impact on the spot market. The result is even stronger if one accepts that changes in spot rates are serially correlated and that there are periods of relatively greater or lesser volatility. Since these three days are consecutive days, the fact that the middle date exhibits this pattern of greater volatility is an indication that something unusual is occurring.

The variance results are not as supportive. Two of the variances, for the Canadian dollar and the British pound, are statistically different and larger on $D - 1$. They are also statistically different on $D - 2$, as is the variance

Table 13–1
Results of Mean and Variance Tests

	D		D-1		D-2	
	n = 28	n = 1,974	n = 28	n = 1,974	n = 28	n = 1,974
Canadian dollar						
μ	0.0001	− 0.00013	− 0.00098	− 0.00016	− 0.0002	− 0.00012
σ	0.00205	0.00258	0.0033*	0.00255	0.0033*	0.00256
German mark						
μ	0.00088	− 0.0001	0.0028*	− 0.00013	0.00083	− 0.000105
σ	0.00405*	0.00658	0.00699	0.00654	0.009159*	0.00651
Japanese yen						
μ	− 0.00051	0.000124	0.00292*	0.000075	0.000878	0.0001
σ	0.00366*	0.00649	0.00644	0.00646	0.00717	0.00646
Swiss franc						
μ	0.00143	0.00017	0.0038*	− 0.000016	0.0019	0.00001
σ	0.00612	0.00819	0.00877	0.00815	0.00990	0.00814
British pound						
μ	0.000575	− 0.000144	0.00379*	− 0.00019	− 0.0014	0.00012
σ	0.0052	0.00612	0.00814*	0.00606	0.00837*	0.00607

Note: μ = mean, σ = variance.
*Statistically significant at the 5 percent confidence level.

for the mark. The variances for the mark and yen are statistically different on delivery day, but are smaller, which is inconsistent with the hypothesis of greater volatility.

The third hypothesis is that the price movements on the interbank spot market are a function of the activity on the futures market which could generate transactions on the spot market. Testing this hypothesis, like testing the first one, is made difficult by the inability to directly measure the spillover transactions. Again, the tests that are performed use the near delivery dates as the sample of observations. For this test OLS regressions were run with the dependent variable the squared percentage change in prices and the independent variable the number of contracts that were delivered, C.

$$(P_2^i)^2 = a + b \, (C^i) + e^i \text{ for } i = 1\text{–}5 \text{ currencies} \qquad (13.1)$$

The transaction hypothesis suggests that $b > 0$.

The regressions were run for D, $D − 1$, and $D − 2$; results are shown in table 13–2. None of the coefficients was statistically different from zero at the 5 percent confidence level although two were statistically different at the

Table 13–2
Settlement Volume and Price Change for
Five Currencies

	a	*b*
Canadian dollar		
D	0.0000041	−3.9080E−11
	(2.61)	(−0.04)
D-1	0.0000131	−1.1970E−9
	(2.07)	(−0.32)
D-2	0.0000136	−2.3587E−9
	(2.61)	(−0.76)
German mark		
D	0.0000139	1.9083E−9
	(1.64)	(1.64)
D-1	0.0000441	−7.9450E−9
	(1.55)	(−0.51)
D-2	0.0000821	−3.5124E−9
	(2.21)	(−0.02)
Japanese yen		
D	0.0000105	1.7498E−9
	(1.93)	(0.70)
D-1	0.0000323	1.0379E−8
	(1.61)	(1.12)
D-2	0.0000434	−4.4245E−9
	(2.38)	(0.53)
Swiss franc		
D	0.0000462	−5.7592E−9
	(1.87)	(−0.40)
D-1	0.0000325	4.1049E−8
	(0.819)	(1.79)
D-2	0.0000657	2.4744E−8
	(1.60)	(1.04)
British pound		
D	0.0000214	2.5334E−9
	(1.98)	(0.63)
D-1	0.0000133	3.2607E−8
	(0.29)	(1.91)
D-2	0.00007	6.1456E−10
	(2.78)	(−0.07)

Note: t-statistics are given in parentheses.

10 percent level. Both of those cases, for the Swiss franc and the British pound, were for $D - 1$. In four of the cases for $D - 1$, the signs of the coefficients were positive, whereas in five of the ten cases for $D - 2$ and D the coefficients were negative. The values in the table are small because the dependent variable is small, being percentage change squared. These results support the hypothesis that delivery-related activities have an impact on spot price.

Conclusion

This research is related to a broad and important question: does trading in foreign-currency futures contracts increase the volatility of the spot price of the underlying currency? Popular opinion holds that the answer is yes. If that were true, it would have important economic and policy implications. This chapter has argued that because the spot markets in currencies are larger and less restricted than futures markets, and because the same groups trade in both, it is unlikely that trading in futures leads trading in the spot currency and, in general, increases the volatility of the spot market. It seems likely that if futures markets affect the volatility of spot markets, this will occur because of specific circumstances linking the two markets.

The evidence presented in this chapter focuses on one such specific inter-relationship between the futures market and the spot market, the delivery date. A study of the means and variances of spot price changes indicated that there are unusual price changes in the currency spot markets on the day prior to delivery. This is the last day on which spot trades in European currencies can be transacted in order to satisfy delivery on a futures contract. Therefore, we conclude that in this instance, the trading in futures markets influences trading in spot markets and tends to increase the volatility of spot prices. Whether futures markets exert a more pervasive influence than measured here is still an open question. This research indicates that the potential for influence is there and suggests the need for further study of the interactions between the two markets.

Notes

1. "World Currency Prices Become More Volatile, Increase Trading Risks," *Wall Street Journal,* July 30, 1985.
2. "Dollar Again Strengthens," *Wall Street Journal,* August 28, 1985.

References

Clifton, E. V. "The Currancy Futures Market and Interbank Foreign Exchange Trading," *Journal of Futures Market* (Fall 1985).

Eaker, M. R. "Covered Interest Arbitrage: New Measurement and Empirical Results," *Journal of Economics and Business,* vol. 32, no. 3 (Spring/Summer 1980).

Goldstein, H. N. "Foreign Currency Futures: Some Further Aspects," *Economic Perspectives.* Federal Reserve Bank of Chicago (November/December 1983).

McRae, T. W., & D. P. Walker. *Foreign Exchange Management.* London: Prentice-Hall International, 1980.

Rogalski, R. J. "The Dependence of Prices and Volume," *Review of Economics and Statistics* (May 1978).

Tauchen, G. E., & M. Pitts. "The Price Variability–Volume Relationship on Speculative Markets," *Econometrica,* vol. 51, no. 2 (March 1983).

14
Recursion Models For Warrant Pricing

Peter H. Ritchken
Michael G. Ferri

ABSTRACT

In order to value warrants it is often assumed that the warrant proceeds are handled in a way that leaves the current stock price unchanged or the total value of the firm unaltered. One way to achieve this is for the warrant income to be passed through to existing shareholders. This simplifying assumption is made so that investment decisions remain unchanged and so that the after-conversion stock price does not depend on the warrant proceeds. This chapter examines the problem of warrant pricing when the firm retains a fraction or all of the proceeds to expand the scale of existing projects. As such, this model extends some of the existing warrant pricing models. The models that are developed allow managers to investigate alternative warrant issuance policies and to assess their impact on shareholders' wealth and preferences.

The theoretical valuation of call options involves making assumptions about the future dividend policy and capital structure of the firm. Subject to these and other assumptions, options can be uniquely priced (Black & Scholes, 1973). These prices are independent of the number of options issued because each option is a separate side bet. Moreover, if it is optimal to exercise one option, then it is optimal to exercise all options. Sequential exercising strategies are never appropriate.

Unlike a call option, a warrant is a security issued by the firm. Numerous U.S. and foreign firms issue stock purchase warrants, usually through bond and warrant packages, in both the U.S. and international capital markets. The valuation of warrants is thus an important topic in international finance. A key feature of warrants and a point of difference between them and options is that when warrants are exercised, the firm receives income in exchange for creating new shares. These transactions lead to reinvestment decisions for the firm and to changes in the capital structure; this, in turn, impacts the value of outstanding warrants. Thus, unlike call options, the value of warrants depends on exercise strategies adopted by warrantholders (Cox & Rubinstein, 1985; Emanuel, 1983). A simplifying assumption that all warrants will be exercised in one block is often made (Galai & Schneller, 1978). Constantinides (1984) shows that if the objective is to price warrants in a competitive market, rather than to investigate the path of warrant exercise, then the block constraint, with its inherent simplicity, leads, at worst, to an upper bound on the warrant.

Although simpler to analyze, European warrants are still nontrivial to value because their issuance raises funds by an unknown quantity. These funds alter the capital structure of the firm, which, in turn, impacts the value of the postconversion stock prices, upon which the warrantholders have a claim. Thus, the future value of the warrantholders' claims depends on how much they initially paid for their claims. To avoid this circularity, Galai and Schneller (1978) assume that the proceeds from selling the warrant are immediately distributed to the current shareholders in the form of cash dividends. As a result, the investment policy of the firm is unaffected and the value of the firm at the expiration date is independent of the size of the premium generated by issuing the warrants (Cox & Rubinstein, 1985). Under this assumption, an explicit warrant price can be derived.

The purpose of this chapter is to extend the Galai-Schneller warrant pricing model to cases where cash dividends may not be paid to the shareholders. Specifically, we allow the income generated by the sale of the warrants to be used by the firm to expand the scale of its existing projects. The model we develop to price warrants contrasts with the usual application of option pricing approaches requiring the underlying security price to be taken as exogeneous. In the next section, we review the role of warrants in current capital markets. Then, we present the Galai-Schneller warrant model and illustrate its application using a two-period binomial model. A binomial approach is then used to value warrants under the assumption that the warrant income is retained by the firm. The third section develops a closed-form solution for the price of a European warrant, with the Galai-Schneller model obtaining as a special case. A few properties of these prices are then presented. The final section investigates the impact of warrant issuance on the wealth of the shareholders and provides management with a mechanism to assess different warrant issuance policies.

Warrants in Today's Capital Markets

Warrants come in a variety of types. Some are warrants to purchase stock and some give owners the right to purchase bonds from the issuing company.

Table 14–1
Dilution Factors of Selected U.S. Stock Purchase Warrants

1. Total in sample = 99

2. Dilution factor or ratio of warrant shares to outstanding shares:

   a. Range: Lowest = 2 percent, Highest = 320 percent

   b. Average = 22.64 percent

   c. Intervals:

Dilution	Number
0 – 5%	16
6%–10%	17
11%–20%	32
21%–30%	10
31%–40%	11
Above 40%	13

3. Typical maturity at issue = 5 years

4. Typical exchange ratio = 1 share/warrant

Source: *Value Line Convertibles*, February 3, 1986.

Warrants often have strike prices that adjust over time, or they may have call provisions.

According to *RHM Survey*, more than 400 U.S. firms have warrants outstanding. About a quarter of these firms have their shares listed on organized exchanges. *Value Line Convertibles* follows the most prominent warrants. Table 14–1 provides some summary information on these warrants. The average dilution factor is 22.64 percent with a range extending from 2 percent to over 100 percent. As table 14–1 indicates, a substantial number of warrants have factors above 100 percent.

Table 14–2 provides summary data on warrants outstanding in international markets. Extel International Bond Service in London provides reports on 157 warrants that were issued with bonds. Over 80 percent of the warrants were issued after 1982. The number of new warrants has increased yearly. Japanese firms account for over 60 percent of the stock warrant group that Extel follows, with German firms making up the next largest group.

Valuation of Warrants: A Binomial Approach

To focus on the issues of warrant pricing, we shall, for simplicity, consider the case of an all-equity firm that has n shares outstanding. We shall assume that this firm is considering a particular warrant issuance policy. Specifically, the firm is considering issuing m warrants. Each warrant provides the holder

Table 14–2
Stock Purchase Warrants on Selected International Bonds

1. Total in sample = 157

2. By year of issue:

1982 or Sooner	1983	1984	1985	1986 to Date
17	29	45	56	10

3. By currency of underlying stock:

Yen	Deutsche Mark	Swiss Franc	U.S. Dollar	Sterling	Other
94	27	13	8	6	9

4. Typical maturity at issue = 5 years

5. Average dilution factors by currency of underlying stock[a]

Yen	Deutsche Mark	Sterling
5.59%	6.12%	8.07%

Source: Extel International Bond Service, March 12, 1986. Dilution factor data come from *Moody's International Manual 1985*.

[a]The average dilution factors, by currency of underlying stock, are seen to be less than the dilution factor of the U.S. firms followed by *Value Line Convertibles*. Indeed, the average dilution factor across warrants of foreign firms is about 6 percent.

with the option of purchasing one share of stock at price X at time T. Let q represent the ratio of warrants issued to outstanding stock. Then, we have

$$V_0 = nS_0 \tag{14.1}$$

where V_0 is the current value of the firm and

$$q = m/n \tag{14.2}$$

Galai and Schneller (1978) assume that the investment policy of the firm is unaffected by the financing decision, with the proceeds of the sale of the warrants being immediately distributed to the shareholders. Under this assumption, they show that a European warrant would only be exercised whenever the value of the firm is sufficiently large to cause call options to be exercised on the stock of an identical firm with no warrants. Moreover, they show that the value of a European warrant, W_0 is equal to the current value of a call option on the stock of an equivalent firm with no warrants, multiplied by a term that depends on the dilution factor. Specifically, they show that

$$W_0 = C_0/(1 + q) \qquad (14.3)$$

where C_0 is the price of a call option on the stock of the all-equity firm. The assumption that the firm distributes the warrant proceeds as dividends to the shareholders is not supported by corporate practice. Indeed, more than half the firms that issue warrants do not pay dividends at all. The assumption is made to simplify the analysis, for, if the warrant income is retained by the firm, then the capital structure is altered. Specifically, the proceeds increase the value of the firm and alter the future stock price. The alteration impacts the warrant price itself.

To illustrate this complexity, consider a binomial approach to the pricing of warrants. Assume an all-equity firm exists with five shares outstanding. Assume one warrant is issued that converts into one share for $18 after two years. The current value of the firm is $100. The value of the firm is assumed to follow a binomial process as shown in figure 14.1.

The stock price of an equivalent firm with no warrants outstanding is given in figure 14–2.

Using the two-period binomial call pricing equation and the risk-free rate of 5 percent per year, the price of a call option with strike $18 and time to expiration of two years can be computed. The value is $C_0 = \$3.78$. Thus, from equation 14.3 we have:

$$W_0 = C_0/(1 + q) = \$3.78/1.2 = \$3.15$$

The $3.15 is assumed to be immediately passed through as a dividend to the existing shareholders. In essence, the $3.15 can be viewed as a payment or "entrance fee" by the warrantholders directly to the shareholders for the right to participate in the future wealth of the firm, provided the wealth of the firm exceeds a critical value at expiration.

If the warrant income is not paid out to the shareholders but instead is retained by the firm and used to increase the scale of existing projects, then, with an initial value of $103.15, the future value of the firm would be given by figure 14–3.

Notice that with this change, the stock price on an equivalent firm with no warrants would be given by figure 14–4.

Using these stock prices, the call price on the stock is given by $C_0 = \$4.38$. Hence the warrant price is $W_0 = 4.38/1.2 = \$3.65$.

If the warrant price is $3.65 and not $3.15, then the initial value of the firm is $103.65 and not $103.15. Using $103.65 as the initial value of the identical firm with no warrants leads to a new call price and hence a new

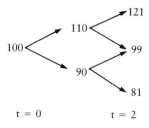

Figure 14–1. Value of the Firm Path

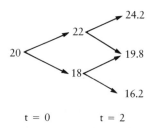

Figure 14–2. Share Price Path (Firm with No Warrants)

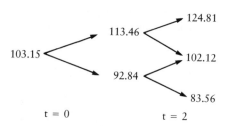

Figure 14–3. Future Value of the Firm Path (Income from Warrants Retained)

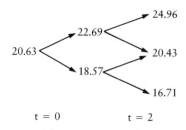

Figure 14–4. Share Price Path (Firm with Warrants, Income from Warrants Retained by Firm)

warrant price. This next price is $3.72. Table 14–3 illustrates the sequence of warrant prices derived by this iterative argument.

The binomial example suggests that an iterative technique can be used to establish a warrant price when the firm retains the income from the sale of the warrant.

Let $(W_j, j = 0, 1, 2, \ldots)$ be the sequence of warrant prices produced in successive iterations with $W_0 = 0$. The sequence of prices obtained is a nondecreasing sequence. To see this, notice that warrant income, when added to the value of the firm, instead of being distributed to the shareholders, can only increase the share price of the identical firm with no warrants and thus the warrant price. Since this nondecreasing sequence of warrant prices is bounded above by the current stock price, the iterative procedure converges in value.

Moreover, under the assumption that the warrant income is retained by the firm, we have:

$$W_0 > \frac{1}{(1 + q)} C_0 \qquad (14.4)$$

That is, the Galai-Schneller price is a lower bound for the warrant price in this example.

A European Warrant Pricing Model

To obtain further insight into the European warrant pricing problem with capital structure considerations, assume V_0^* is the value of the firm after European warrants have been issued. Then

$$V_0^* = nS_0 + mW_0. \qquad (14.5)$$

Table 14–3
Sequence of Stock Prices Derived by an Iterative Argument

Iteration Number	Initial Firm Value	Call Value	Value of European Warrant
1	100	3.78	3.15
2	103.15	4.38	3.65
3	103.65	4.47	3.72
4	103.72	4.48	3.73
5	103.73	4.48	3.73

Under the Galai-Schneller assumptions, the warrant income is distributed to the shareholders. In essence, the warrantholders have paid an entrance fee to the shareholders for contingent claims on the postconversion stock price of the original firm. Here, we assume no dividends are paid out and that the firm cannot declare any stock dividends or issue new stock. In this case, the warrantholders can be viewed as investing mW_0 dollars into the firm in exchange for contingent claims whose value depends on the postconversion stock price of this expanded firm.

Let $\tilde{V}_T$ be the future value of the firm without warrants. Then

$$\tilde{V}_T = V_0 \tilde{R}_v \tag{14.6}$$

where $\tilde{R}_v$ is the price relative for the firm with no warrants. If we assume the income from the warrants is used to increase the scale of existing projects, we then have:

$$\tilde{V}_T^* = V_O^* \tilde{R}_v \tag{14.7}$$

where $\tilde{V}_T$ is the future value of the firm with warrants. Then,

$$\tilde{V}^*T = (nS_0 + mW_0)\, \tilde{V}_T/V_0$$

or

$$\tilde{V}_T^* = na\, \tilde{S}_T \tag{14.8}$$

where

$$a = 1 + qW_0/S_0 \tag{14.9}$$

The final stock price $\tilde{S}_T^*$ of the firm with warrants depends on whether the warrants are exercised or not. If exercised, the stock price, $\tilde{S}_T^*$, is given by $\tilde{S}_{TE}^*$ where

$$\tilde{S}_{TE}^* = (\tilde{V}_T^* + mX)/(m + n) \tag{14.10}$$

Substituting 14.8 into 14.10 we obtain:

$$\tilde{S}_{TE}^* = (a\tilde{S}_T + qX)/(1 + q) \tag{14.11}$$

If unexercised, the stock price, $\tilde{S}_{TU}^*$ is given by:

$$\tilde{S}_{TU}^* = \tilde{V}_T^*/n$$
$$= a\, \tilde{S}_T \tag{14.12}$$

Since the warrantholders always act in their own interests, we have:

$$\breve{W}_T = \max \left(0, \frac{V_T^* + m\,X}{(m + n)} - X\right) \tag{14.13}$$

The warrantholders will exercise if the afterconversion stock price exceeds the strike price; that is, if

$$\frac{\tilde{V}_T^* + mX}{(m + n)} > X$$

or

$$\tilde{V}_T^* > nX \tag{14.14}$$

Now, substituting 14.8 into 14.14, we obtain the following condition for exercise:

$$\tilde{S}_T > X/a \tag{14.15}$$

Let $F(W_0)$ be the probability that the warrants are exercised. Then:

$$\begin{aligned} F(W_0) &= Pr\,(\tilde{S}_T > X/a) \\ &= Pr\,[\tilde{S}_T > XS_0/(1 + qW_0)] \end{aligned} \tag{14.16}$$

Then, the postconversion stock price can be summarized by the following mixture distribution:

$$\begin{aligned} \tilde{S}_T &= \tilde{S}_{TE} \text{ with probability } F(W_0) \\ &= \tilde{S}_{TU} \text{ with probability } 1 - F(W_0) \end{aligned} \tag{14.17}$$

Equation 14.17 illustrates the fact that even if the value of the firm follows a geometric Wiener process, then, with European warrants, the postconversion stock price will not be lognormal.

Notice from equation 14.13, however, that the warrant price at expiration is:

$$\breve{W}_T = \text{Max} \left(0, \frac{\tilde{V}_T^* + mX}{(m + n)} - X\right) \tag{14.18}$$

Substituting equation 14.8 into 14.18, we obtain:

$$\breve{W}_T = \text{Max} \left[0, \frac{an\tilde{S}_T}{(m + n)} - X\right]$$

which simplifies to:

$$\tilde{W}_T = \frac{1}{(1 + q)} \text{Max} (0, a\tilde{S}_T - X) \qquad (14.19)$$

Equation 14.19 indicates that the final payout of the warrant is determined by the value of the stock price at expiration if the firm issued no warrants, the value a, and the dilution factor $(1 + q)$. Notice that a depends on the initial warrant premium. If this premium was paid out the shareholders, then $a = 1$, and we obtain the Galai-Schneller result. Redefining a as:

$$1 + \delta q W_0/S_0 \qquad (14.20)$$

Then $\delta = 1$ corresponds to full retention of warrant income, while $\delta = 0$ corresponds to full distribution of warrant income to shareholders.

Since the future value of the warrant, $\tilde{W}_T$, is perfectly correlated with the future value of a call option on the firm with no warrants (for $\delta = 0$), their current prices should be proportional. That is, for $\delta = 0$,

$$W_0 = C_0/(1 + q) \qquad (14.21)$$

However, in general, $\delta \neq 0$, and hence, by the usual arbitrage argument:

$$W_0 = C_0^*/(1 + q) \qquad (14.22)$$

where C_0^* is the value of an option on the stock of a firm identical to the firm with no warrants, except for "leverage." This leveraged firm has the same equity as the original firm, namely nS_0, but may be viewed as having borrowed an additional amount equal to the value of the warrant issue retained by the firm. That is:

$$a = \frac{nS_0 + \delta m W_0}{nS_0} \qquad (14.23)$$

Equation 14.22 provides the pricing relationship between warrants and call options on the stock of an equivalent firm with no warrants. If, for example, we assume the value of the all-equity firm follows a geometric Wiener process, then, at the expiration date, T, the stock price $\tilde{S}_T$ will have a lognormal distribution. Let σ be the instantaneous volatility of this process. For a given W_0, $a\tilde{S}_T$ is lognormal with the same volatility. Hence, under the usual Black-

Scholes assumptions, options on the "leveraged" stock price aS_T can be computed. Specifically, from equation 14.22 we have:

$$W_0 = \frac{1}{(1 + q)} [aS_0 N(d_1) - X \exp(-rT) N(d_2)] \qquad (14.24)$$

where

$$d_1 = [\ln(aS_0/X) + (r + \sigma^2/2) T] / \sigma \sqrt{T}$$
$$d_2 = d_1 - \sigma \sqrt{T}$$
$$a = 1 + \delta q W_0/S_0$$

$N(x)$ is the cumulative normal distribution value up to x, and r is the riskless rate.

Notice that since W_0 appears on the right-hand side of 14.24, an iterative procedure is necessary to solve the equation. Only if $\delta = 0$, will the iterative procedure simplify.

Let $[W_j, j = 0, 1, 2, \ldots]$ be the sequence of successive warrant prices. W_j is obtained from its predecessor W_{j-1} by using an *a* value, a_j, where:

$$a_j = 1 + \delta q W_{j-1}/S_0$$
$$a_0 = 1 \qquad (14.25)$$
$$\text{and } W_0 = 0$$

These warrant prices $[W_j]$ form a nondecreasing sequence. A simple upper bound to this sequence is obtained by recognizing that:

$$W_0 < \frac{1}{(1 + q)} [aS_0 N(d_1)] \qquad (14.26)$$
$$< \frac{1}{(1 + q)} aS_0$$

from which, after substituting for *a*, we obtain:

$$W_0 \leq S_0$$

Since the sequence of prices is bounded above, the sequence must converge.

Empirical Properties

The value of the warrant depends critically on the value of a call option on the leveraged stock and on the dilution factor. Table 14–4 compares the Galai-Schneller warrant prices ($\delta = 0$) to the warrant prices produced under the assumption of full retention of the warrant income ($\delta = 1$) for different dilution factors.

Table 14–4 clearly illustrates the fact that with no dividends the warrant prices are significantly higher than in the case when a dividend is declared. As the dilution factor increases, the difference between the two models ($\delta = 0$ and $\delta = 1$) increases.

The Impact of Warrant Issuance on the Price of the Shares

Equation 14.15 provides the condition whereby warrantholders exercise their warrants. Table 14–5 summarizes the stock prices of the firm with and without warrants.

Notice that if the warrants are not exercised, then the shareholders will be better off than if the firm had not used the warrants. Specifically, if the stock price of the firm with no warrants is below X/a, then the warrants will not be exercised, and the share price of the firm will be aS_T ($a \geq 1$).

The warrants will be exercised only if the stock price of the firm with no warrants exceeds X/a. In this case, from table 14–5, we have:

$$\tilde{S}_T^* - \tilde{S}_T = [a \, \tilde{S}_T + qX - (1 + q) \, \tilde{S}_T]/(1 + q) \qquad (14.27)$$

This value is nonnegative if:

$$\tilde{S}_T \leq dX \qquad (14.28)$$

where:

$$d = q/(1 + q - a) \qquad (14.29)$$

Since $dx > X/a$, there exists an interval of stock prices between X/a and dX for which the shareholders will have no regret in issuing the warrants even though the warrantholders exercise their claims and dilute the stock. Table 14–6 summarizes the regret table.

For $\delta = 1$, shareholders will approve this issuance of warrants if the

Table 14–4
Comparison of Warrant Prices

Dilution q	Warrant Prices		Percent Difference
	$\delta = 0$	$\delta = 1$	
0	14.29	14.29	0
0.1	12.99	13.78	6.12
0.2	11.91	13.33	11.98
0.3	10.99	12.93	17.63
0.4	10.20	12.56	23.08
0.5	9.52	12.22	28.35
0.6	8.93	11.92	33.46
0.7	8.40	11.63	38.43
0.8	7.94	11.37	43.27
0.9	7.52	11.12	47.98
1.0	7.15	10.9	52.58

Note: Case parameters: $S_0 = 100$, $X = 105$, $T = 2$, $r = 0.10$, $\sigma = 0.3$.

Table 14–5
Stock Prices of a Firm with and without Warrants

	$\bar{S}_T < X/a$	$\bar{S}_T > X/a$
Share price with no warrants	$\bar{S}_T$	$\bar{S}_T$
Share price with warrants	$\bar{S}_T^* = a\bar{S}_T$	$\bar{S}_T^* = (a\bar{S}_T + qX)/(1 + q)$

Table 14–6
Share Prices and Warrants

	$\bar{S}_T \leq X/a$	$X/a < \bar{S}_T \leq dX$	$\bar{S}_T > dX$
Do not issue warrants	$a\bar{S}_T - \bar{S}_T$	$\dfrac{(a\bar{S}_T + qX)}{(1 + q)} - \bar{S}_T$	—
Issue warrants	—	—	$S_T - \dfrac{(a\bar{S}_T + qX)}{(1 + q)}$

probability that the stock price exceeds the value dX is "small." This probability, R, is

$$R = Pr\,(\tilde{S}_T \geq dX) = Pr\,[\tilde{S}_T \geq qX/(1 + q - a)] \qquad (14.30)$$

Upon substituting for a, we obtain:

$$R = Pr[\tilde{S}_T \geq S_0X/(S_0 - W_0)] \qquad (14.31)$$

Since the warrant value W_0 depends on decision variables, q, X, and T, we write:

$$R = R(X, T, q) \qquad (14.32)$$

Equation 14.31 together with 14.24 allows management to establish warrant-issuing policies that minimize "regret." Moreover, the amount of income generated by the issuance of any warrant package can be established.

Conclusion

A common assumption in warrant pricing models is that the issuance of warrants does not alter the size of the firm. The firm achieves this goal by passing the warrant premium to existing shareholders. In essence, the warrant holders are paying the shareholders for the right to participate in the afterconversion stock price of the existing firm. This payment can be viewed as an entrance fee to the existing firm. In this chapter, we have assumed that the income from the warrants (all or part) is used to increase the scale of its existing projects and that no dividends are declared. The options granted in exchange for this income are options on the afterconversion stock price of this larger firm. The larger the fraction of warrant income retained by the firm, the more valuable the warrant. A simple closed-form solution that uses the Black-Scholes equation has been derived. A sensitivity analysis of this price shows that its value is quite sensitive to the fraction of income retained. Moreover, as the dilution factor increases, the difference between this model and the Galai-Schneller price expands. Empirical comparisons of warrant prices with the simple dilution-adjusted Black-Scholes price indicate that warrants are significantly undervalued. Using the adjusted model, the size of these undervaluations will decrease.

The method of analysis presented here is equally applicable to other types of securities. A convertible bond issued by an all-equity firm, for example, could be valued using similar methods. Of more interest, however, would be extensions of this recursive approach to value warrants (or convertibles) in firms with more complex capital structures. Finally, it should be pointed out that whenever the value of the firm (upon which the contingent claim is to be priced) cannot be taken to be exogeneous, a recursive (or simultaneous) solution to the value of the claim and firm is required. This situation will always occur when a firm is considering increasing its size by issuing warrants, convertibles, or other types of debt.

Notes

1. See J. Cox and M. Rubinstein (1985) for the analysis of the binomial call option pricing model.

References

Black, F., & M. Scholes, "The Pricing of Options and Corporate Liabilities," *Journal of Political Economy* (May 1973), 637–54.

Constantinides, G. M., "Warrant Exercise and Bond Conversion in Competitive Markets," *Journal of Financial Economics*, 13 (September 1984), 371–97.

Cox, J., & M. Rubinstein, *Option Markets*. Englewood Cliffs, N.J.: Prentice-Hall, 1985.

Emanuel, D. C., "Warrant Valuation and Exercise Strategy," *Journal of Financial Economics*, 12 (August 1983), 211–35.

Galai, D., & M. I. Schneller, "Pricing of Warrants and the Value of the Firm," *Journal of Finance*, 33 (December 1978), 1333–42.

Smith, C., "Applications of Option Pricing Analysis," chapter 4, *Handbook of Financial Economics*, J. Bicksler, editor. Amsterdam, N.Y.: North-Holland, 1979, 80–119.

Name Index

Subject Index

About the Contributors

Bajis Dodin is assistant professor at the Graduate School of Management, University of California, Riverside.

Mark R. Eaker is a professor at The Colgate Darden Graduate School of Business Administration of the University of Virginia.

Cheol S. Eun is an assistant professor of finance at the College of Business and Management at the University of Maryland, College Park.

Michael G. Ferri holds the Edward J. and Louise E. Mellen Chair in Finance at John Carroll University.

William R. Folks, Jr., is professor of international business at the University of South Carolina.

J. Orlin Grabbe is assistant professor at The Wharton School of the University of Pennsylvania.

Michael R. Granito is managing director at J.P. Morgan Investment Management Inc.

Dwight M. Grant is the Presidential Professor of Finance at the Robert O. Anderson School of Management, University of New Mexico.

Jack Guttentag is professor of finance and Robert Morris Professor of Banking at The Wharton School of the University of Pennsylvania.

Richard Herring is a member of the Finance Department and director of the Program in International Banking and Finance at The Wharton School of the University of Pennsylvania.

Shyam J. Kamath is assistant professor of economics at California State University, Hayward.

Michael Kelley is with J.P. Morgan Investment Management Inc.

Chuck C. Y. Kwok is assistant professor of international business at the University of South Carolina.

J. Huston McCulloch is professor of economics and finance at The Ohio State University.

Lars Oxelheim is a research fellow at the Industrial Institute for Social and Economic Research (IUI) in Stockholm and a senior partner in Foreign Risk Advisory Services, Stockholm.

Krishna Ramaswamy is associate professor at The Wharton School of the University of Pennsylvania.

Bruce G. Resnick is associate professor of finance at Indiana University.

Peter Ritchken is an assistant professor in the Operations Research Department, Weatherhead School of Management, Case Western Reserve University.

Alan M. Rugman is director of the Center for International Business Studies and professor of business administration at Dalhousie University.

Ole Christian Sand is a Ph.D. candidate at the UCLA Graduate School of Management.

Hans Schollhammer is associate professor and chairman of the International Management Program at the UCLA Graduate School of Management.

Suresh M. Sundaresan is assistant professor at the Graduate School of Business, Columbia University.

Hirokazu Takada is an assistant professor of marketing at the Graduate School of Management, University of California, Riverside.

Clas Wihlborg is an associate professor of finance and international business at the University of Southern California and an associate of the Center for Economic Policy Studies at the Claremont Graduate School.

About the Editors

Sarkis J. Khoury is an associate professor of finance at the University of California, Riverside. He earned his Ph.D. in international finance/finance at The Wharton School, the University of Pennsylvania, in 1978. He taught at Bucknell University for three years before joining the faculty at Notre Dame in 1980 and the University of California, Riverside, in 1984. He has conducted several seminars on banking, financial planning, and international finance. Dr. Khoury is the author of eight books and monographs dealing with international finance, international banking, investments, and the mathematics of finance, and of several articles, some of which have been published in leading journals in the United States. Dr. Khoury has lectured on various topics all over the world and is now serving as a consultant to many organizations.

Alo Ghosh is currently with the consulting firm of McKinsey & Co., New York. He previously served as assistant professor of finance at the University of California, Riverside. His field of expertise is options and option-like instruments. Dr. Ghosh received his Ph.D. from The Wharton School, the University of Pennsylvania, in 1985.